Preface

The Competition Act 1998 has been described as the 'europeanisation' or 'modernisation' of UK competition law. It will sweep away most of the existing patchwork of UK competition law which dates back to the 1970s. In its place, the UK will have a regime which is in tune with the EU rules and those of most other EU Member States. The Labour Government also views this legislation as integral in its policies to increase the competitiveness of UK plcs and to give UK consumers a better deal.

Will the Act make a difference? We think it will. The Act will bring focus and bite to enforcement of competition law. In announcing the new regime, Mr Bridgeman, DGFT, said:

> 'The Competition Act will radically change the OFT's powers of investigation and enforcement. From 1 March 2000, the UK will move from having one of the most permissive competition regimes in the world to one of the toughest. The new law gives my officials the power to enter premises and require the production of documents. I will be able to impose penalties on those who abuse a dominant market position or enter secret deals to destroy competition in order to keep prices high for UK consumers. The days of anti-competitive activity such as price fixing and market sharing are numbered.'

The Act should be recognised as a 'framework Act' since much of the detail is contained in EU case law guidelines, statutory instruments and procedural rules. For this reason, the Act is not an easy piece of legislation to understand. We have sought to produce a guide of the Act which draws together these various sources in a way which will enable readers to understand the real implications of the Competition Act 1998.

We are tremendously grateful to all those who assisted with this book and would mention Andrew Johnston, Swapna Sachdev, Julia Sharp, Hugh Stokes, Maria Webb and Angela Worsfold.

Contents

Contents

Contents

1 – Overview of the Act

Aims and Objectives [1.1]

For many years, business and government have criticised the way competition law operates in the UK. The first indications of reform appeared in the 1988 green paper, *Review of Restrictive Trade Practices Policy: a consultative document* and the 1989 white paper, *Opening Markets: New Policy on Restrictive Trade Practices*. Despite a number of false dawns, real progress was not achieved until a consultation paper and draft bill were published in August 1996.

The Competition Bill finally became law on 9 November 1998, although it will not come into full effect until 1 March 2000 (subject to transitional provisions).

There were three main drivers for change:

○ the perceived inadequacy of the existing UK competition law system;
○ the Government's desire for the UK to fall in line with the EU competition rules, consistent with its general Treaty obligations and the principle of subsidiarity; and
○ the Government's perception of the Act as a tool in its drive to make UK business more competitive and deliver a better deal to UK consumers.

Inadequacies of the Existing Law [1.2]

UK competition law is currently spread between four main statutes:

○ *Restrictive Trade Practices Act (RTPA) 1976;*
○ *Resale Prices Act 1976;*
○ *Fair Trading Act 1973;* and
○ *Competition Act 1980.*

(Existing UK competition law, as it will survive under the new regime, is described in **Chapter 3:** EXISTING LEGISLATION.)

The main criticisms of the old legislation are that:

○ the *RTPA 1976* is:
  ● the principal tool to regulate restrictive agreements, yet it lacks focus;
  ● directed at the form of an agreement but ignores its effect, which in the past has resulted in many benign commercial agreements being subject to needless regulation;
  ● poorly drafted;
  ● not able to catch some seriously anti–competitive agreements and even if agreements are caught, the registration system is not an effective way of uncovering cartels – the DGFT has limited investigatory powers and no power to impose fines;
○ in addition:
  ● the institutional system for regulation of anti–competitive activity is slow and inflexible – there is considerable duplication between the Office of Fair Trading (OFT) and the Competition Commission (CC) (formerly the Monopolies and Mergers Commission (MMC));
  ● there is no prohibition of anti–competitive behaviour or abuse of dominance – the OFT has had to seek court rulings or an MMC enquiry before effective action could be taken to help victims, with the result that in some cases victims were no longer in business by the time the procedure had run its course;
  ● in general customers or competitors injured by anti–competitive behaviour had no adequate redress and no realistic prospect of damages;
  ● the application of competition law to different sectors of the economy is patchy – some are excluded altogether, others, such as the utilities, are subject to regulatory control which overlaps with competition regulation and may produce different outcomes.

Interaction with EU Law and Policy [1.3]

Companies doing business in the UK are subject to the EU competition rules. Articles 81 and 82 (formerly Articles 85 and 86) of the EC Treaty have direct effect in the UK and throughout the EU, and have applied since the accession of the UK to the European Economic Community in 1973.

Existing UK law makes little attempt to fall into line with the EU rules or to avoid or reduce 'double jeopardy' for UK undertakings. The whole analytical and institutional approach of the UK is at odds with the EU rules. One of the primary objectives of the Act is to bring UK competition law into line with the EU rules.

The Act effectively mirrors EU competition rules, with the result that the UK authorities are now more likely to be regarded by the European Commission as being in a position to deal effectively with anti-competitive conduct. The practical result of this is that the Commission will be able to reserve its scarce resources for those cases with an international element and may, therefore, interfere less with more domestic issues in the future.

This change also brings the UK into line with other Member States. The UK will be one of the last of the fifteen EU Member States to adopt competition laws specifically modelled on the EC Treaty. Effectively, the same, or very similar, substantive and procedural rules will soon be applied in nearly all Member States.

UK Government Policy   [1.4]

The Labour Government perceives the Act as a key part of its strategy to make UK business more competitive. When kick-starting the consultation process, Margaret Beckett, the then President of the Board of Trade, commented:

> 'Effective and fair competition is essential to ensure value and choice for customers. In the global market place, competition provides a spur to British companies to innovate and invest. Competitiveness, both at home and overseas, is enhanced by competition in the domestic market.'

The Government is also promoting the Act as an important weapon in its drive to give consumers in the UK a better deal. In statements following the Budget in March 1999, Stephen Byers, Secretary of State for Trade and Industry, stated:

> '[t]his Government is putting the needs of consumers at the heart of our competitiveness agenda. Knowledgeable consumers stimulate businesses to innovate and so contribute to competitiveness. But equally, we won't allow consumers to be ripped off.'

The Government is expecting the OFT to use its enhanced powers and greater resources under the Act to destroy cartels and other practices which result in the UK consumer paying allegedly higher prices than consumers in the United States and elsewhere.

Structure of the Act [1.5]

The Act is in four parts:

O *Part I*: Competition.
O *Part II*: Investigations in relation to Articles 81 and 82.
O *Part III*: Monopolies.
O *Part IV*: Supplemental and Transitional.

In addition, there are 14 Schedules.

The bulk of this guide concentrates on *Part I*. This Part contains the key prohibitions and powers of investigation and enforcement. *Part II* is discussed in **Chapter 6: INTERACTION WITH EU LAW**. *Part III* makes consequential amendments to the monopoly provisions of the *Fair Trading Act 1973* and is discussed in **Chapter 3: EXISTING LEGISLATION**. The elements of *Part IV* are discussed where appropriate.

The Act is a framework act. Key elements of procedure and substance are, or will be, the subject of orders made by statutory instrument.

OFT Guidelines [1.6]

The DGFT has also published a number of non-binding guidelines which he has identified as being core to the successful implementation of the Act. These cover:

O The Major Provisions (OFT 400);
O The Chapter I Prohibition (OFT 401);
O The Chapter II Prohibition (OFT 402);
O Market Definition (OFT 403);
O Powers of Investigation (OFT 404);
O Concurrent Application to Regulated Industries (OFT 405);
O Transitional Arrangements (OFT 406);
O Enforcement (OFT 407)
O Trade Associations, Professions and Self Regulating Bodies (OFT 408);

O   Assessment of Individual Agreements and Conduct (OFT 414);
O   Assessment of Market Power (OFT 415); and
O   Mergers and Ancillary Restraints (OFT 416).

The following guidelines are also expected:

O   Vertical Agreements and Restraints;
O   Intellectual Property Rights;
O   Land Agreements;
O   General Economic Interest;
O   Application in the Telecommunications Sector;
O   Application in the Energy Sectors;
O   Application in the Railways Sector; and
O   Application in the Water and Sewerage Sectors.

Timetable for Implementation   [1.7]

Certain provisions of the Act commenced automatically at Royal Assent on 9 November 1998 (*sections 71, 75, 76, Schedule 13, paras 1–7* and *para 35*).

Other sections will be the subject of Commencement Orders. At the time of writing three Commencement Orders have come into effect:

O   *The Competition Act 1998 (Commencement No 1) Order 1998 (SI 1998 No 2750)*;
O   *The Competition Act 1998 (Commencement No 2) Order 1998 (SI 1998 No 3166)*;
O   *The Competition Act 1998 (Commencement No 3) Order 1999 (SI 1999 No 505)*.

The two new prohibitions will not come into force until 1 March 2000 (the starting date) when the new regime is launched by means of a fourth Commencement Order.

In addition, a programme of secondary legislation under the Act will be necessary in the run up to 1 March 2000. At the time of writing four statutory instruments have been made:

O   *The Competition Act 1998 (Competition Commission) Transitional, Consequential and Supplemental Provisions Order 1999 (SI 1999 No 506)* (under *section 45*) establishing the Competition Commission, came into force on 1 April 1999;

O   *The Competition Act 1998 (Provisional Immunity from Penalties) Regulations 1999 (SI 1999 No 2281)* (under *section 41*) describing the meaning of 'provisional immunity', will come into force on 1 March 2000;

O   *The Competition Act 1998 (Definition of Appropriate Person) Regulations 1999 (SI 1999 No 2282)* (under *section 73*) defining the meaning of 'appropriate person', will come into force on 1 March 2000; and

O   *The Compmetition Act 1998 (Application for Designation of Professional Rules) Regulations 1999 (SI 1999 No 2546)* (under *Schedule 4, para 3*) setting out the procedure for professional bodies to apply for immunity, came into effect on 1 October 1999.

Interpretation – *Section 60*   [1.8]

Unusually, the Act contains a 'guiding principles' clause in *section 60*. The purpose of *section 60* is to achieve harmony, if not complete consistency, between the Act and EU competition law on which it is based. Whilst the theory is straightforward, the reality is that those charged with enforcing the Act will be faced with potentially unfamiliar and tricky principles of EU and economic law.

Section 60 imposes a double obligation on UK authorities in considering the application of *Part I*. Firstly, the authorities must ensure that there is 'no inconsistency' with principles of the EC Treaty and the European Court or relevant decisions of the European Court. Secondly, the authorities are under a lesser obligation to 'have regard to' any relevant decision or statement of the European Commission.

In the guideline *The Major Provisions*, the DGFT states that, in his view, this obligation is limited to:

> 'decisions or statements which have the authority of the European Commission as a whole, such as, for example, decisions on individual cases under Articles 85 and 86 [now Articles 81 and 82]. It would also include clear statements about its policy approach which the European Commission has published in the Annual Report on Competition Policy.'

The Government expects that UK authorities – and, presumably, also UK undertakings when considering the Act – will 'be able to produce a sensible translation of EC rules into the domestic system'. However, this statement may underestimate real problems with how *section 60* will work in practice.

Consistency with EU Law [1.9]

The general principle is one of consistency, except where there exist 'relevant differences between the provisions concerned'. So, for example, where the Act on its face departs from EU law, then the authorities are not bound to follow the EU precedent. It is, therefore, clear that the principle of consistency will be overridden to the extent necessary to give effect to, say, the exclusion for vertical agreements to be made pursuant to *section 50*.

Similarly, as there is no requirement in the UK prohibitions for an effect on trade between Member States, as there is in the EU provisions, this element of EU decisions will not be relevant to interpretation of the Act.

However, there are other differences in the drafting of the Act where it is unclear whether the difference is intended to be a 'relevant' difference. An obvious example is in the wording of the Chapter II Prohibition on the use of dominance. *Section 18* talks about 'any conduct on the part of one or more undertakings' whereas Article 82 simply prohibits 'any abuse by one or more undertakings'. Is the inclusion of the term 'conduct' intended to limit the scope of the Chapter II Prohibition to sins of commission but not omission? It would seem not, as the guidelines specifically identify a refusal to supply as a potential abuse of the Chapter II Prohibition.

'In Relation to Competition' [1.10]

The consistency principle applies only 'in relation to competition'. It is clear from statements made in the House of Lords by the Government Minister, Lord Simon, that the intention is not to restrict *section 60* purely to interpretation of the meaning of the terms or concepts of Articles 81 and 82 of the EC Treaty. The aim is that those Articles must be understood in the context of general principles of Community law, such as proportionality, non-discrimination and fundamental rights.

These principles have proved pivotal in a number of appeals of major competition cases in the EU but may be unfamiliar to UK authorities. It is clear, however, that the application of these principles does not go as far as to replicate the procedural rules of the European Commission. The UK will have its own distinct procedural rules.

In considering the EU precedents, the UK authorities face a practical problem in separating out competition motives and other motives which lie behind a given decision. For example, one of the basic tenets of EU law as set out in the EC Treaty is the creation of an internal market characterised by the free movement of goods and services. This motive often lies behind decisions taken under Art 81 in relation to agreements which contain restrictions on inports and exports. However, this is not a relevant factor in relation to interpreting the Act. Again, in the House of Lords, Lord Simon clarified this point in emphasising that single market considerations are not relevant to interpretation of the UK prohibitions.

Unclear Concepts [1.11]

As will be seen in the following chapters, some key concepts of the EU Prohibitions are unclear. The effect of *section 60* is, therefore, to import into UK law concepts such as joint dominance under Article 82 which are not settled as a matter of EU law.

Section 60 presents a real practical problem to the uninitiated seeking to apply the Act. The Government's adherence to *section 60* means that even some of the most basic provisions of the Act do not necessarily mean what they say.

For example, the Chapter I Prohibition states that agreements which restrict competition are void. However, this is not the case. If the offending provisions can be severed as a matter of UK law, then the rest of the agreement will not, in fact, be prohibited. This result is derived from case law under Article 81 and so flows through to the interpretation of the UK Prohibitions by virtue of *section 60*. The net result of this is that the Act cannot be read as a stand alone document.

The guidelines issued by the DGFT (see **1.6** above) are helpful but even these contain a health warning that they 'should not be regarded as a substitute for or as an authoritative interpretation of Community law'. In other words, to understand the Act one needs also to become expert in EU competition law.

Case Law [1.12]

There is no guarantee that decisions under the Act will develop in tandem with, and consistently with, decisions under the EC rules. For example, the territorial ambit of the Chapter I Prohibition extends to agreements which are implemented, or are intended to be implemented, in the UK. This principle is taken from the current position under EU Law, as set down by the European Court in [*Woodpulp*]. However, the Government has made it clear, in statements in Hansard, that if EU Law subsequently diverges from this position, the UK will not follow.

Understanding the Act [1.13]

As the preceding paragraphs illustrate, this particular piece of legislation cannot simply be interpreted on the basis of the ordinary meaning of the words in the Act. Litigation under the Act is likely to involve lawyers poring over EU textbooks and also over Hansard, since the Government relied very heavily on statements made in both Houses of Parliament as to the Act's interpretation as a means of avoiding making changes to the drafting of the Prohibitions.

In this book, we begin in **Chapter 2:** THE REGULATORS with a description of the regulators who will have power to enforce the Act. **Chapter 3:** EXISTING LEGISLATION summarises the limited continuing role of the existing competition legislation. **Chapters 4** and **5** describe in detail the Chapter I and II Prohibitions respectively. **Chapter 6:** INTERACTION WITH EU LAW considers the relationship with EU law. **Chapter 7:** PROCEDURE AND ENFORCEMENT deals with the procedure for investigation and enforcement under the Act. Finally, **Chapter 8:** COMPLIANCE concludes with some practical pointers as to how to comply with the Act.

2 – The Regulators

Introduction [2.1]

This chapter introduces the authorities involved in enforcing the Act and explains how they will work together.

The table below lists the relevant sections of the Act covered in this Chapter.

Section No.	Description of Section
45	The Competition Commission
46–49 (incl.)	Appeals
51–53 (incl.)	DGFT's rules, guidance and fees
54	Regulators
71	Regulations, orders and rules
Sch 7	The Competition Commission
Sch 8	Appeals
Sch 10	Regulators
Sch 11	Interpretation of *section 55*

Relevant Authorities [2.2]

The relevant authorities are the:

○ Director General of Fair Trading (DGFT) – has the principal enforcement role under the Act, supported by the OFT;

○   Regulators – share concurrent powers under the Act with the DGFT in respect of the regulated sectors e.g. utilities;

○   Competition Commission – hears appeals from decisions of the DGFT or sectoral regulators under the Act and assumes role of MMC under *Fair Trading Act 1973* and other legislation;

○   Secretary of State – overall responsibility for competition policy and regulation-making role; and

○   courts – Court of Appeal will hear appeals from the Competition Commission. The prohibitions in the Act may also be pleaded in civil litigation either as a claim for breach of statutory duty or as a 'competition defence'.

Director General of Fair Trading [2.3]

The DGFT acquires very considerable new powers under the Act. He will have the central enforcement role in the UK competition regime.

Most of the DGFT's powers are to be exercised pursuant to procedural rules made under *section 51* of the Act and approved by the Secretary of State. A set of procedural rules was published in March 1999 and these are discussed further in **Chapters 7: PROCEDURE AND ENFORCEMENT** and **8: COMPLIANCE**.

The DGFT, who is appointed by the Secretary of State, is independent and has a range of statutory duties and responsibilities. The present DGFT is John Bridgeman. The DGFT heads the OFT, which is a non-ministerial government department. In addition to his responsibilities for competition law enforcement, he also has responsibilities in the consumer protection field. Implementing the new legislation will require a radical overhaul of the OFT. The diagram opposite sets out the OFT's revised structure of the OFT.

By the time the Act comes fully into effect on 1 March 2000, it is expected that the OFT will have approximately 200 staff working within the Competition Policy Division. This represents the addition of about 50 staff specifically to deal with its increased role. A specialist cartel unit has also been established. It is expected that the casework branches will be allocated sectoral responsibilities in much the same way as units and direct-orates operate within Directorate General IV of the European Commission.

The DGFT will lead enforcement of the Act. The OFT will lead investigations and dawn raids as well as acting as the postbox for notifications and complaints under the Act.

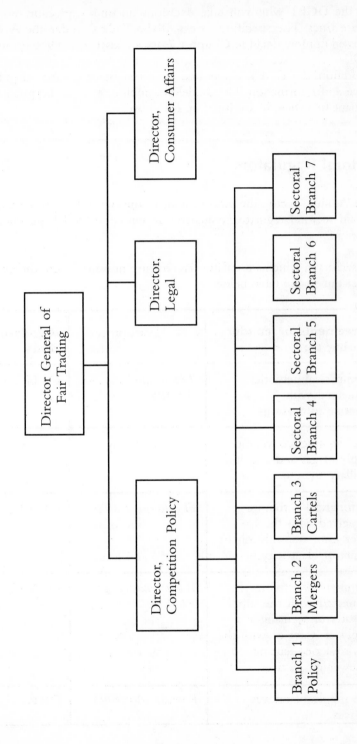

It is the DGFT who will take decisions under the prohibitions and impose fines. The specific powers of the DGFT under the Act are discussed in more detail in **Chapter 7:** PROCEDURE AND ENFORCEMENT.

In addition, the DGFT is required by *section 52* of the Act to publish advice and information. The guidelines published (or to be published) pursuant to *section 52* are listed at **1.6** above.

Sectoral Regulators [2.4]

In the utilities sector, the enforcement of the Act is carried out by the relevant sectoral regulator, concurrently with the DGFT, pursuant to *section 54*.

The sectors in which a regulator has concurrent powers with the DGFT are set out in the table below.

Agreements or conduct relating to:	Statute	Regulatory Body
Commercial activities connected with telecommunications.	*Telecommunications Act 1984*	OFTEL
The shipping, conveyance or supply of gas and activities ancillary thereto.	*Gas Act 1986*	OFGAS[1]
Commercial activities connected with the generation, transmission or supply of electricity.	*Electricity Act 1989*	OFFER[1]
Commercial activities connected with the supply of water or securing a supply of water or with the provision or securing of sewerage services.	*Water Industry Act 1991*	OFWAT
The supply of railway services.	*Railways Act 1993*	ORR

Commercial activities connected with the generation, transmission or supply of electricity in Northern Ireland.	*Electricity (Northern Ireland) Order 1992*	OFREG
The conveyance, storage or supply of gas in Northern Ireland.	*Gas (Northern Ireland) Order 1996*	OFREG

[1] The functions of OFGAS and OFFER are now merged into a new regulator OFGEM (the Office for Gas and Electricity Markets) and this change will be formalised in the forthcoming Utilities Bill.

In relation to its sector, each regulator has all the powers of the DGFT to apply and enforce the Act, except that only the DGFT has the power to issue guidance on penalties and to make and amend procedural rules.

The aim of concurrency is to achieve a seamless application of the Act to all sectors. In other words, the Act should be applied in the same way in, say, the electricity industry as it is in any other industry.

The topic of concurrency was the subject of protracted debate in Parliament, resulting in some important amendments to the Act. The OFT was opposed to the concept and the regulated industries lobbied hard to make changes to address their concerns about the way the system would work. Debate centred on two key issues:

○ the relationship between regulatory powers and duties and *Competition Act* powers and duties; and
○ concurrency in practice – joint working between the DGFT and the regulators.

Regulation Versus Competition [2.5]

Sectoral regulators will retain their powers and duties under the relevant sectoral legislation. In general, regulators are under a duty to:

○ ensure there is sufficient provision of the regulated goods or service throughout the UK;
○ promote or facilitate competition; and

○ protect the interests of customers and consumers.

The duty to promote or facilitate competition, although important, is one of a number of duties to be balanced with other duties under each sectoral statute.

Schedule 10 of the Act, which sets out a number of amendments to utility statutes, effectively disapplies the regulator's statutory duties when that regulator is exercising concurrent functions under the Act.

In some circumstances, a particular agreement or course of conduct may fall both within the regulator's specific legislation as well as within the prohibitions contained in the Act. For example, many regulated companies operate under licences which prevent them from showing undue preference to, or undue discrimination against, any class of persons. Such discriminatory behaviour might, for example, also infringe the prohibition in Chapter II of the Act, where the regulated company is in a dominant position.

In this case, *Schedule 10* specifically amends the relevant sector's specific legislation, which would otherwise have required a regulator to enforce a licence condition, to the effect that where he considers it more effective or more efficient to use his powers under the Act, then his duty to take licence enforcement action no longer applies.

It is also open to the regulator to switch from one regime to the other during an investigation, if he considers it appropriate to do so. In these circumstances, the relevant parties will be informed. This is important because the rights and remedies under the sector's specific legislation differ from those available under the Act. For example, a decision of a regulator under the Act may be appealed in law or in fact to the Competition Commission Appeal Tribunals. However, a decision under the sector specific legislation may only be challenged by means of a judicial review, which is likely to be a more difficult hurdle. Attempts to review decisions of regulators in the past have, for the most part, failed.

In *R v Director General of Telecommunications ex parte Cellcom Ltd & Others (QBD, 26 November 1998, Lightman J)*, a number of mobile operators challenged the DGFT *inter alia* for failure to act in accordance with his duty to maintain effective competition under its sectoral statute. The court rejected the application, holding that (at para 27):

> 'the Court may interfere with a decision if satisfied that the
> director has made a relevant mistake of fact or law. But a
> mistake is not established by showing that on the material

before the director the Court would reach a different conclusion.
The resolution of disputed questions of fact is for the decision
maker and the Court can only interfere if his decision is
perverse e.g. if his reasoning is logically unsound . . .'.

Another crucial difference alluded to above is that many situations of
overlap will concern the Chapter II Prohibition. This only applies to
companies in a dominant position, whereas the licence conditions under
the sector's specific legislation apply to a regulated company whether
or not it is dominant within the meaning of Chapter II.

Joint Working [2.6]

Under the *Fair Trading Act 1973*, concurrency already exists. Under
this regime, the DGFT and the relevant sectoral regulator are required
to consult when either intends to take any action under that Act and
would be prevented from doing so if the other were already taking
similar action (the so called 'first past the post' system).

Amendments made by *Schedule 10* to the sectoral statutes mean that this
system does not apply in relation to the exercise of functions under the
Act. The 'first past the post' system was rejected as being too rigid, as it
precludes joint working between regulators and also the transfer of cases.

A guideline on concurrent application to regulated industries sets out
the basis upon which joint working is envisaged to work in practice. In
relation to case handling, the guideline states that an agreement or
conduct which falls within the industry sector of a regulator will be
dealt with by that regulator (although in some cases the DGFT will
deal with such a case). The general principle will be that a case would
be dealt with by whichever of the DGFT or the relevant regulator is
better placed to do so.

Relevant factors will include the sectoral knowledge of the regulator;
previous contacts with the parties; and recent relevant experience.

The guideline, therefore, offers little practical guidance as to the basic
question, 'Who is my regulator?'. It is thought that in practice the
industry regulator will generally run cases within its sector.

The authority dealing with a case will handle all investigation, decision
making and enforcement but will consult with other regulators as
appropriate and the case may be transferred at any stage.

The DGFT acts as a postbox for all notifications, although complaints may be made either to the DGFT or direct to the relevant regulator (see further **Chapter 7:** PROCEDURE). Applications for interim measures may also be made either to the regulator or to the DGFT.

It is generally recognised that the guideline on concurrent application of the Act does not give business a transparent or detailed guide as to the procedures which will be followed by the DGFT and the regulators.

It is intended that additional guidelines as to the application of the Act to the telecommunications sector, the energy sector, the water and sewerage sector and the railways sector will be issued. These guidelines may also shed further light on the way concurrency will work in general.

Making Concurrency Work [2.7]

A Concurrency Working Party has been established in order to facilitate joint working and promote consistency in decision making. This is an informal body meeting monthly, on which each regulator is represented. It is chaired by a representative of the OFT. The Concurrency Working Party is intended to be a forum for discussion of general principles, as well as allocation of particular cases and sharing of information.

It is anticipated that the onus of making concurrency work will fall on the OFT. This may prove to be a heavy burden to discharge, given that experience to date suggests that sectoral regulators can take personal and highly publicised positions in relation to their sectors. There is also the alarming prospect that different regulators might, as a matter of policy, use their powers under the Act to a greater or lesser extent. For example, some regulators might prefer always to proceed by means of licence conditions under the sectoral statute.

Concern about the prospect of joint working prompted the Government to amend the Act at a late stage of committee in the Commons. This amendment to *section 54* gives the Secretary of State the power to make regulations for the purpose of co-ordinating the exercise of concurrent powers and the procedures to be followed. The Department of Trade and Industry has issued a consultation paper and draft regulations in October 1999. If adopted, these may necessitate substantial revision of the guideline on *Concurrent Application to Regulated Industries*.

Not least amongst the problems of joint working is the issue of disclosure of information. This is discussed in more detail in **Chapter 7:** PROCEDURE.

Information can be shared between regulators 'for the purpose of facilitating the performance of any relevant functions of a designated person [i.e. a regulator]' *(section 55(2))*. Arguably, the DGFT could not refer documents to a regulator to determine whether that regulator has jurisdiction. Alternatively, if a document concerns two regulated sectors, would the document need to be amended to delete information not relevant to the sectoral regulator in question? Also discussion of specific cases within the Concurrency Working Party may be inhibited.

Competition Commission [2.8]

The Act created a new body with effect from 1 April 1999, to be known as the Competition Commission. The Monopolies and Mergers Commission (MMC) has been dissolved and its functions transferred to the Competition Commission. Like the MMC, the Competition Commission will act as an independent tribunal but will have no power to initiate enquiries itself.

The diagram below summarises the membership of the Competition Commission.

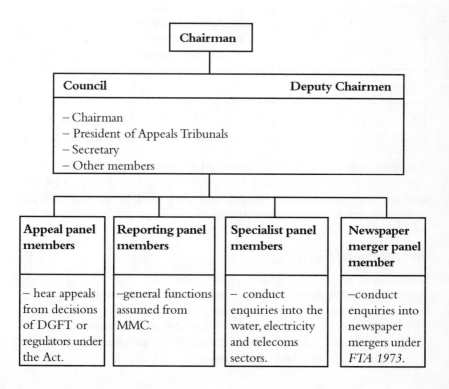

The Chairman is appointed by the Secretary of State from among the reporting panel membership. He may have a number of Deputy Chairmen, also drawn from the Reporting panel. The first Chairman and Deputy Chairman and Secretary are the holders of comparable positions in the MMC.

The Council manages the Competition Commission which actually carries out its functions through groups comprising at least three members.

The Appeals Tribunal is headed by a President appointed by the Secretary of State. The first President is Christopher Bellamy QC. Individual appeal tribunals will be appointed by the President and will comprise the President, or another chairman, and two other appeal panel members. The procedure for appeal is set out in **Chapter 7: PROCEDURE AND ENFORCEMENT.**

The Reporting panel members will initially comprise the existing membership of the MMC. Their functions will include:

Statute	Investigation
Fair Trading Act 1973	Monopoly references Merger references General references Restrictive labour practices reference
Competition Act 1980	Public Sector references
Broadcasting Act 1990	Channel 3 networking references

Specialist panel members will initially be those members of the MMC appointed under the relevant utility statutes in the water, electricity and telecommunications sectors and they will be responsible for references made under these statutes.

Secretary of State   [2.9]

The functions of the Secretary of State under the Act include:

○ appointment of members of Competition Commission;
○ making of orders under *section 50* – exclusions for vertical agreements and land agreements;

- approval of rules of DGFT (*section 52*);
- making of regulations in relation to concurrency (*section 54*);
- making of orders in connection with the dissolution of the MMC (*section 45*);
- approval of the DGFT's guidance in relation to penalties (*section 38*);
- amending the scope of *Schedules 1, 3* and *4* – exclusions from the prohibitions;
- making block exemption orders (*section 6*) and *section 11* exemption orders; and
- making regulations in relation to procedures in notification (*section 12*).

The Courts [2.10]

The role of the courts is twofold. First, a decision of the appeal tribunal of the Competition Commission is appealable to the Court of Appeal either on a point of law or as to the amount of a penalty. There is also the possibility of judicial review.

Secondly, a third party may bring a civil action in the UK courts against an undertaking for breach of the Chapter I or Chapter II Prohibitions.

The role of the courts is discussed further in **Chapter 7:** PROCEDURE AND ENFORCEMENT.

3 – Existing Legislation

Introduction [3.1]

The Act repeals much of the existing UK competition legislation. This chapter explains which legislation will go, which will stay and what amendments will be made to make the existing legislation work alongside the Act.

The table below summarises the relevant provisions of the Act.

Section No.	Description of Section
1	Repeals
17	Enactments replaced
66–69 (incl.)	Monopolies
70	Contracts as to patented products etc.
Sch 2	Exclusions: Other Competition Scrutiny
Sch 10	Utilities: Minor and consequential amendments
Sch 12	Minor and consequential amendments
Sch 13	Transitional provisions and savings
Sch 14	Repeals and revocations

Repeals [3.2]

With effect from 1 March 2000, the Act repeals the following legislation:

○ *Restrictive Trade Practices Act 1976 (RTPA 1976)*;

- O   *Restrictive Practices Court Act 1976*;
- O   *Restrictive Trade Practices Act 1977*;
- O   *Resale Prices Act 1976 (RPA)*; and
- O   most of the *Competition Act 1980*.

Limited parts of the *Fair Trading Act 1973 (FTA)* are repealed but, notably, the provisions relating to mergers and scale and complex monopolies are retained and investigation powers are enhanced (see further **3.1** and **3.1** below).

Minor amendments are also made to the *Patents Act 1977* and the *Broadcasting Act 1990*.

Restrictive Trade Practices Act 1976   [3.3]

The *Restrictive Trade Practices Act 1976 (RTPA)* will continue to apply in a limited form until it is repealed on 1 March 2000. The way in which it applies will depend on whether the agreement in question was made before or after the enactment date of the Act (9 November 1998).

Agreements made Prior to 9 November 1998   [3.4]

Agreements made before 9 November 1998, which are notifiable under the *RTPA 1976*, should have been furnished to the DGFT as required by that Act. The normal time limit for notification is three months from the date of the making of the agreement. Similarly, variations to such an agreement, even if made after 9 November 1998, should be notified to the OFT in accordance with *sections 24* and *27* of the *RTPA 1976*.

The principal consequence of failing to notify a notifiable agreement or variation is that the restrictions in that agreement or variation, as the case may be, will be void pursuant to *section 35* of the *RTPA 1976*. The passing of the *Competition Act 1998* will not 'cure' this voidness and the infringing restrictions will continue to be void and unenforceable.

Agreements made in the Interim Period   [3.5]

The *RTPA 1976* applies in a more limited form to agreements made in the interim period from 9 November 1998 to 29 February 2000 (the day before the Act will come fully in to force) inclusive. The only agreements which remain notifiable under the *RTPA 1976* are registerable agreements in which one of the relevant restrictions or information provisions relates to price (i.e. price fixing agreements within the meaning of *section 27(3)* of the *RTPA 1976*). All other agreements, and variations to agreements made in the interim period, will be non-notifiable under the *RTPA 1976*.

This concession is likely to mean that the vast majority of commercial agreements entered into in the interim period will not be notifiable. However, the DGFT has been at pains to stress that this concession does not represent a moratorium on enforcement of the competition rules. The DGFT retains a discretion pursuant to *section 36* of the *RTPA 1976* to call in for investigation certain anti-competitive agreements. He also has a discretion to institute proceedings before the Restrictive Practices Court at any time up to 1 March 2000.

Special rules apply to the very few agreements (or variations) which are made in the final three months before 1 March 2000. Parties to such agreements will not have to notify them to the OFT. If the agreements are not notified, then the normal sanctions of voidness and potential third party liability will not arise. However, if the parties do notify the agreements before 1 March 2000, then the agreements will be eligible for a one-year transitional period.

The last possible day on which agreements or variations can be notified under the *RTPA 1976* will be 29 February 2000.

Restrictive Practices Court [3.6]

During the interim period, Orders of the Restrictive Practices Court will remain in force and breach of such Orders will be a contempt of court. However, from 1 March 2000, most Orders of the Restrictive Practices Court will cease to have effect. This includes, in particular, restraining Orders made under *section 35* of the *RTPA 1976*. The DGFT's guidelines on transitional arrangements state that undertakings given in lieu of orders also lapse.

It is important to note that the repeal of the *RTPA 1976* will not effect either:

○ liability for contempt of court in respect of breach of Orders committed before 1 March 2000; or

○ liability in actions for breach of statutory duty brought by third parties who have suffered loss as a result of a breach committed before 1 March 2000.

The right to bring civil proceedings under *RTPA 1976* is expressly preserved (*Schedule 13, para 13*).

Proceedings before the Restrictive Practices Court may be instituted at any time before 1 March 2000. The detailed provisions governing proceedings which have not been determined as at 1 March 2000 are set out in *Schedule 13, para 15*.

Applications under *RTPA 1976, section 3* for interim orders of the court will continue after 1 March 2000 and the whole of the machinery of *RTPA 1976* is preserved for this purpose. The same is true for applications under *RTPA 1976, section 26* (rectifications) made before 1 March 2000.

The position in respect of other 'continuing proceedings' is as follows: enforcement proccedings under *sections 2(2), 35(3), 37(1), 40(1)* and *Schedule 4, para 5* of *RTPA 1976* cease on 1 March 2000 if not determined at that date. Other proceedings under *RTPA 1976*, e.g. *section 4* (variations of the court's decision) continue.

Public Register [3.7]

The public register of restrictive trading agreements will continue to be maintained after 1 March 2000. However, the DGFT will only add certain agreements to it, i.e:

○ agreements which have been notified but not put on the register before 1 March 2000;
○ agreements subject to continuing proceedings determined after 1 March 2000; and
○ agreements in relation to which a court gives directions to the DGFT after 1 March 2000 as to the application of the *RTPA 1976* prior to its repeal.

The reason for maintaining the register is to enable parties to discover the effect of the *RTPA 1976* on an agreement. This may be important since, for example, a direction under *section 21(2)* of the *RTPA 1976* excludes an agreement from the application of the Chapter I Prohibition (see **Chapter 4:** THE CHAPTER I PROHIBITION).

Therefore, for an initial period after 1 March 2000, the register will remain accessible to the general public at Field House, Bream's Buildings. However, at some stage in the future, it is likely that regulations reducing access will be made.

Winding Down [3.8]

Application of RTPA 1976		
Agreements	Enactment date (9 November 1998)	Starting date (1 March 2000)
Made prior to the enactment date. (9 November 1998)	*RTPA 1976* continues to operate as before, until its repeal (variations remain notifiable).	*RTPA 1976* repealed on the starting date, but continuation of: −pre-repeal voidness; −pre-repeal rights for breach of statutory duty; −certain undetermined Restricted Practices Court applications; −*RTPA 1976* register (but only added to or varied in limited circumstances).
Made in the interim period. (9 November 1998 to 1 March 2000)	*RTPA 1976* applies but: − all agreements except price-fixing non-notifiable; − The DGFT's duty to refer to Restrictive Practices Court replaced by discretion. − *s21(2)* directions not possible.	
Made after the starting date (1 March 2000)		*RTPA 1976* repealed.

Resale Prices Act 1976 [3.9]

The winding down of the *RPA 1976* will follow a similar pattern to that for the *RTPA 1976*.

The right to bring civil proceedings is expressly reserved (*Schedule 13, para 13*). Generally, proceedings under the *RPA 1976* which are not determined by 1 March 2000 will continue although enforcement proceedings under *s25(2)* cease on 1 March 2000 (*Schedule 13, para 8*).

Competition Act 1980 [3.10]

The bulk of the *Competition Act (CA) 1980* will be repealed by the Act, including *sections 2–10* which relate to the investigation of anti-competitive practices by single undertakings. These powers have been little used in recent years.

Fair Trading Act 1973 [3.11]

The two main areas of competition law covered by the *FTA 1973* are the investigation of mergers and monopolies. The provisions relating to mergers are not materially affected by the Act, whilst the monopoly powers are substantially retained but are likely to be used in future largely as a 'fall-back' power.

Monopoly Provisions [3.12]

The *FTA 1973* gives the Secretary of State (and often the DGFT) the power to refer monopolies to the Competition Commission for investigation. Two types of monopoly situations are defined in the *FTA 1973* – complex monopolies and scale monopolies. A scale monopoly is where 25% or more of all the goods or services of a particular type which are supplied in the UK, or a part of it, are supplied or purchased by one company. A complex monopoly exists where 25% or more of all the goods and services of a particular type which are supplied in the UK, or a part of it, are supplied by or to two or more companies who so conduct their respective affairs as in any way to prevent, restrict or distort competition.

The Act retains both provisions allowing the Competition Commission to investigate complex and scale monopolies. There was a considerable amount of debate during the passage of the Competition Bill as to why it was necessary to retain these provisions since the Chapter II Prohibition covers abuse of a dominant position and there are no similar provisions under EU law.

During the Committee stage, Lord Simon of Highbury explained the Government's reasons for keeping these provisions as follows.

> 'This is a new bill and at this stage we believe that there is a very strong case for retaining the Fair Trading Act monopoly provisions to enable investigations to be conducted into markets in cases where competition issues arise from the structure of the market rather than from anti-competitive agreements or specific abuses by a dominant company. The current regime under the Fair Trading Act enables wide-ranging and impartial investigation of such as situations by the MMC. It also provides scope for a wide range of remedies . . . I believe it is widely recognised that the complex monopoly provisions fill a gap between the two prohibitions. The Chapter I prohibition will deal very effectively with anti-competitive agreements and the Chapter II prohibition with abuses by a single dominant company. But the complex monopoly provisions will continue to be a more effective tool for dealing with anti-competitive parallel behaviour by companies where there is no agreement between them.'
>
> (Lords 13.11.97, col 300)

Although it has been generally accepted that the retention of the complex monopoly provisions is a good thing to give the competition authorities flexibility in investigating whole industries, there has been considerable debate regarding the reasons for retaining the scale monopoly provisions. It has been argued that this betrays a belief that the Chapter II Prohibition will not be effective. However, the Government has said that these provisions will only be used:

> 'in circumstances where there has already been proven abuse under the prohibition and where the DGFT believes that there is a real prospect of future abuses by the same firm'.
>
> (Lords 13.11.97, col 300 (Lord Simon))

The *FTA 1973* provisions will in any case not be used in parallel with the prohibitions and will in general be used as reserve powers to deal with situations where the problem is market structure rather than abuse or where divestment orders may be the only effective means of preventing further abuses.

Powers of Inquiry and Investigation [3.13]

Section 66 of the Act gives the DGFT (and the sectoral regulators) new powers to obtain information for the purpose of deciding whether to make a monopoly reference. These powers enable the DGFT to require the production of documents, to enter premises and to take copies of documents. The powers are backed by criminal sanctions in *section 67* and the Act represents a substantial strengthening of information gathering powers under *FTA 1973*.

Services Relating to the Use of Land [3.14]

Section 68 of the Act provides for the Secretary of State by order to modify the definition of supply of services under FTA 1973. This enables him to extend the scope of what can be investigated under FTA 1973 and is designed to address past difficulties in applying that Act to situations involving the use of land.

Patents Act 1977 [3.15]

Section 70 of the *Competition Act 1998*, repeals *sections 44* and *45* of the *Patents Act 1977*. These sections provide broadly that certain terms of a contract for the supply of a patented product or a licence to use a patented invention are void and render the licensed patent unenforceable, so long as the offending contract continues. These provisions are no longer appropriate in light of the new rules and by virtue of *section 70* will cease to have effect.

Other Competition Scrutiny [3.16]

Schedule 2 of the Act provides for certain matters, that are subject to seperate competition scrutiny, to be excluded from the Chapter I Prohibition.

These include the:

O   *Financial Services Act 1986*;
O   *Companies Act 1989*;
O   *Broadcasting Act 1990*; and
O   *Environment Act 1995*.

See further **4.36** below.

4 – The Chapter I Prohibition

Introduction [4.1]

This chapter deals with the Chapter I Prohibition on restrictive agreements and concerted practices. The Chapter I Prohibition effectively replaces the *Restrictive Trade Practices Act 1976* and *Resale Prices Act 1976*, as described at **1.2** above *et seq*. However, there is little point in a detailed comparison between the 'old' and the 'new' since they are so totally different in approach.

Instead, this chapter explains the:

O key elements of the Chapter I Prohibition;
O effects of the Prohibition;
O specific exclusions from the Chapter I Prohibition (of which there are many);
O concept of exemption under the Act;
O transitional provisions under which the Chapter I Prohibition is phased in; and
O application of the Prohibition to specific types of agreements (summarised in the form of checklists).

The Chapter I Prohibition is closely based on Article 81 and most of the key words and phrases are identical between the two provisions. Those familiar with Article 81 will recognise these concepts. Departures from the EU precedent are highlighted where appropriate in the text.

This chapter features the provisions in the Act summarised in the table below.

Section No.	Description of Section
2	The Chapter I Prohibition
3	Excluded agreements
4	Individual exemption
5	Cancellation etc. of individual exemption
6	Block exemption
7	Block exemption: opposition
8	Block exemption: procedure
9	The criteria for individual and block exemption
10	Parallel exemption
11	Exemption for certain other agreements
50	Special treatment for vertical and land agreements
Sch 1	Exclusions: mergers and concentrations
Sch 2	Exclusions: other competition scrutiny
Sch 3	General exclusions
Sch 4	Professional rules
Sch 13, paras 1–7 & 35	Transitional provisions

The Prohibition [4.2]

The Chapter I Prohibition is set out in *section 2* of the Act, the full text of which is reproduced below.

'**2**.–(1) Subject to section 3, agreements between undertakings, decisions by association of undertakings or concerted practices which –

    (a)   may affect trade within the United Kingdom, and

    (b)   have as their object or effect the prevention, restriction or distortion of competition within the United Kingdom,

are prohibited unless they are exempt in accordance with the provisions of this Part.

(2) Subsection (1) applies, in particular, to agreements, decisions or practices which –

    (a)   directly or indirectly fix purchase or selling prices or any other trading conditions;

    (b)   limit or control production, markets, technical development or investment;

    (c)   share markets or sources of supply;

    (d)   apply dissimilar conditions to equivalent transactions with other trading parties, thereby placing them at a competitive disadvantage;

    (e)   make the conclusion of contracts subject to acceptance by the other parties of supplementary obligations which, by their nature or according to commercial usage, have no connection with the subject of such contracts.

(3) Subsection (1) apples only if the agreement, decision or practice, is, or is intended to be, implemented in the United Kingdom.

(4) Any agreement or decision which is prohibited by subsection (1) is void.

(5) A provision of this Part which is expressed to apply to or in relation to, an agreement is to be read as applying equally to, or in relation to, a decision by an association of undertaking or a concerted practice (but with any necessary modifications).

(6) Subsection (5) does not apply where the context otherwise requires.

(7) In this section "the United Kingdom" means, in relation to an agreement with operates or is intended to operate only in a part of the United Kingdom, that part.

(8) The prohibition imposed by subsection (1) is referred to in this Act as "the Chapter I prohibition".'

Purpose [4.3]

The purpose of the Chapter I Prohibition is to ensure that undertakings determine their market behaviour independently. It catches anti-competitive transactions or practices involving two or more businesses. It is not important to identify particular forms of transaction in applying the prohibition. The important distinction is between arrangements involving two or more undertakings which are caught and unilateral conduct which is not.

Key Terms [4.4]

Most of the key terms used in *section 2* are not defined in the Act itself. The mechanism of the *section 60* filter (see **1.8** above *et seq.*) results in these terms being interpreted in a manner which is consistent with Article 81.

Agreements, Decisions and Concerted Practices [4.5]

It is not strictly necessary to distinguish between an agreement, a decision or a concerted practice. In any event, the three concepts are very widely interpreted and overlap. The OFT will be interested in any arrangement that results in an appreciable restriction on competition, whatever its form.

'Agreements' [4.6]

The concept of 'agreement' is extraordinarily wide and embraces almost any form of consensus between two or more parties. Whether it is called an agreement or not is immaterial as to whether it falls within the concept of an 'agreement' for the purposes of the Chapter I Prohibition.

The Chapter I Prohibition potentially catches both *horizontal agreements* i.e. those made between competitors and *vertical agreements* i.e. those made between undertakings at different levels of the supply chain such as a manufacturer and distributor or a retailer and end user.

The concept of an agreement includes, but is not confined to, legally binding contracts. It also extends to 'gentlemen's agreements', oral agreements, and other informal understandings between undertakings, such as:

- ○ arrangements which are made by exchange of telephone calls or correspondence – it is not necessary for the parties to have met in person;
- ○ agreements taking the form of a series of meetings or correspondence;
- ○ agreements entered into unwillingly – e.g. where an undertaking participates in a cartel as a result of commercial pressure;
- ○ standard terms and conditions of sale (e.g. those applied by a manufacturer to sales to its distributors – together with other elements of the continuing commercial relations between the parties – may in some circumstances be regarded as an agreement;
- ○ intellectual property licences, including assignments;
- ○ arguments relating to land – transfers, leases and licences in relation to interests in land are also agreements for the purposes of *section 2*, however, most such arguments benefit from an exclusion from *section 2*;
- ○ trade association documents – both the constitution of trade associations and their recommendations may be agreements falling within *section 2*.

'Undertakings' [4.7]

The concept of an 'undertaking' is not a familiar one in UK law and is another term borrowed from EU law. The concept is very wide and includes any natural or legal person capable of carrying on commercial or economic activities relating to goods or services, irrespective of its legal status. It includes companies, firms, businesses, partnerships and individuals operating as sole traders, sporting bodies, professional bodies, agricultural co-operatives, non-profit making organisations and in some cases public bodies. A public body, even if operating under direct supervision of government, may be an undertaking provided it carries some form of economic or commercial activity.

Corporate Groups [4.8]

Members of the same corporate group will generally be treated as being a single undertaking for the purposes of *section 2* and so an agreement between them will not be caught. The approach taken under Article 81 is likely to be followed. Article 81 does not apply to agreements or concerted practices between undertakings belonging to the same group in the form of parent company and subsidiary, if the undertakings form an economic unit within which the subsidiary does not have real autonomy in determining its line of conduct on the market and if the agreements have the aim of establishing an internal distribution of tasks between the undertakings.

If a parent wholly owns a subsidiary and appoints its board, then it is almost certainly a single economic entity as the parent will inevitably direct the subsidiary's commercial behaviour. A parent need not own all the shares in a subsidiary to exercise control, 51% typically suffices. A lower shareholding may also result in a single entity where the other shareholdings are widely held, provided that in practice the subsidiary has no real freedom to determine its own conduct in the market, either strategically or on a day-to-day basis.

Essentially, whether or not undertakings form a single economic entity will depend on the facts of each case.

'Decisions by Associations of Undertakings' [4.9]

There are two parts to this concept. Firstly the meaning of a 'decision' and secondly the meaning of an 'association of undertakings'. Both limbs need to be satisfied to come within the ambit of the Chapter I Prohibition.

Decision [4.10]

A decision can be binding or non-binding as long as it reflects the association's desire to co-ordinate its members' conduct in accordance with its statutes. It is mostly likely to be a resolution of the management committee of an association, or of the full membership in general meeting, the effect of which is to limit the commercial freedom of the members.

The concept also extends to the rules of an association e.g. a rule preventing members from soliciting business from customers of another member, and recommendations of an association e.g. as to prices or terms and conditions of sale.

Associations of Undertakings [4.11]

An association of undertakings is not limited to any particular type of association, but most commonly will be a trade association. However, an association may also be an agricultural co-operative, an association without legal personality, a non-profit making organisation and a statutory body entrusted with certain public functions.

'Concerted Practices' [4.12]

A concerted practice is a form of informal co-operation or collusion between undertakings which does not have all the characteristics of an agreement. Therefore, it is a lesser form of co-operation than an agreement, although the concepts overlap.

A concerted practice can exist where the parties have not even spelled out the terms of an agreement but simply where each infers commitment from the other. There must be some co-ordination between undertakings which replaces the risks of competition with a practical form of co-operation.

The OFT's Guideline on *The Chapter I Prohibition* states that two main elements need to be established to prove a concerted practice:

'O the existence of positive contacts between the parties; and
O the contact has the object or effect of changing the market behaviour of the undertakings in a way which may not be dictated by market forces.'

Parallel conduct on its own will not in principle constitute a concerted practice. For example, simultaneous price rises by two competitors might have been made independently because of a rise in raw material costs. The DGFT recognises that in markets with few players, similar behaviour by undertakings may occur without any type of collusion.

The following are factors which the DGFT lists as relevant in establishing whether a concerted practice exists in a particular market:

'O whether the parties knowingly enter into practical co-operation;
O whether behaviour in the market is influenced as a result of direct or indirect contact between undertakings;
O whether parallel behaviour is as a result of contact between undertakings which leads to conditions of competition which do not correspond to normal conditions of the market;
O the structure of the relevant market and the nature of the product involved;

○ the number of undertakings in the market, and where there are only a few undertakings, whether they have similar cost structures and outputs.'

'May affect trade within the United Kingdom'   [4.13]

This form of wording, as with other areas of the Act, is borrowed from Article 81 under which an agreement must have an effect on trade between Member States. The Act is only concerned with effects in the UK rather than inter-state trade. Once jurisdiction is reduced to a single Member State in this way, competition becomes a subject of trade within that State so that any restriction on competition will always amount to an effect on trade as well.

Arguably this test is therefore redundant. However, the test may be useful insofar as it introduces the requirement that trade must be affected. The concept of trade is wide, and covers all economic activity involving the supply of goods and services, including the financial sector and public utilities.

Implementation in the UK   [4.14]

Section 2(3) of the Act provides an important limitation on the territorial scope of the Chapter I Prohibition. The agreement must be implemented, or intended to be implemented, in the UK.

The wording mirrors the decision of the European Court of Justice in the *Woodpulp* case [*1988*] *5193* whereby an agreement would only be caught by Article 81(1) if it were implemented or intended to be implemented in the European Community.

The fundamental test under the Act therefore falls short of the so-called 'effects doctrine', as practised, for example, in the USA. Under that doctrine, the US authorities have claimed jurisdiction in relation to economic conduct outside the USA but which has produced substantial and foreseeable effects within the USA. In contrast, the extra-territorial reach of the Act could catch agreements made outside the UK between non-UK undertakings but only if implemented or intended to be implemented, in the UK.

'Part of the United Kingdom' [4.15]

Section 2(7) states that 'the United Kingdom' means, in relation to an agreement which operates or is intended to operate only in part of the UK, only that part. There is no requirement that the relevant part of the UK be a substantial part.

The Prohibition is clearly intended to apply to agreements which may operate only within local markets in the UK. There is therefore no need to show an effect on the movement of trade between different parts of the UK.

'Object or Effect' [4.16]

The Chapter I Prohibition applies where the object or effect of the agreement, decision or concerted practice is to prevent, restrict or distort competition in the United Kingdom.

The words object or effect are read disjunctively. Where the object is so blatantly anti-competitive the effect of the agreement does not need to be considered. Therefore, it is not necessary to show that an agreement has been put into practice or that it has achieved its anti-competitive objects. The types of agreement that are likely to have such a clear object include price-fixing and market sharing.

Where there is no clear anti-competitive object, the OFT will need to analyse the economic effect of the agreement, decision or concerted practice to see whether it restricts competition. To do this, the OFT will consider the operation of the agreement, decision or concerted practice in its market and economic context. It will consider the structure of competition in that market (and possibly upstream or downstream markets) and the behaviour of competitors.

Prevent, Restrict or Distort Competition [4.17]

In order for an agreement, decision or concerted practice to fall under the Chapter I Prohibition, it must prevent, restrict or distort competition within the UK. It does not matter which of the three terms are satisfied. The scope of the prohibition turns on there being an appreciable impact on competition.

Examples of Anti-competitive Agreements [4.18]

Given the need to assess the impact of a given agreement in its full market context, it is not possible to draw up a definitive list of types of agreement which are prohibited.

Section 2(2) sets out a non-exhaustive list of types of agreements, decisions or practices which would be caught by *section 2(1)* as long as they appreciably restrict competition (see **4.2** above). The list mirrors verbatim the examples set out in Article 81(1). It is important to recognise that the Chapter I Prohibition could be applied to agreements not specifically mentioned on this list.

Price Fixing [4.19]

Price fixing can be found in both horizontal and vertical agreements (for a definition of these see **4.6** above). Agreements which explicitly and directly fix the price or the resale price of any product or service are highly likely to infringe the Chapter I Prohibition.

The guidelines on the Chapter I Prohibition elaborate on other ways in which the OFT considers prices might be fixed in breach of it:

○ resale prices;
○ setting a minimum price which the goods are not to be sold below;
○ setting the range of discounts or allowances to be granted and the percentage by which prices can be increased; or
○ controlling discounts or rebates to be charged or other commercial terms such as credit terms.

Limiting or Controlling Production [4.20]

An agreement between competitors to restrict production is also likely to have a detrimental effect on competition.

The agreement may relate to production levels or quotas, specialisation in certain products or ranges, co-ordination to address structural over-capacity or future investment policy.

Sharing Markets [4.21]

If competitors agree to share their market, either by carving up the territory, sharing out customers by size or type or in some other way, the agreement will be likely to infringe the Chapter I Prohibition. A market sharing arrangement may be employed instead of, or as well as, a price fixing cartel.

'Specialisation' or research and development arrangements between competitors in which market sharing is a consequence of the agreement but not its principle objective, may be legitimate. Such an agreement is caught by the Chapter I Prohibition where there is an appreciable effect on competition. However, there may be the possibility of an exemption.

Collusive Tendering (bid-rigging) [4.22]

Tendering procedures are not likely to be caught by the Prohibition provided that prospective suppliers prepare and submit tenders or bids independently. Any collusion on bids will be likely to be a serious infringement of the Chapter I Prohibition.

Information Sharing [4.23]

As a general rule, the wider information is made publicly available, the more effective competition is likely to be. Indeed, information exchange for the purpose of compiling statistics on an industry or benchmarking can be pro-competitive. However, some exchanges of information may lead to price co-ordination or other co-operation between competitors, thus eliminating or blunting competition which would otherwise have taken place between them. This is particularly so when the information concerns prices.

Appreciable Effect [4.24]

The Chapter I Prohibition will apply only where an agreement has an appreciable effect on competition. This is a key feature of the Act, yet there is no mention in the Act itself of the requirement that an agreement must have, or be capable of having, an 'appreciable effect'. Early drafts of the Competition Bill referred to a 'substantial' effect on competition. However, this wording was dropped so as to promote consistency with the wording of Article 81 which does not expressly refer to an 'appreciable effect'. The requirement of an 'appreciable effect' is therefore imported into the Chapter I Prohibition by the operation of *section 60* (see **1.8** above *et seq.*), since it also forms part of Article 81 according to the case lawof the European Court of Justice.

In response to prolonged debate as to the desirability of expressly including a reference to 'significant' or 'appreciable effect' in the wording of the Act, Lord Simon for the Government stated:

> 'I remain convinced that an express significance test might inadvertently create so high a threshold for action that we could impede the effective tackling of anti-competitive agreements'.

OFT Guidelines [4.25]

The OFT has issued draft guidelines: *The Chapter I Prohibition* which set out the DGFT's views on the meaning of 'appreciable effect'.

Para 2.19 states:

> 'The Director General takes the view that an agreement will generally have no appreciable effect on competition if the parties' combined share of the relevant market does not exceed 25%, although there will be circumstances in which this is not the case'.

Paragraph 2.20 of *The Chapter I Prohibition* guidelines gives examples where the 25% threshold cannot be relied on.

> 'The Director General, will in addition, generally regard any agreement between undertakings which:
>
> O directly or indirectly fixes prices or shares markets; or
> O imposes minimum resale prices; or
> O is one of a network of similar agreements which have a cumulative effect on the market in question.'

As regards other agreements below the 25% guidelines, it is clear that the DGFT is not in general interested in receiving notifications. However, he does not preclude himself from acting in other cases where the market structure is such that in fact an appreciable restriction of competition occurred. An example might be where one party held a 24% share but its competitors were fragmented with none having more than a 5% share.

There are a number of other legal and practical issues which also reduce the value of the DGFT's guidance and in practice businesses may find that the 25% threshold cannot be used as 'a bright line' test for deciding which agreements fall outside the Chapter I Prohibition for lack of an appreciable effect.

Firstly, the guidelines are not formally binding in the courts and, therefore, there is no guarantee that the court will take the same view of the market or the concept of appreciability in a particular case.

Secondly, the courts and the DGFT are, in principle, required by *section 60* to interpret the Chapter I Prohibition consistently with Article 81 (see **1.8** above *et seq.*). For example, they must have regard to statements of the Commission. The most recent guidelines issued by the Commission (*Commission Notice on Agreements of Minor Importance (1997 OJC 372)*) take a different line from that adopted by the DGFT. That Notice determines the question of appreciability on the basis of market share but adds special rules for small and medium-sized enterprises. The Notice states that vertical agreements involving a combined share of 10% of the relevant market will not have an appreciable effect on competition unless they involve price fixing or territorial protection. For horizontal agreements the figure is 5%, provided the agreement does not involve price fixing or market sharing.

Thirdly, practical problems result from the use of market share as the relevant measure. Many companies may find it difficult to define the relevant product and geographic markets in which they operate. It may also be difficult to be confident of market size and shares, since these may vary over time. See the DGFT guideline on market definition for an explanation on how to approach market definition under the new regime.

Consequences of Infringement [4.26]

The main consequences of infringing the Chapter I Prohibition are voidness (*section 2*), the risk of financial penalties (*section 36*) and the risk of third party actions.

Voidness [4.27]

Section 2(4) provides that:'any agreement or decision which is prohibited by (1) is void'. The language of *section 2(4)* is similar to that in Article 81(2). Agreements that infringe the Chapter I Prohibition will be void. This means that the offending restrictions will be unenforceable and so can have immense significance to the parties to infringing agreements.

Although the wording of *section 2(4)* talks of an agreement being void, infact the UK courts will apply the doctrine of severance with the result that only those parts of an agreement which restrict competition within the meaning of the Chapter I Prohibition will be void if they can be severed from the rest of the agreement. This is the way in which the European Court of Justice has interpreted the equivalent provision in Article 81(2) and so by action of *section 60*, the same interpretation will apply to *section 2(4)*.

The English law contract rules on severance are complex. Broadly, the so called 'blue pencil test' for severance means that a UK court should consider whether the contract would be so changed in its character as not to be the sort of contract the parties intended to enter into at all. In other words, severance will not be possible if severing the offending clauses would result in a contract entirely different in scope or intention from what the parties had originally agreed.

In Gibbs Mew v Gemmell [1998] Eu LR 588, the Court of Appeal concluded that an agreement that infringes Article 81(1) is not only void and unenforceable but is also illegal. The result of this conclusion is that a party to an illegal agreement cannot recover money paid under that agreement nor can it claim damages from the other party. The Chapter I Prohibition will presumably be interpreted in the same way.

Financial Penalties [4.28]

Section 36 empowers the DGFT to require an undertaking which is party to an agreement to pay a penalty in respect of infringement of the Chapter I Prohibition by that agreement of up to 10% of its turnover in the United Kingdom. The definition of turnover will be set out in a statutory instrument, but no Order has been made at the time of writing.

Section 38 requires the DGFT to prepare and publish guidance as to the appropriate amount of any penalty. This will set out the steps and considerations to be taken by the DGFT when setting the level of a penalty. In particular, it is expected that this guidance will make clear whether relevant turnover is that in respect of all goods and services or only those affected by the agreement or concerted practice. A consultation draft of this guidance was published in August 1999. See **Chapter 7:** PROCEDURE AND ENFORCEMENT for further details.

The Act contains a limited concession to non price-fixing agreements which fall within the Chapter I Prohibition but which have a minimal impact on competition by reason of the low combined turnover of the parties involved (precise figures have yet to be specified). Such agreements would still be void and may be subject to third party actions, but the undertakings concerned would be immune from the penalties which could otherwise be imposed. The DGFT may however remove this immunity by directions in individual cases.

Third Party Actions for Damages [4.29]

An undertaking in breach of the Chapter I Prohibition is also at risk of a third party, who has suffered loss as a result of the infringement, claiming damages.

Exclusions [4.30]

The Act specifically provides for certain categories of agreements to be excluded from the Chapter I Prohibition. The purpose of these exclusions is to ensure that the Act does not interfere with routine commercial activity but instead efficiently and effectively targets areas of real concern.

Details of the exclusions, and where they are to be found in the Act are set out in the **Appendix** and detailed below.

Section 3 [4.31]

Section 3 provides for certain categories of agreements to be excluded from the Chapter I Prohibition. These are set out in *Schedules 1–4* of the Act.

Power to Vary [4.32]

Section 3 provides for the exclusions in Schedule 1 and some of the exclusions in Schedule 3 to be amended by additional exclusions or by removing any provision by Order. For example, there is a need for this power in respect of the exclusion for agricultural products in Schedule 3, para 9 (see **4.46** below) as there may be a time in the future when the European institutions decide to alter the manner in which agricultural products are treated under EU law. If this were to happen it would be logical to ensure that the changes flow through to the UK exclusion. An amending Order may also provide for the exclusion to cease to apply to a particular agreement.

Clawback [4.33]

The exclusions are generally widely drawn. In order to limit the application of the exclusions, the DGFT has the power to withdraw some of the exclusions in certain circumstances, namely under Sch 1, Sch 3, paras 2 and 9, Sch 4 and the Orders made under s50.

Mergers [4.34]

The purpose of this exclusion is to ensure that a merger agreement is not subject to double scrutiny under both the Act and either the Fair Trading Act 1973 or the EC Merger Regulation. The effect of Schedule 1, para 1, is that in principle an agreement is outside the Chapter I Prohibition (and also the Chapter II Prohibition) to the extent that it results, or if carried out would result, in any two enterprises ceasing to be distinct for the purposes of the Fair Trading Act 1973. It is important to note that a merger is therefore outside the context of the Act if it results in enterprises ceasing to be distinct irrespective of whether that merger actually 'qualified for investigation' within the meaning of the Fair Trading Act 1973.

The exclusion also extends to any provision directly related and necessary to the implementation of the merger, commonly known as ancillary restraints.

The phrase 'directly related and necessary' is taken from EU law and the Commission Notice on Restrictions Ancillary to Concentrations (OJ

1990 No C203/5) provides some guidance as to when a restriction will be considerd ancillary.

The guidelines to be published by the DGFT also give examples of ancillary restraints.

The sorts of provision typically regarded as ancillary include:

○ intellectual property licences;
○ purchase and supply contracts (for goods or services) – these are often necessary for a transition or start-up period to enable the parties to continue to run the relevant business without disruption;
○ non-competition covenants given by the vendor on the sale of a business as a going concern, or by parents to a joint venture (vendor non-competes).

In relation to vendor non-competes, the rule of thumb at EU level is a maximum of five years if goodwill and know-how are being transferred and two years if only goodwill is transferred. This rule is not immutable and the duration permitted in a particular case may be less. In any event the restrictions must be strictly limited to the scope of the undertaking being sold and its geographic extent.

The OFT's Mergers Secretariat will decide the question of whether a restriction will be ancillary in relation to a given merger. The provision in question will be regarded as 'necessary' insofar as the merger:

○ could not be implemented without it; or
○ could be implemented only at:
  ● much greater cost;
  ● over an appreciably longer period; or
  ● with considerably less likelihood of success.

Furthermore the provision must be no more restrictive than is necessary to achieve its objective.

Clawback Power for Mergers [4.35]

Under *Sch 1*, the DGFT may give a direction (without retrospective effect) withdrawing the benefit of a particular exclusion. Before doing so, the DGFT may serve a written notice requiring a party to provide information to assist him in deciding whether or not to give a direction.

The Director may give a direction if:

○ the party fails to provide the information required; or
○ he considers that, if not excluded, an agreement will infringe a prohibition; and
○ that he is not likely to grant an unconditional individual exemption; and
○ the agreement is not a protected agreement (i.e. it has been cleared or referred for investigation).

The DGFT's clawback power may only be applied in certain circumstances. *Sch 1, para 5* specifies the circumstances in which the DGFT may not withdraw the exclusion as being where the:

○ Secretary of State has announced his decision not to refer the merger to the Competition Commission under *s64* of the *FTA 1973*;
○ Secretary of State has made a merger reference under *s64* of the *FTA 1973*.
○ merger results in the acquisition of a controlling interest under *s65* of the *FTA 1973*.
○ Secretary of State has made a reference to the Competition Commission under *s32* of the *Water Industry Act 1991*.

In summary, the clawback power is likely to be rarely exercised. Jurisdiction can be clawed back only in relation to mergers which do not involve the acquisition of a controlling interest (i.e. merely the acquisition of a material influence or control over policy) and only then if not reviewed by the competition authorities under the merger rules.

Other Competition Scrutiny [4.36]

Schedule 2 of the Act allows certain matters that are the subject of separate competition scrutiny to be excluded, thereby avoiding unnecessary overlap with the Chapter I Prohibition (although there is no equivalent exclusion from the Chapter II Prohibition).

The Prohibition will not apply to :

○ agreements constituting bodies regulated under the *Financial Services Act 1986*, nor to certain other arrangements made by such bodies or their members;

○   agreements for the constitution of certain supervisory or qualifying bodies under the *Companies Act 1989* nor to arrangements made by them;

○   certain agreements relating to the broadcasting sector such as network agreements which are regulated under the *Broadcasting Act 1990*;

○   regulations made under the *Environment Act 1995* imposing an obligation on producers to recover and recycle packaging waste.

Planning Obligations [4.37]

Under *Sch 3, para 1*, the Chapter I Prohibition will not apply to agreements to the extent to which they are planning obligations under the *Town and Country Planning Act 1990* or which are made under the *Town and Country Planning (Scotland) Act 1997* or the *Planning (Northern Ireland) Order 1991*.

Section 21(2) Agreements [4.38]

The Chapter I Prohibition will not apply to agreements which benefit from *s21(2)* directions under the *Restrictive Trade Practices Act 1976*. In other words, agreements which have been blessed by the DGFT as not containing restrictions which are significant pursuant to that Act will be granted a permanent exclusion from the Chapter I Prohibition. However, this exclusion will cease to apply if such agreements are materially varied in the future or if the DGFT examines the power of clawback in relation to a particular agreement.

Material Variation [4.39]

Schedule 3, para 2(2) provides that the exclusion shall cease to apply automatically if an agreement is subject to a material variation. This raises the possibility that the exclusion would be lost even if the variation has no material competitive impact. In fact the DGFT has indicated in his guideline on transitional arrangements that a material variation would be one that has a material effect on competition.

Changes such as different delivery dates, modes of transportation, credit terms or methods of payment would generally not be considered material. Converting a joint marketing area into partitioned markets or the addition of a significant competitor or the conversion of recommended resale prices to mandatory prices, would be likely to be material.

Under *Sch 3, para 2* and *s21(2)* of the Act, the DGFT may give a direction (without retrospective effect) withdrawing the benefit of a particular exclusion. Before giving a direction, the DGFT may serve a written notice requiring a party to provide information to assist him in deciding whether or not to give a direction. The Director may give a direction if:

O   the party fails to provide the information required; or
O   the DGFT thinks the agreement will, if not excluded, infringe the Chapter I Prohibition; and
O   he is not likely to grant it an unconditional individual exemption.

EEA Regulated Markets   [4.40]

Under *Sch 3, para 3* of the Act, the Chapter I Prohibition does not apply to an agreement for the constitution of an European Economic Area (EEA) regulated market, regulatory decisions, or agreements or practices of that market. An EEA regulated market is an investment market which is listed by another EEA State under Council Directive 93/22/EEC, Art 16 and does not require a dealer to have a physical presence in the EEA State or on any trading floor of that market.

Services of General Economic Interest etc.   [4.41]

Under *Sch 3, para 4* of the Act, the Chapter I Prohibition does not apply to an undertaking entrusted with the operation of services of general economic interest, or having the character of a revenue producing monopoly insofar as a prohibition would obstruct the performance of the particular task assigned to that undertaking.

This exclusion paraphrases Article 86(2) (formerly Article 90(2)) of the EC Treaty and as such its definitions are likely to be strictly interpreted as they are at the EU level. A 'revenue producing monopoly' would be likely to include some of the public utility networks and uniform letter pricing by the Post Office (Commons 8.7.1998 1175).

The DGFT aims to publish guidelines on the interpretation of this important exclusion.

Compliance with Legal Requirements [4.42]

Under *Sch 3, para 5* of the Act, the Chapter I Prohibition (and the Chapter II Prohibition) does not apply to agreements to the extent to which they are made in order to comply with a legal requirement. This means a requirement imposed by or under:

O a UK Act;
O the EC Treaty;
O the EEA Agreement; or
O the law enforced in another Member State and having legal effect in the UK.

During the passage of the Act through the House of Lords, the Government specifically stated that this exclusion would benefit utility companies entering into agreements to the extent that they are required to do so pursuant to the conditions of their relevant utility licence. (HL Committee, 13 November 1997, col 334.)

The purpose of this exclusion is to ensure that no-one can be required to do something for example, by a regulation or by a licence condition, and at the same time be prohibited from doing it under the Act.

An agreement is excluded only to the extent to which it is legally required, so that which goes beyond the legal requirement falls to be considered under the Act. For example, undertakings in the telecoms sector are often legally required to enter into agreements governing the connection of their networks. However, the terms of the agreement are subject to commercial negotiations and could result in one company gaining an unfair advantage over a smaller rival. These terms should not be excluded merely because the agreement itself is made pursuant to a legal requirement.

Conflict with International Obligations [4.43]

Under *Sch 3, para 6* of the Act, the Secretary of State can make an order excluding an agreement or class of agreement from the Chapter I Prohibition (or Chapter II Prohibition), in order to avoid a conflict with an international obligation of the UK. This covers both formal treaties and also agreements (such as those in the aviation sector made pursuant to inter-governmental arrangements but which fall short of Treaty status).

Public Policy [4.44]

Under *Sch 3, para* 7 of the Act, the Secretary of State can by Order exclude an agreement or class of agreement from the Chapter I Prohibition (and also the Chapter II Prohibition), if he is satisfied that there are exceptional and compelling reasons of public policy to do so. This is a higher burden of proof than a public interest test and is only likely to be exercised in rare circumstances. It may be used, for example, in relation to the defence industry. When the Act passed through the House of Commons, the Government said that at that time they had no plans to exercise this power, but that it should be available to them (Commons 8.7.1998 Column 1175).

Coal and Steel [4.45]

Under *Sch 3, para* 8 of the Act, the Chapter I Prohibition (and Chapter II Prohibition) will not apply to an agreement that relates to a coal or steel product, in line with the rules under the European Coal and Steel Community (ECSC) Treaty which reserves exclusive jurisdiction to the European Commission.

The ECSC Treaty is due to expire in 2001 and the Government intend the exclusion to expire automatically with it.

Agricultural Products [4.46]

Under *Sch 3, para* 9 of the Act, the Chapter I Prohibition will not apply to certain specified agreements to the extent to which they relate to the production of or trade in agricultural products and would fall outside Article 81 of the EC Treaty. (EC Regulation 26/62 – which, broadly, gives special treatment to agricultural co-operatives, national market organisations and agreements necessary for the attainment of Common Agricultural Policy objectives.)

Under *Schedule 3, para* 9, the DGFT may give a direction (without retrospective effect) to withdraw the benefit of the exclusion from a particular agreement.

Before giving a direction, the DGFT may serve a written notice requiring a party to provide him with information to assist him in deciding whether or not to give a direction. The director may give a direction if:

○ the party fails to provide the information required; or
○ the DGFT thinks that an agreement (whether or not he considers that it infringes the Chapter I Prohibition) is likely, or is intended, substantially and unjustifiably to prevent, restrict or distort competition in relation to an agricultural product.

It is intended that the exclusion will be removed where the European Commission finds that an agreement breaches Article 81(1) and where the DGFT has given a direction to remove the exclusion. The two differences between the UK exclusion and the EC exclusion for agricultural products are that:

○ the exclusion under the UK system can be clawed back in respect of all such agreements, whereas the European Commission can only do so in respect of agreements relating to agricultural co-operatives;
○ the competition test is different – under the EU system it is whether competition is excluded by the agreement whereas under the UK system the test is lower, the test being that the agreement is likely or is intended unjustifiably and substantially to prevent, restrict or distort competition in relation to an agricultural product.

Professional Services [4.47]

Schedule 4 provides for the exclusion of certain professional rules. It is a hangover from the list of professional services excluded under *Schedule 1* from the *Restrictive Trade Practices Act 1976.* The list has been criticised for being arbitrary and the terms used are internally inconsistent. Having said that, during debate in the House of Lords, the Government steadfastly resisted claims for changes to the description of professions on the list.

One important change, however, is that the exclusion under the Act only relates to the rules of professional bodies involved in the regulation of the listed professional services. The previous exclusion under the *RTPA 1976* was wider, in that it extended to agreements relating to such professional services. Such agreements will not be excluded under the Act.

The rationale for excluding only professional rules is apparently that their purpose is to protect the public and that they may contain certain disciplinary provisions subject to judicial review.

Application for designation of rules relating to the listed professional services must be made to the Secretary of State. Any alterations to professional rules which are on the list must be brought to the attention of the Secretary of State.

The Secretary of State and the DGFT have to keep the exclusion under review and the DGFT may recommend to the Secretary of State that a designated professional service be revoked. Where the Secretary of State considers that he would be justified in doing so, he can make an order to revoke designation, thereby removing the professional service from the list.

Vertical and Land Agreements [4.48]

Section 50 of the Act provides a wide power to introduce secondary legislation to provide for exclusions or exemptions or otherwise provide for the prescribed provisions not to apply to vertical agreements or land agreements. The definitions of a vertical agreement and a land agreement is to be set out in the 'Disapplication Orders' issued under this power.

Vertical Agreements [4.49]

A vertical agreement is one between undertakings at different levels in the supply chain (e.g. manufacturer and distributor; wholesaler and retailer). The Government decided that there was significant merit in special treatment for vertical agreements under the Chapter I Prohibition, since most vertical agreements do not harm competition.

The Government introduced a mechanism for the exclusion of vertical agreements by Order (Commons 25.6.98, col 629). This was because of problems in framing the wording of the exclusion and also because the Government wished to achieve consistency with EC law which is currently under review in this area. The Government did not wish to jump the gun by attempting to define vertical agreements on the face of the Act before the European Commission had concluded its review of the treatment of the vertical agreements.

In the House of Lords, the Government stated that the Government intended to follow the Commission's approach, and copy the Commission's definition of a vertical agreement (Lords 20.10.1998, col 1379) .

EC Review [4.50]

The European Commission has been conducting a review of its treatment of vertical restraints, and have issued a Communication setting out proposals for the adoption of one wide umbrella block exemption based on market share thresholds and a black list of prohibited restrictions.

The new block exemption regulation is likely to be adopted on 1 January 2000 and will come into force on 20 June 2000. The regulation marks a shift in European Commission policy and at least a partial recognition that many vertical agreements are benign in competition terms.

The position under European competition rules under the new regime is likely to be as follows.

Some vertical agreements will not have an appreciable effect on competition and so fall outside Article 81(1) altogether. The Commission's notice on agreements of minor importance (OJC 372, 9.12.97, p13) provides that a vertical agreement between undertakings with a combined market share of less than 10% would normally fall outside Article 81(1) altogether. Even above this figure, it remains possible that, depending on the circumstances, Article 81(1) may not apply. For agreements entered into between undertakings with a combined share of between 10% and 30%, the Block Exemption Regulation will apply, subject to the agreement not containing any blacklisted clauses. For undertakings with a share above 30%, there is no block exemption and agreements will be evaluated on a case by case basis.

The Draft Disqualification Order [4.51]

The Government has postponed publication of an order until the EU rules have been finalised and therefore no order is likely until January 2000. A draft order was published in February 1999 which broadly provided for a blanket exclusion for vertical agreements other than those which set fixed or minimum resale prices. The definition of 'vertical agreement' is likely to follow that adopted in the EU Block Exemption Regulation.

The treatment of vertical agreements under the Act is likely to be more lenient than that under Article 81(1) as:

○ there is no market share threshold; and
○ there is no black list (other than price fixing).

However, this apparent leniency is counter-balanced in three ways:

○ the Chapter II Prohibition is not excluded and potentially applies to all vertical agreements entered into by undertakings in a dominant position;
○ the complex monopoly provisions of the *Fair Trading Act 1973* remain in force and are likely to be used to investigate sectors in which competition appears not to be operating effectively (e.g. the investigation into new motor vehicles);
○ the Disapplication Order will include a clawback provision (this would not have retrospective effect)

Land Agreements [4.52]

The Government has also produced a draft Order under *section 50* excluding from the Chapter I Prohibition agreements relating to land.

The Disapplication Order for land agreements will be introduced at the same time as the order for vertical agreements. A draft order was also published in February 1999. The purpose of the order is to address concerns expressed in the property industry, that the Chapter I Prohibition might apply to restrictive covenants and other clauses in property dealings and so lead to a flood of precautionary notifications.

The draft order is widely drafted and broadly diaspplies the Chapter I Prohibition to any agreement between undertakings which:

'creates, alters or terminates, an interest in land or an agreement or enter into such an agreement together with any obligation or restriction which in accordance with Article 3 is to be treated as part of the agreement.'

The DGFT intends to publish a guideline on land agreements.

Exemptions [4.53]

The Act specifically provides for certain agreements and categories of agreements which are caught by the Chapter I Prohibition to benefit from an exemption where the resulting benefits for consumers outweigh any anti-competitive effects in the same way as under Article 81.

The exemptions available are summarised in the table below.

Section No.	Exemption
4	Individual exemption
6	Block exemptions
10	Parallel exemptions
11	Exemption for certain other agreements

Each form of exemption is discussed in detail below after a review of the criteria for exemption as specified in *section 9* of the Act.

Section 9 Criteria [4.54]

The wording of *section 9* is based on Article 81(3) save that the first condition expressly applies to both goods and services.

9.   This section applies to any agreement which –
      (a) contributes to –
            (i) improving production or distribution, or
            (ii) promoting technical or economic progress,
      while allowing consumers a fair share of the resulting benefit; but
      (b) does not –
            (i) impose on the undertakings concerned restrictions which are not indispensable to the attainment of those objectives; or
            (ii) afford the undertakings concerned the possibility of eliminating competition in respect of a substantial part of the products in question.

In order to satisfy the exemption criteria, all four conditions must be satisfied. It is up to the parties to the agreement to show that all the conditions are met, but the DGFT's staff dealing with an individual agreement will be prepared to discuss changes to an agreement that would enable the conditions to be satisfied.

Improving Production or Distribution   [4.55]

Any improvement must be clearly identified and justified, even though any benefits may be in the future. In order to satisfy the DGFT of the improvements, parties will need to show that they outweigh any possible harm to competition that would otherwise be regarded as infringing the Chapter I Prohibition. Examples would include:

○ lower costs as a result of:
  ● longer production or delivery runs; or
  ● changes in the methods of production or distribution brought about as a result of a co-operative agreement;
○ improvement in product quality; or
○ increases in the range of products produced or services provided, with unchanged inputs.

Contribution to promoting technical or economic progress would include efficiency gains from economies of scale and specialisation in research and development with the prospect of an enhanced flow or speed of innovation, and technical progress promoted by the development of industry-wide technical standards.

Allows Consumers a Fair Share of the Benefits   [4.56]

While the ultimate purpose of competition policy is to advance the interests of consumers, the second *section 9* condition is not limited to final consumers (who may be too far removed from the market where the agreement takes place to benefit directly) but it must be shown that the customers of the parties to the agreement share in the benefits.

If an improvement, say a cost reduction, is seen as benefiting only the shareholders of the parties to the agreement, the condition would not be satisfied. The views of customers and consumers are likely to be important in the consideration of the case for exemption, and in appropriate cases, will be sought.

An agreement may restrict competition significantly in the short term but enhance it in the future, if it leads, for example, to the faster development of new products or of new markets or better distribution systems. The DGFT takes account of the dynamics of market conduct and competition in assessing whether or not this condition for exemption is satisfied.

No Restrictions Beyond those Necessary [4.57]

Agreements may not include restrictions beyond those necessary for the attainment of the benefits which the parties can demonstrate to the competition authorities are likely to flow from the agreement. The DGFT will look carefully for any restrictions beyond those necessary to securing the benefits which add, directly or indirectly, to the anti-competitive effects of the agreement.

Given the variety of agreements that may be candidates for exemption, it is not possible to list categorically the terms of an agreement which may be found not to be indispensable. Some guidance may be found in the various block exemption Regulations. These Regulations include so-called 'black lists' of terms the inclusion of which will mean that the agreement does not qualify for block exemption (though the possibility of an individual exemption is not thereby ruled out, but remains unlikely). These would typically include price restrictions and non-competition covenants beyond certain stated periods.

No Elimination of Competition [4.58]

The DGFT's assessment will consider this condition and if, after an appropriate market analysis, he concludes that it is not satisfied, there can be no possibility of an exemption. An application for an individual exemption is unlikely to succeed if the parties are unable to show that, notwithstanding the adverse effects on competition of the agreement, there will continue to be effective competition in the market or markets for the goods or services with which the agreement is concerned.

Individual Exemption [4.59]

Under *Section 4(1)*, the DGFT may grant an individual exemption if an agreement has been notified to him asking him to do so, and the criteria for exemption set out in *section 9* are satisfied (see **4.54** above). A candidate for exemption might be, for example, a joint venture between competitors to produce an improvement in their existing product lines. This might have benefits for the consumer in terms of increasing the range of products available.

The exemption may be granted subject to such conditions and obligations as the DGFT considers appropriate and would have effect for such period as the DGFT may specify. Importantly the DGFT can backdate any exemption decision to the date of the agreement in question.

The DGFT may cancel an individual exemption or vary or remove conditions or obligations attached to it.

Block Exemptions [4.60]

Section 6 empowers the DGFT to recommend to the Secretary of State to make an Order creating block exemptions in respect of a particular category of agreement which satisfies the *section 9* criteria (see **4.54** above). If an agreement falls within any such category it is exempt from the Chapter I Prohibition and there is no need to notify the agreement to the DGFT.

A block exemption may have conditions or obligations attached to it, subject to which the block exemption is to have effect.

As in the case of an individual exemption, a block exemption may be cancelled where a condition is breached or an obligation is not complied with, or the DGFT considers that an agreement is not one to which *section 9* applies.

It remains to be seen what block exemptions will eventually be adopted by the Secretary of State. Given that most vertical agreements will be outside the Chapter I Prohibition by means of the Disapplication Order for vertical agreements (see **4.48** above), it is unlikely that many block exemption regulations will be made. It is clear that the intention is not the intention simply to replicate block exemptions which already exist at the EU level. One possible sector where block exemptions might be used is the utility sector where, for example, connection agreements in the electricity industry might merit a block exemption.

Parallel Exemption [4.61]

An agreement is automatically exempt from the Chapter I Prohibition if it is covered by an EC block exemption or would be covered if the agreement had an effect on trade between Member States, or has been granted an individual exemption by the EC Commission (*s12*). This avoids parties having to notify their agreement to the DGFT and reduces the burden on business. It should be noted, however, that the parallel exemption will not apply to agreements which benefit from a comfort letter from the European Commission (see **6.15** below).

If the EC exemption ceases to have effect or is cancelled, the parallel exemption also ceases to have effect.

Where the DGFT finds that an agreement which benefits from a parallel exemption has produced, or may produce, significantly adverse effects on a market in the United Kingdom, he can impose conditions or obligations subject to which the exemption is to have effect. He can also vary or remove any such condition or obligation, impose one or more additional conditions or obligations, or cancel the exemption.

This power begs the question as to what extent the DGFT can deviate from an EU decision as it is not clear as a matter of EU law whether he may impose stricter standards than those applied by the Commission under Article 81(3). This power is likely to be invoked rarely, if ever, and then probably only with prior consultation with the European Commission.

Exemption for Certain Other Agreements [4.62]

Section 11 provides for exemptions of 'other' agreements but is likely to be used rarely in practice. It is necessary because a few sectors exist for which exemptions are given by the Commission by virtue of Article 84 (formerly Article 88) of the EC Treaty. Therefore, this section is an extension of *section 10*.

Timetable [4.63]

The timetable for the implementation of the Chapter I Prohibition is detailed below.

Early Guidance [4.64]

The Chapter I Prohibition does not come into force until 1 March 2000. Parties to an agreement entered into during the interim period (i.e. 9 November 1998 to 29 February 2000) can, if they so choose, apply to the DGFT for early guidance as to whether the agreement is likely to infringe the Chapter I Prohibition when it comes into force and, if so, whether it would be likely to be exempt. (See **4.53–4.62** above.)

The procedure for making an early guidance notification is set out in the DGFT's directions on early guidance which were issued in November 1998 (see **Chapter 7: PROCEDURE AND ENFORCEMENT**).

Transitional Periods [4.65]

For agreements made before 1 March 2000, there will be a number of transitional periods provided after the start date of 1 March 2000, during which the Chapter I Prohibition will not apply (the effect for their duration being similar to that of the exclusions provided for in *Section 3* of the Act).

The General Rule [4.66]

The general rule is that all agreements below entered into before the starting date (1 March 2000) will receive a one year transitional period. The Chapter I Prohibition does not apply to the agreement to the extent that a transitional period applies. In practice, the two main examples of agreement benefiting from this one year transitional period will be non-notifiable agreements made during the interim period, and agreements made prior to the starting date to which the *RTPA 1976* did not apply at all.

No Transitional Period [4.67]

Exceptionally, agreements will receive no transitional period to the extent to which, immediately before the starting date, under the *RTPA 1976* they are void or subject to a restraining order, or a person has unlawfully given effect to restrictions prior to duly furnishing particulars of an agreement or variations. Similarly, agreements receive no transitional period to the extent to which, immediately before the starting date, they are unlawful or void under the *RPA 1976*.

Agreements and variations for which the deadline for furnishing particulars under the *RTPA 1976* falls after the starting date, but particulars are not furnished by that date, will receive no transitional period.

Five Year Period [4.68]

Agreements will receive a five year transitional period to the extent to which, immediately before the starting date, they have been found not to be contrary to the public interest by the Restrictive Practices Court or relate to goods which fall within the scope of an exemption order under *section 14* of the *RPA 1976*.

In the special case of certain agreements which have been subject to scrutiny under the *Financial Services Act 1986* or the *Broadcasting Act 1990*, there will be a five year transitional period.

Certain agreements in the electricity, gas and railway industries will receive transitional periods of up to five years:

○ in the electricity sector, agreements covered by orders under *s100* of the *Electricity Act 1989*;
○ in the gas sector, agreements covered by orders under *s62* of the *Gas Act 1986*; and
○ in the railway sector, agreements covered by *section 131* or directions thereunder.

Agreements after the Starting Date [4.69]

Except in the limited case of certain utilities agreements, there will be no transitional period available for agreements made after the starting date: the Chapter I Prohibition has immediate effect.

Application of Chapter I Prohibition		
Agreements	**Enactment date (9 November 1998)**	**Starting date (1 March 2000)**
Made prior to the enactment date (9 November 1998)		Chapter I comes into force on starting date, but: – exclusion for *s21(2)* agreements; – transitional periods available (generally 1 or 5 years from starting date; – termination/extension of transitional periods possible.
Made in the interim period	Early guidance possible	
Made after the starting date (1 March 2000)	N/A	Chapter I applies immediately.

Operation of the Transitional Periods [4.70]

Generally, transitional periods will begin on the starting date. There are two exceptions to this rule: first, for certain agreements relating to the utilities and, secondly, for agreements subject to certain Restrictive Practices Court proceedings continuing after the starting date. In the case of these latter agreements, any transitional period available will begin when the proceedings end. This is important, as the outcome of continuing proceedings may affect the transitional period applicable to the agreement. For example, to the extent to which an agreement were found by the Restrictive Practices Court in continuing proceedings not to be contrary to the public interest, it would receive a five year transitional period, starting from the end of those proceedings. Conversely, to the extent to which an agreement were found to be contrary to the public interest, it would receive no transitional period, and would instead be immediately subject to the Chapter I Prohibition at the conclusion of the proceedings.

The Chapter I prohibition will not apply 'to the extent to which' a transitional period is available. Similarly, a number of the transitional periods will apply 'to the extent to which' an agreement meets the relevant criteria. Therefore a particular transitional period may apply only to certain provisions of an agreement rather than its entirety. Consequently, it will be possible for some provisions in an agreement to benefit from transitional periods of different lengths to others. For example, those provisions of an agreement made before the enactment date and duly notified within the time limits under the *RTPA 1976* which were found by the Restrictive Practices Court not to be contrary to the public interest would receive a five year transitional period, whereas the rest of the agreement would receive a one year transitional period.

Where an agreement is only partly covered by a transitional period and the DGFT has competition concerns about the provisions not covered, he will still be able to have regard to the whole agreement in order to assess whether the Chapter I prohibition has been breached (rather than assess only the provisions not covered by a transitional period in an artificial vacuum which does not take account of the surrounding circumstances). However, in the event of an infringement finding, those provisions benefiting from a transitional period will not be prohibited or subject to the consequences of infringement for the duration of that period.

5 – Chapter II Prohibition

Introduction [5.1]

The Chapter II Prohibition of the Act deals with 'abuse of a dominant position' and largely incorporates the provisions of Article 82 (formerly Article 86) of the EC Treaty into UK legislation.

The Chapter II Prohibition is contained in *section 18* of the Act. The section prohibits any conduct by one or more undertakings which amounts to the abuse of a dominant position in a market and which may affect trade within the UK.

Section No.	Description of Section
18	Prohibition – abuse of dominant position
19	Excluded cases
20–24 (incl)	Notification
73	Crown application

OFT Guidance [5.2]

The OFT has produced two useful guidelines: *The Chapter II Prohibition* and *Market Definition*. These guidelines are available from the Office of Fair Trading (Tel: 0870 6060321) and are intended as a practical guide for business rather than legal practitioners.

Influence of European Community Case Law [5.3]

UK undertakings will also be able to look to European case law to seek guidance on the interpretation of the Chapter II Prohibition. This is because English Courts must generally follow established European jurisprudence.

Section 60 of the Act states that English Courts will have to have regard to any relevant decision or statement of the European Commission (see **1.8** above). Furthermore, English Courts must, as far as possible, deal with cases brought under the Act 'in a manner which is consistent with the treatment of corresponding questions arising in Community law in relation to competition within the Community' (see further **Chapter 6: INTERACTION WITH EU LAW**). Therefore, established European Court of Justice and Court of First Instance decisions dealing with Article 82 will provide an important guide as to the DGFT's likely interpretation of the Chapter II Prohibition.

Coming into Force [5.4]

There are no transitional provisions relating to the implementation of the Chapter II Prohibition and, therefore, it will come into force on the 'starting date', 1 March 2000 (see further **Chapter 1: INTRODUCTION TO THE ACT**). Meanwhile, Article 82 will continue in full force with UK and EU legislation running in parallel from the starting date.

Constituent Elements [5.5]

There are five constituent elements of the Chapter II Prohibition:

- one or more undertakings involved;
- a dominant position;
- the market in which the dominant position exists must be identified;
- abuse of that dominant position; and
- that abuse must affect trade within the UK.

One or More Undertakings [5.6]

One of the crucial differences between the Chapter I and Chapter II Prohibitions is that only the latter may be infringed by the activities of a single undertaking. Unlike the Chapter I Prohibition, it is not necessary to have an agreement between two or more undertakings, although any such agreement could, in theory, fall foul of both the Chapter I and

Chapter II Prohibitions.

In practice, an undertaking is most likely to be a company or firm, but may also include partnerships, sole traders or other businesses as well as health authorities, education bodies, NHS trusts and quangos.

There can be joint or collective dominance by two or more undertakings if there are 'economic links' between them (*Societa Italiano Vetro SpA v Commission [1992] II ECR 1403; 5 CMLR 302)*. Undertakings which are linked by common ownership obviously fall within this definition. Further, two or more legally independent undertakings who adopt the same conduct in the market may collectively breach the Chapter II Prohibition where there is some form of economic link between them.

Joint dominance could be used as an alternative to the Chapter I Prohibition either when agreements enjoy the benefit of exemptions, or where it was hard to prove that there was a concerted practice between undertakings which would be caught by the Chapter I Prohibition (see **4.12** above).

Throughout this chapter, the term product is used but should be read to include services as well.

Dominant Position [5.7]

Generally speaking, a dominant position is a position of economic strength enjoyed by an undertaking, which enables it to hinder the maintenance of effective competition on the relevant market, by allowing it to behave, to an appreciable extent, independently of its competitors and customers and ultimately of consumers (*Michelin v Commission [1983] ECR 3461*).

Whether an undertaking holds a dominant position in the relevant market (see **5.11** below) will depend largely on two factors – market share and entry barriers.

Market Share [5.8]

There is no definitive test of whether an undertaking is in a dominant position or not according to the percentage of their market share.

However, as a general guide, undertakings with less than 20–25% of the market share for their particular product will not be in danger of breaching the Chapter II Prohibition.

Undertakings which enjoy a market share of over 50% will nearly always be in a dominant position unless there is clear evidence to the contrary. In addition, undertakings with a share between 40% and 50% may also be found to be in a dominant position. Where share is below 40%, the OFT's guidelines to the Chapter II Prohibition indicate that it is unlikely that an undertaking would be found to be dominant, although dominance might be established if, for example, the position of competitors in the relevant market was weak.

In addition to market share, whether undertakings are found to occupy a dominant position, will largely depend on the conditions of the relevant market and, in particular, barriers to entry (see **5.9** below).

The size of the nearest competitors may also influence whether a business is in a dominant position or not. If the next biggest competitor is proportionately far smaller than the main business in the market, then the main business may well find itself in a dominant position despite having a low percentage of the market share. This may occur, for example, when the competitors are fragmented so none are individually strong enough to challenge abusive behaviour by the market leader.

Similarly, the reverse is true. An undertaking may enjoy a fairly large market share in percentage terms but still not be in a dominant position because there are two or three main competitors of a similar size who would be able to prevent abusive behaviour.

Entry Barriers [5.9]

The existence of entry barriers into the market faced by new entrants will be another factor in deciding whether an undertaking occupies a dominant position. If there are no, or very few, barriers to entry, the undertaking is less likely to be in a dominant position notwithstanding a high percentage market share. This is because any anti-competitive behaviour by the undertaking will result in new suppliers rapidly entering the market and taking its custom away.

The reverse is also true. If there are substantial entry barriers facing new entrants, it is far more likely that an established undertaking within the market will be in a dominant position even if it only enjoys a low percentage of the market share.

Examples [5.10]

Examples of such entry barriers may include the following.

○ Initial start-up or investment costs (also known as 'sunk' costs) necessary to establish a new undertaking in the market which are so high as to be likely to deter new entrants. For example, computer hardware production, which requires extensive research and initial production costs prior to production commencing.

○ Situations where the market is effectively 'branded', making it hard for new entrants to establish a reputation. For example, the markets for nappies and washing powders are dominated by a few household names which their manufacturers have spent considerable time and money promoting. Any new entrant would find it very expensive to conduct the intense advertising campaign necessary to establish a foothold in the market.

○ Markets in which there are regulations requiring licences or permits for new entrants.

○ Copyright, patents and other intellectual property rights already subsisting in favour of the incumbent undertaking. However, note that the exercising of the intellectual property rights alone will not normally constitute an infringement of the Chapter II Prohibition (see **5.31** below).

Market [5.11]

The relevant market must be defined to determine whether the undertaking is dominant in it. The relevant market has two dimensions: product and geographic.

Product Market [5.12]

The relevant product market has been defined as comprising 'all those products and/or services which are regarded as interchangeable or substitutable by the consumer, by reason of the products' characteristics, their prices and their intended use' (European Commission Notice on the Definition of 'Relevant Market' for the purposes of Community competition law (*97/C 372/03*)).

One test that may be used to try and determine the relevant product market is 'would a rise in the price of the product lead to a fall in the level of demand for the product?' and vice versa. If the answer is 'no', then purchasers are essentially trapped in that product market. However, if there are suitable alternative products which most purchasers would decide to substitute for the original product, then the product market would carry a much wider definition.

Example [5.13]

The European Court of Justice (ECJ) considered the definition of the relevant product market in *United Brands v Commission [1978] ECR 207*, which was brought in relation to Article 86 (now Article 82) of the EC Treaty, the European legislative equivalent of the Chapter II Prohibition.

This case concerned the supply of bananas and whether bananas are in a market of their own, or are part of a wider 'fruit' market. Undoubtedly, some purchasers of bananas would easily switch to other fruit should the price of bananas increase. However, a number of purchasers, such as the very young, the very old or infirm, for whom bananas are more suitable than most other fruits, could not. The ECJ also had to consider the fact that during the summer months there are more acceptable substitutes for bananas than during winter. The ECJ found that there were enough purchasers for whom other kinds of fruit were not a substitute, for bananas to be a relevant market.

The 5–10% Rule [5.14]

Guidelines published by the OFT: *The Competition Act 1998: Market Definition* reiterate the established European test known as the '5–10% rule'. This gives a rough guide for calculating whether there are acceptable substitutes for a product and therefore helps to determine the relevant product market.

The test is 'would a non-transitory increase in price of 5–10% above competitive levels lead to a significant number of customers switching to a substitute product?' Note that the number of customers must be 'significant' (i.e. more than a few but not necessarily all or nearly all). However, it must be stressed that this is a general guide and not a hard and fast rule.

Geographic Market [5.15]

The OFT's guidelines on the Chapter II Prohibition refer to the fact that:

> 'The geographic market will sometimes be the area supplied by the complainant, or the party or parties to the conduct concerned, but the Director General also considers whether customers could easily obtain similar products from suppliers in other areas on reasonable terms. If so, those other areas may form part of the geographic market.'

In light of this, and depending on the circumstances of each case, the relevant geographic market may be defined as 'the whole of the UK', 'the North of England', 'South Wales' or even a large town.

In practice, it is likely that the OFT will be prepared to initiate investigations under the Chapter II Prohibition in relation to alleged abuses in relatively local markets within the UK. The OFT's guidelines on market definition indicate that the relevant geographic market could be 'any part of the United Kingdom'.

A number of factors are likely to determine the definition of the relevant geographic market.

Transport Costs [5.16]

The geographic market is the area where the competitive conditions applying to the product in question are the same for all businesses. One of the main factors determining this definition will be transport costs – is it relatively cheap and easy to transport the product to different parts of the UK? If so, then the geographic market is likely to be larger than if the transport costs were higher.

For example, sugar is relatively heavy and bulky compared with its value and this restricts the scope of the geographic market (see *Napier Brown v British Sugar (OJ [1988] L284/41)*). Contrast this with nail cartridges for cartridge guns, which are relatively cheap to transport and therefore have a much wider geographic market (*Hilti v Commission* [*1991*] *ECR II 1439*).

Nature of the Product [5.17]

The geographic market for certain products may be limited by the very nature of the product. For example, a local bus service obviously has a much narrower geographic market than the entire UK.

Ease of Availability of Substitutes [5.18]

Ease of availability of substitute products to consumers will also affect the dimensions of the relevant geographic market. For example, in the outlying Scottish highlands consumers may have to travel much further to find suitable substitute goods than consumers in central England, simply because of the local public transport infrastructure. This factor would indicate a more narrow geographic market.

Further details on the DGFT's approach to market definition are available in the OFT guidelines: *Market Definition*, referred to above.

Abuse of a Dominant Position [5.19]

There is a fine line between abuse and competition. Generally, abuse is behaviour by a dominant business which is detrimental to consumers. This may be evidenced in a variety of ways, for example by removing or excluding competitors. Although the Act does not define 'abuse', *section 18(2)* lists five examples of conduct that may constitute abuse.

These are:

○ raising prices in a captive market;
○ predatory pricing;
○ price discrimination;
○ fidelity rebate; and
○ refusal to supply.

It is important to note that these examples are only indicative and should not be seen as an exhaustive list.

Conduct for which there is an objective justification is not regarded as an abuse even though it may restrict competition. However, it may in practice be very difficult to find and prove such objective justification.

Raising Prices in a Captive Market [5.20]

Raising prices to an excessively high level, with the intention to simply increase profits where there are no corresponding increases in cost to the producer, will normally constitute abuse. 'Excessively high' is higher than would normally be the case in a competitive market. In practice, the OFT acknowledges in its guidelines to the Chapter II Prohibition that there may be objective justification for prices which appear to be excessive. Prices would need to be persistently excessive to amount to an abuse.

Predatory Pricing [5.21]

Predatory pricing is seeking to destroy competition by pricing at an unrealistically low level with the aim of driving a competitor out of the market. Principles of what exactly constitutes a predatory low level were founded in *ECS v AKZO Chemie BV (1986) 3 CMLR 273*, where a distinction was drawn between average variable cost (AVC) and average total cost (ATC).

AVC is the sum of all variable costs, i.e. those which vary with output such as raw materials. ATC is the average cost of production including all initial investment and sunk costs (initial start-up or investment costs). If a product is sold at below AVC, there is a presumption of predatory behaviour (as the producer would be able to increase profits simply by ceasing production) although it might be possible to justify such pricing, for example if it was a short run promotion to move old stock. Selling above AVC but below ATC will normally only indicate predatory behaviour if there is evidence of an intention to eliminate a competitor. Prices above ATC are unlikely to indicate any predatory intentions.

Price Discrimination [5.22]

Price discrimination can take one of two forms. Either charging different prices to different customers for the same product, or charging the same price to all customers where the costs of production and supplying different categories of people are very different.

There may be objective justifications for price discrimination, for example, where the volume of sales to a particular customer justifies a discount because of the cost savings resulting from them, or if there are large fixed costs and low marginal costs in the industry concerned. However, in the *AKZO* case (see **5.21** above), a company was found to be in breach of Article 86 (now Article 82), for cutting prices charged to its competitor's regular customers, while maintaining higher levels for its own established customers.

Fidelity Rebate/Discounts [5.23]

Giving customers a discount for buying all or most of their purchases from the dominant business, where there are no corresponding cost savings to the business itself, is an example of a fidelity discount (see *Hoffmann Law Roche v Commission* [1979] ECR II). This would be considered to be an abuse on the basis that its effect could be to prevent competing suppliers from supplying the customers receiving the discount.

It is not a defence to say that the customer insisted on the rebate (*BPB Commission* [1993] ECR II).

Refusal to Supply [5.24]

Refusal to supply existing or potential customers or competitors *prima facie* constitutes abuse, unless the refusal can be objectively justified. For example, a customer's poor creditworthiness may constitute a valid justification for refusal to supply.

The 'Essential Facilities' Doctrine [5.25]

Denial of access to ports or other methods of obtaining input goods such as raw materials, is known as the 'essential facilities' doctrine, (see further the *Sealink* case (*OJ* [1994] L15/8), and has arisen in EU competition law according to the same principles as refusal to supply (see **5.24** above). The basis for this is that access to the facility concerned is a pre-requisite for any company which wants to compete in the market concerned and that duplicating the facility is either impossible or extremely difficult.

In *Port of Rodby* (*OJ* [*1994*] *L55/52*), it was held that the owner of a port which refused access to an operator that wished to set up competing ferry services, was in breach of Article 86 (now Article 82) of the EC Treaty.

This doctrine was extended in *Port of Roscoff* [*1995*] *5 CMLR 177*, where the owner of that port was held to be abusing its dominant position by refusing access to a new factory operator, even though it did not itself run competing ferry services.

The Mediaprint Case   [5.26]

The essential facilities doctrine was considered recently by the ECJ in *Oscar Bronner v Mediaprint* (*26 November 1998, Case C–7/97*), in relation to an established home-delivery newspaper service. The dominant undertaking, Mediaprint, had invested substantial time and money in establishing its nationwide delivery service. Bronner sought a declaration that Mediaprint's refusal to allow it access to the delivery service for its relatively small publication, was in breach of Article 86 (now Article 82) of the EC Treaty. Bronner was prepared to pay a reasonable sum for access to the service, but failed to convince the European Court of Justice of its case.

Influential factors were that:

○   if Mediaprint allowed access to all newspapers and journals in the territory (Austria), its delivery system would collapse;
○   a postal delivery service was available as a suitable alternative for Bronner; and
○   Mediaprint's behaviour was not intended to drive Bronner out of the market.

The case is significant in that it appears to indicate a restricted view by the European Court of Justice of the circumstances in which the essential facilities doctrine may be applied.

Nevertheless, the doctrine could be extended to cover other facilities which it is essential for competitors in the market to enjoy access to (e.g. a telecommunications network).

Tying-in Retailers or Distributors [5.27]

Tying-in retailers or distributors by making the purchase of the product conditional on purchasing other products, in the absence of any objective justification or common commercial practice, may be an abuse.

In *Hilti v Commission* [1991] *ECR II* (*Case T–30/89*), the tying-in of the purchase of nail guns to the purchase of the same manufacturer's nails and cartridge strips was held not to be justifiable on safety grounds. The UK, where the dispute arose, had existing safety laws which were designed to prevent the wrong type of nails and cartridge strips being sold and used with the manufacturer's nail gun and as a result there was no basis for asserting that the tie was necessary on grounds of safety.

Imposing Unfair Trading Conditions [5.28]

Obliging a competitor to conform to strict quality controls for products or services, which in turn causes it to incur higher production costs, amounts to the imposition of unfair trading conditions.

Extraneous Obligations [5.29]

Insisting that a retailer does not stock products of a rival manufacturer, or making it more difficult for them to do so, may amount to an abuse on the grounds that it limits competitors' ability to compete. This point arose in the European Commission's decision in relation to Van den Bergh Foods Limited (a subsidiary of Unilever plc) *Van der Bergh Foods* (*OJ L246/1/98*).

The company lent ice-cream cabinets to retailers in Ireland, on the condition that they only stocked frozen ice-cream products made and supplied by Unilever. The European Commission found that since there is limited space for a freezer in most shops, this effectively denied market access to other suppliers of 'impulse-bought' ice-cream in the Irish market. This decision is under appeal at the time of writing.

Exclusions [5.30]

There are certain exclusions to the Chapter II Prohibition. These are listed in *Schedules 1* and *3* of the Act.

Cases which are excluded are:

○ mergers which are subject to UK merger control – i.e. any conduct resulting in two enterprises ceasing to be distinct enterprises for the purposes of *Part IV* of the *FTA 1973*;
○ a transfer of a newspaper or of newspaper assets – for the purposes of *section 57* of the *FTA 1973*;
○ concentrations (i.e. mergers) which are subject to EU controls – i.e. conduct giving rise to a concentration with a Community dimension within the meaning of *Articles 1* and *3* of the *Merger Regulation (EEC) No 4064/89* (as amended by *Council Regulation (EC) No 1310/97*) if the *Merger Regulation* gives the Commission exclusive jurisdiction in the matter;
○ undertakings entrusted with the operation of services of general economic interest, or having the character of a revenue-producing monopoly insofar as the prohibition will obstruct the performance of the particular tasks assigned to that undertaking;
○ conduct carried out in order to comply with a legal requirement;
○ those excluded at the discretion of the Secretary of State, in order to avoid a conflict with international obligations of the UK;
○ those excluded at the discretion of the Secretary of State, where there are exceptional and compelling reasons of public policy for the Chapter II Prohibition not to apply; and
○ conduct which relates to a coal or steel product to the extent to which the *European Coal and Steel Community Treaty* gives the Commission exclusive jurisdiction in the matter.

These exclusions are exhaustive and limited in scope. In particular, it is clear that the Secretary of State will not readily grant exclusion on an individual basis on the grounds of public policy.

Under *section 19*, the Secretary of State has the power to amend the list of exclusions at any time.

Intellectual Property Rights [5.31]

The lawful use of valid intellectual property rights will not usually constitute an infringement of the Chapter II Prohibition. Intellectual property rights include copyright, patents, trade marks (both registered and unregistered), design rights (both registered and unregistered) and confidentiality.

For example, in granting a patent, the State is effectively giving the successful applicant a monopoly right to exploit the product or system patented for 20 years. This would not normally give rise to any liability under the Chapter II Prohibition if the rights were being exercised in a *bona fide* manner.

However, in a limited number of cases, the European Commission and European Court of Justice have held that the exercise of intellectual property rights may constitute an abuse.

Refusal to Licence [5.32]

Generally, a refusal to licence an intellectual property right will not amount to an abuse, but in certain exceptional circumstances it has been held to be so.

The leading case in this area is *Magill (RTE and ITP v Commission* [1995] *I ECR 743;* [1995] *4 CMLR 718*), which involved the refusal to licence copyright of weekly TV listings by three TV broadcast companies in Ireland (RTE, BBC and ITV). The European Court of Justice found that there were exceptional circumstances (arising from the fact that the refusal thwarted consumer demand for a new product) which led to their decision that the refusal to licence did amount to breach of Article 86 (now Article 82) of the EC Treaty.

The OFT is likely to adopt a cautious approach to complaints under the Chapter II Prohibition seeking to challenge refusal to licence, not least because of the risk of discouraging investment which would be protected by intellectual property rights.

Other [5.33]

A dominant undertaking may infringe the Chapter II Prohibition in other ways in relation to its intellectual property rights, for example by tying the grant of a licence to obligations which were not objectively justified (see **5.27** above), or in certain circumstances by tying a purchaser of, for example, a piece of machinery to its spare parts or consumables through the use of intellectual property rights.

For agreements involving intellectual property, see **Chapter 4: THE CHAPTER I PROHIBITION** and the DGFT's Guidelines: *Intellectual Property Rights*.

Consequences of Infringement [5.34]

Although procedure and compliance matters generally are dealt with in **Chapters 7: PROCEDURE AND ENFORCEMENT** and **8: COMPLIANCE**, specific matters applicable to the Chapter II Prohibition are summarised here.

The DGFT is able to impose financial penalties of up to 10% of the total UK turnover on businesses which infringe the Chapter II Prohibition. In the event that an undertaking is found to be in breach, the DGFT is also able to 'give directions' requiring the breach to be brought to an end.

The directions may be given to any person in breach of the prohibition whom the DGFT considers it appropriate to give them, and in any form he considers appropriate. This is in addition to the DGFT's power to impose fines.

Notification [5.35]

For those undertakings that are uncertain as to whether their behaviour or conduct may infringe the Chapter II prohibition, *sections 20–24* of the Act may be relevant. *Section 20* provides that any person may apply to the DGFT if they fear they may be infringing the Chapter II Prohibition, either requesting guidance or a decision. (See further **Chapter 7: PROCEDURE AND ENFORCEMENT**.) In practice, it is not clear how widely these decisions will be relied on.

There is no immunity period from the date of application so businesses must be aware that they may be found liable for breaching the Chapter II Prohibition in relation to conduct carried out between applying to the DGFT for either guidance or a decision and receiving the result of their unsuccessful application.

Relationship with the Chapter I Prohibition [5.36]

As is the case with Articles 81 and 82, certain behaviour, practices or conduct may infringe either the Chapter I Prohibition, the Chapter II Prohibition or both. Although individual commercial agreements (such as distribution agreements) are more likely to be caught under the Chapter I Prohibition, undertakings should be aware that both Prohibitions may apply to the same set of facts.

Relationship with Existing Legislation [5.37]

The Chapter II Prohibition will become the main UK legislation regulating the abuse of a dominant market position. Nevertheless, the monopoly provisions of the *FTA 1973* will remain in force and run concurrently.

These provisions provide for the Competition Commission (formerly the Monopolies and Mergers Commission (MMC)) to investigate following a reference from the OFT.

The key market share threshold for the monopoly provision of the *FTA 1973* is 25%, either where a single company has a share equal to or greater than this (a scale monopoly), or where two or more companies with a share equal to or greater than 25%, conduct their affairs so as to prevent or distort competition (a complex monopoly). The purpose of this latter provision is to enable particular economic sectors to be investigated even if there is no suggestion of collusion. The retention of these provisions aroused a certain amount of opposition during the drafting of the Act, but was justified on the ground that they were particularly suited to a situation where the structure of a particular industry hampered competition and structural remedies were required.

(See further **3.11** and **3.12** above.)

Exemptions [5.38]

There are no powers in the Act to grant individual exemptions from the Chapter II Prohibition on the basis that it produces benefit. In other words, the DGFT has no power to decide that the abusive effects of particular behaviour are outweighed by certain beneficial consequences where he gives guidance or a decision and that conduct is not abusive.

However, there will be limited immunity for conduct of minor significance (see **7.64** below) under which the Act gives immunity from penalties for the abuse of a dominant market position under the 'conduct of minor significance' exemption.

This reflects the Government's concern that small and medium-sized undertakings should not be overburdened by the application of the Act. However, the DGFT will consider removing immunity from penalties 'in appropriate cases' involving conduct of minor significance. Therefore, even a small undertaking, with a small annual turnover who abuses its dominant position in a small market cannot necessarily hide behind the 'conduct of minor significance' exemption.

It should be noted that this exemption applies only to penalties imposed by the OFT and does not prevent third parties from claiming damages for such conduct.

6 – Interaction with EU Law

Introduction [6.1]

Articles 81 and 82 (formerly Articles 85 and 86) of the EC Treaty have direct effect in the UK. Many agreements and practices entered into by companies operating in the UK are potentially subject to the EU rules.

For this reason the Act is designed to align UK competition law and procedure with the EU equivalents so as to reduce the regulatory burden on business. This chapter looks at the practical implications of the interaction of the Act with EU law.

Section 60 – Guiding Principles [6.2]

Section 60 is designed to achieve consistency between EU competition law and the Act (see further **1.3** and **1.8–1.11**). The importance of this section cannot be overstated. It remains to be seen whether the rather ambiguous wording of *section 60* will be sufficient to ensure that UK law develops in tandem with EU law.

One important consequence of the Government's decision to follow Articles 81 and 82 almost to the letter, is that in cases of doubt as to the relevant EU law, parties litigating under the Act in the UK courts may seek a reference to the European Court of Justice under Article 234 (formerly Article 177) of the EC Treaty.

Article 234 provides:

> 'The Court of Justice shall have jurisdiction to give preliminary rulings concerning:
>
> (a) the interpretation of this Treaty;
> (b) the validity and interpretation of acts of the institutions of the Community and of the ECB;
> (c) the interpretation of the statutes of bodies established by an act of the Council, where those statutes so provide.

> Where such a question is raised before any court or tribunal of a Member State, that court or tribunal may, if it considers that a decision on the question is necessary to enable it to give judgment, request the Court of Justice to give a ruling thereon.
>
> Where any such question is raised in a case pending before a court or tribunal of a Member State against whose decisions there is no judicial remedy under national law, that court or tribunal shall bring the matter before the Court of Justice.'

A reference may be made from any UK court but in practice is most likely from the Court of Appeal. It is not possible to make a direct reference from the DGFT or Appeals Tribunal.

It is for the court to identify and frame the question of EU law in issue. A reference will only be made in cases in which the question is determinative of the outcome of the case.

The precedent for references of EU principles under domestic law under Article 177 (now Article 234) of the EC Treaty was set by the Dutch courts in the *Leur Bloem v Inspecteur ce Belastingdienst (Case C-28/95 (1997) ECR 1-4161)*. Most observers feel that the UK courts will follow this precedent in relation to the Act.

Jurisdictional Tests for Articles 81 and 82 [6.3]

Article 81 prohibits agreements, decisions and concerted practices which restrict competition and affect trade between Member States. Article 82 prohibits abuse of a dominant position in a substantial part of the common market which affects trade between Member States.

The definition in this context of an 'effect on EU trade' is of considerable importance, since it effectively determines the scope of EU competition law. In practice, both the European Commission and the European Court of Justice have adopted an extremely wide-ranging definition of this phrase, with the result that an effect on trade is readily found in many cases. In particular, even where the effects of an agreement or practice appear to have been largely or wholly confined to a particular Member State, the requisite effect has still been established. For example, in one decision the European Commission held that the relevant test was satisfied in relation to an agreement between two UK companies to set up a joint venture. It considered that without the agreement it was likely that each company would otherwise have sold the product concerned in other EU Member States. (*Re Vacuum Interrupters Ltd (OJ [1997] L48/32)*).

At one end of the spectrum, the issue is likely to be fairly clear cut e.g. where an undertaking prevents a UK distributor from selling outside the UK. The distorting effect of the agreement on EU trade in such a case is normally readily apparent. However, the test has also been held to be satisfied in other circumstances where the effect on trade is more subtle and indirect.

In the leading case on this point, *Société Technique Minière v Maschinenbau Ulm (Case 56/65 (1966) ECR 235)*, the European Court of Justice held that it must be established:

> 'with a sufficient degree of probability on the basis of a set of objective factors . . . that the agreement in question may have an influence, direct or indirect, actual or potential, on the pattern of trade between Member States'.

This definition has been applied in a number of subsequent cases. Its key element is that there is no need to establish an actual effect on trade, but merely that there might potentially be one.

It follows that an agreement concluded between two companies within the UK, and whose effects are apparently confined to the UK, may have an effect on interstate trade in the light of this definition. This might occur where an exclusive purchasing obligation in an agreement made it more difficult for foreign companies to penetrate the UK market for the product concerned, for example where a distributor was obliged to obtain all of their supplies of a particular product from a UK producer. Similarly, price fixing or market sharing agreements between UK producers, whose effect was to exclude foreign producers from the UK, would normally be seen to have this effect.

Therefore, in many circumstances it is likely that both the Act and EU laws will apply to the same agreement or practice. In general, an agreement capable of infringing Article 81 is likely also to infringe the UK Chapter I Prohibition if the parties, or at least one of them, operates in the UK and/or the goods or services in question are sold in the UK. Similarily, if the conduct of a business in a dominant position has an effect on trade between Member States and within the UK, it is likely that both Article 82 and the Chapter II Prohibition will apply.

At the same time, it should be borne in mind that there may be instances where Article 81 will applies but the Chapter I Prohibition does not, given that the exclusions under the Act are more generous than the EU rules. For example a 'vertical' agreement may well not be subject to the Chapter I Prohibition by virtue of an Order under *section 50* of the Act but still be caught by Article 81.

In addition, the DGFT's guidance as to appreciability (see **4.24** and **4.25** above) under the Chapter I Prohibition appears to set the threshold for the application of the prohibition at a higher level *(25% market share)* than equivalent guidance from the Commission in relation to Article 81 (5–10% market share).

The possibility of 'double jeopardy' opens the door to action in national courts under both the EU and UK rules and also to complaint or notification to either or both of the European Commission or the OFT. In principle there is no reason why the same company cannot be fined by both the European Commission and the OFT for the same infringement, although *section 36(9)* of the Act provides that the DGFT must take into account any penalty imposed by the European Commission or any court/body in another Member State when setting the level of the fine.

Who will Investigate? [6.4]

When will the European Commission investigate and when will it leave a case to the UK authorities? Even though a large number of infringements occurring in the UK may also fall for consideration in relation to EU law, it does not follow that the European Commission will wish to become involved in every case where jurisdiction arises under Articles 81 and 82. It simply does not have the resources or the political will to do so.

In fact, in recent years the European Commission has increasingly emphasised its desire to delegate the implementation of competition law to national competition authorities, and to restrict its role to dealing with those cases which raise specific EU–wide issues. This reasoning was adopted in relation to a case in which the European Court rejected a complaint, *Automec (No 2) (Case T-24/90, 1992 SCMLR 341)*. It indicated that the role of the European Commission should be confined to dealing with issues of particular political or legal significance for the Community.

The objective behind this is, broadly, to focus the Commission's limited resources on cases with an 'EU dimension', and to allow others to be dealt with by national competition authorities. This is justified on the basis that national competition authorities are equally well, if not better, placed to deal with many 'domestic' cases.

Main Jurisdictional Differences

Competition Act 1998	Arts 81 and 82 of the EC Treaty
Effect on trade within the UK	Effect on trade between EU Member States
25% market share test guideline in relation to appreciability for Chapter I Prohibition. (**NB** An agreement may infringe the Chapter I Prohibition where the market share is below 25% if it fixes prices, imposes minimum resale prices, or is part of a network of similar agreements which appreciably restrict competition.	5–10% market guideline in relation to appreciability for Article 81, although agreements which fix prices may infringe Article 81 where relevant market share is below this level.
Wide exclusion covering most vertical agreements (i.e. those between companies at different levels in the supply chain) in relation to the Chapter I Prohibition. (**NB** This exclusion will not cover agreements which fix prices.) Exclusion in principle for land agreements.	Vertical agreements subject to Article 81 in principle, although subject to appreciability and availability of the Vertical Agreements Block Exemption, which imposes stricter conditions than the exclusion under the Act.
Certain specific exclusions in relation to the Chapter I Prohibition: – mergers (subject to clawback provisions); – competition scrutiny under other enactments; – planning obligations; – professional rules.	Mergers with a Community dimension subject to the EU Merger Regulation and not Articles 81 and 82.
Certain specific exclusions in relation to the Chapter II Prohibition: – mergers; – compliance with legal requirements; – avoidance of conflict with international obligations; – exceptional and compelling reasons of public policy.	See above in relation to mergers.

The Commission's Policy [6.5]

The European Commission's policy in this regard, and the criteria it considers relevant to determine which authority should deal with a given case, are set out in two explanatory Notices, the Commission Notice on co-operation between national courts and the Commission in applying Articles 81 and 82 of the EC Treaty and the Commission Notice on co-operation between national competition authorities and the Commission in handling cases falling within the scope of Articles 81 and 82. The second Notice, which was published in 1997, notes the disadvantages of:

> 'parallel proceedings before the Commission and a national competition authority [which] are costly for businesses'.

Further, it expressly acknowledges that certain cases which fall within the scope of EU law may be better dealt with at a national level.

Allocation of Cases [6.6]

Territorial Impact [6.7]

Under para 26 of the 1997 Notice, national authorities should handle cases '. . . the effects of which are felt mainly in their territory'. In other words, if a particular case impacts solely on the UK market, even though it may affect inter-state trade, the Commission would normally leave it for the OFT to investigate.

On the other hand, if the effects of an infringement impact across a number of EU Member States, the Commission will almost certainly wish to conduct its own investigation particularly if access to a national market is impeded. So, if a Europe-wide price fixing cartel were suspected, and some of the members were based in the UK, the Commission would want to be the appropriate investigating body.

Possible Exemption under Article 81(3) [6.8]

It would also be appropriate for the European Commission to become involved, where there is a possibility of an exemption under Article

81(3) of the EC Treaty. This might apply, for example, in relation to a co-operation agreement, where the benefits arising from the agreement might outweigh any negative consequences for competition.

Since the European Commission is the only body which may grant an exemption under Article 81(3), it follows that such cases must be dealt with by it. Note that the same point does not apply in relation to Article 82, since there is no provision for an exemption from its application under EU law.

Community Interest   [6.9]

The Commission has indicated that it will wish to become involved in cases which involve a 'Community interest', even where such cases would otherwise be suitable for handling by the OFT. For example, where the case raised a novel point of law.

The Commission is also likely to be anxious to deal with (or at least oversee) cases which involve a public undertaking engaging in anti-competitive activity, on the grounds that these may raise issues of general concern such as whether a Member State is complying with its treaty obligations.

Avoidance of Parallel Proceedings   [6.10]

The Act is designed to promote the decentralisation of enforcement to Member States and avoiding, or at least minimising, 'parallel proceedings', and ensuring consistency between UK and EU competition law.

To promote co-operation between EU and national authorities, the European Commission requests that national authorities inform it of proceedings which they intend to initiate. In turn, the European Commission passes this information onto other Member States. In the same way, the OFT may request confirmation in a given case from the Commission of whether it has started proceedings.

The Commission's view is that where it has begun proceedings then any national proceedings should be stayed pending resolution of the European Commission proceedings.

In summary, there is no brightline distinction as to when the European Commission will act and when it will defer to the OFT. It is really a case of policy. However, the European Commission only acts on its own initiative in a relatively small proportion of cases. The majority of cases that the Commission deals with are as a result of complaints or notifications made to it.

Important tactical considerations therefore arise in deciding whether to complain to or notify an agreement or practice to the European Commission or to the OFT, or both.

Notification Strategy [6.11]

In any circumstances where the effect on interstate trade test is likely to be satisfied, there will be clear benefits in notifying the European Commission.

The OFT's Guidelines, referred to above, identify the following.

○ The European Commission has sole authority to grant an exemption from the prohibition of Article 81(1) further to Article 81(3)
○ Exemption from the Chapter I Prohibition will not prevent Article 81(1) applying.
○ By definition, an EU exemption will be effective throughout the EU, rather than just in the UK. This is of particular relevance where an agreement may impact upon other EU Member States apart from the UK.
○ the current position regarding backdating of exemptions is different under UK and EU law. The European Commission generally does not have power to grant retrospective exemption or immunity from fines, although exceptions are where an agreement does not relate to imports or exports between Member States, or if it is a vertical agreement. For most other agreements, in order to fully protect their position in relation to Article 81(1), companies should consider notifying the European Commission at a relatively early stage. If the OFT is subsequently notified under the Competition Act, the UK exemption may be backdated. Moreover, a penalty cannot be imposed under the Chapter I prohibition where an agreement has been notified to the European Commission until the Commission has determined the matter.

These reasons may appear strong arguments in support of a notification to the European Commission where a retrospective exemption is not available. One further reason that might be added is the making of a tactical notification to the European Commission in order to stall proceedings in a national court – which would stay proceedings pending the outcome of the European Commission's investigation.

The most common circumstances in which parties to an agreement tend to make notification to the European Commission are where:

○ legal certainty of the key restrictions is paramount (and there is no possibility of obtaining an exemption);
○ the parties anticipate challenges from third parties and wish to get their story in first to the Commission; or
○ the parties consider that there is a real risk of fines.

In his guidelines, the DGFT suggests that the question of making a notification to both the European Commission and the DGFT will only arise in 'borderline' cases.

However, where legal certainty is paramount, it is likely that in practice parties will need to consider very carefully the benefit of notifying both authorities. Dual notification gives greatest legal certainty that the arrangement would benefit from exemption under both regimes. Dual notification might be appropriate in circumstance where there was an effect on trade between Member States but the main anti-competitive effect was in the UK. In such a case the OFT would be the more natural regulator and the European Commission may not move swiftly to close the file if the case is not considered priority. Similar considerations might apply where market conditions in the UK differ materially from those in the Member States.

In other cases, it should normally be commercially acceptable not to notify the OFT at the outset. Notification can always be made at a later date and backdated to the date of the agreement. Also the DGFT's guidelines on the Chapter I Prohibition have specifically stated that 'as a general policy the Director General will follow the EC Commission's assessment of the agreement'. Notification is the only way to get an exemption. In most cases, the Commission will in fact close the file by means of an administrative letter – a 'comfort letter' and not take a full decision. A comfort letter is not binding in national courts or authorities but is persuasive. So if the parties have received a comfort letter from the European Commission, they have a high level of security that even though this does not confer a parallel exemption, the agreement should not be struck down under the Act.

The DGFT's guidelines helpfully state that where an agreement in respect of which the European Commission was granted a comfort letter is challenged in an English Court under the Chapter I Prohibition, the DGFT will give priority to the case and an agreement if capable of exemption would be likely to receive exemption with retroactive effect.

The DGFT's stance appears to be to deter what it considers to be unnecessary notifications – and that is likely to be many dual notifications. It expects to defer to the European Commission and will not generally attach any priority to an investigation in most cases. Two exceptions to this general rule are identified in the guidelines. Where:

◯ it raises particular competition concerns in the UK (although it concedes that this is likely to be unusual); or
◯ the agreement involves important legal, economic, or policy developments. The meaning of this exception is not entirely clear, and it is not evident how it would relate to the above.

Complaints [6.12]

Similar tactical considerations to those for notification apply in respect of complaints. Neither the European Commission nor the OFT (or regulators) are obliged to take up a complaint. Relevant consideration as to whom to complain include:

◯ the nature of the complaint – is it a domestic issue or a European one;
◯ does the action restrict access to the UK market i.e. raise single market issues;
◯ is this a sector in which either authority (i.e. the OFT or the regulator) has experience or interest; and
◯ how quickly is a response required?

As a general rule it is expected that the OFT will be in a position to respond quicker to complaints. The OFT has additional resources and does not suffer from the same backlog of cases which have constrained the European Commission in the past.

Substance and Conflict [6.13]

The principle of supremacy of EC law, as set out in *section 2* of the *European Communities Act 1972* imposes an overriding obligation on the UK that any conflict between Community law and UK law be resolved in favour of Community law. These general rules will apply in respect of decisions by the UK courts, the OFT or a regulator.

Given that the Act is so closely modelled on the EU rules, it is hoped that different substantive outcomes will be rare. However, the Act expressly recognises that there are relevant differences between EU and UK law and there is no guarantee that the rules will develop in tandem in the future. There is real potential for conflict of outcome in certain cases.

General Rules [6.14]

In an attempt to avoid conflict between Community and UK law the following general rules apply.

○ An agreement or practice which is prohibited under both the UK and EU rules should not give rise to a situation of conflict. Investigation and enforcement procedures may well be applied concurrently and this will require some practical co-operation between the OFT and the European Commission. Any penalty or fine imposed by the European Commission must be taken into account by the UK authorities in determining the proper penalty under the Act.

○ Where an agreement is prohibited under the EU rules but is not prohibited under the Act (for example, a distribution agreement which confers territorial protection) again no conflict should arise. The agreement will be void under the EU rules and the Act will have no bearing on this.

○ An agreement or practice which is prohibited under the UK rules but is not caught by the EU rules should not give rise to conflict. This will be the case where there is an insufficient effect on trade between Member States. This will be rare.

○ Where an agreement or practice is exempted under the EU rules either by means of a block exemption or an individual exemption, it will enjoy parallel exemptions from the Chapter I Prohibition under *section 10* of the Act. The Act does, however, allow the DGFT to cancel a parallel exemption or to impose conditions in certain circumstances. It is not settled law the extent to which a national authority may derogate from the effect of a Community exemption in this way. However, further to an amendment in June 1999 to the EU Regulation governing the Commission's power to grant block exemptions, it is now possible for the OFT to withdraw the benefit of a block exemption in certain circumstances. This would be applicable where, for the purposes of the agreement or agreements concerned, the UK (or part of it) had the characteristics of a 'distinct market', and the criteria for exemption under Article 81(3) were not met. That said, it is expected that the situation will arise only rarely. The OFT has already informally indicated that it does not expect to use its powers to impose conditions or cancel a parallel exemption other than in very extreme cases. In such cases, for example where the situation in the UK raises particular competition concerns which are not present in other Member States, the OFT would first consult with the European Commission before taking action.

○ Where an agreement has been 'approved' by the European Commission by means of a comfort letter (and about 95% of cases are still closed in this way), the position is less clear-cut. Comfort letters do not have the same force as Commission decisions. The DGFT has indicated in its guidelines that 'as a general policy the Director General will follow the EC Commission's s assessment of the agreement' (see above). That said, the publication of a comfort letter will not prevent an agreement being prohibited under the Act.

Comfort Letters [6.15]

There are different types of comfort letters.

A comfort letter which concludes that the agreement does not infringe Article 81 on the grounds that it has an insufficient effect on trade between Member States will in no way constrain the UK authorities or courts.

Where the comfort letter states that an agreement falls within Article 81(1) but would qualify for exemption under Article 81(3), the European Commission has requested the national authorities to consult it before adopting an incompatible decision under national law. As stated above, the OFT would only be likely to take a contrary decision in circumstances where particular competition concerns were raised in the UK.

The Commission also sometimes issues 'discomfort letters' which indicate that the agreement infringes Article 81. Such a letter will in no way constrain the UK authorities from taking action under the Act.

EU Reform [6.16]

The Act borrows from EU law the concept of prohibitions backed by procedures for notification and exemption. However, this model has received criticism over the years. With rather unfortunate timing for the UK legislators, the European Commission issued in April 1999 a white paper proposing radical reform to its procedures for implementing Articles 81 and 82. These proposals, if implemented, would significantly impact on the *Competition Act* procedures and may even require amendment to the Act, on the grounds that they would involve the European Commission giving up its monopoly to grant exemptions and delegating this function to national courts and competition authorities. This would appear to undermine the operation of *section 10* of the Act which deals with parallel exemptions.

The thrust of the Commission's proposals is to move away from a 'centralised authorisation system' in which only the Commission can issue exemption decisions. It considers that the prior notification and exemption system is inefficient in that to function effectively it requires enormous resources and imposes heavy costs on companies.

The proposed reform involves the abolition of the notification and exemption system and its replacement by a new Regulation which would render the exemption rule under Article 81(3) directly applicable without prior decision by the Commission. Article 81 as a whole would be applied by the Commission, national competition authorities and national courts.

The Commission is seeking to create a decentralised system of enforcement with the Member States taking a greater role. At the centre, the Commission would take a leading role in determining policy and setting out the principal rules of interpretation of Articles 81 and 82. The Commission would also continue to consider some individual cases and issue decisions. The Commission's enforcement efforts would be directed in particular against cross border cartels.

The most routine cases would be shifted to the national competition authorities, including the OFT which would grant exemptions. This proposal would however, conflict with the Government's and the OFT's vision of how the two systems interact. First, the concept of 'parallel exemption' would be less useful as the new system does really not envisage individual notification to the European Commission. Second, the European Commission appears to be shifting the burden of dealing with routine cases onto the OFT. In the context of the Act the OFT has been anxious to deter routine notifications so as not to clog up its resources. For example, as noted above, the DGFT's guidelines encourage parties to notify the European Commission rather than the OFT which affect trade between Member States. That option will disappear.

It is unlikely that the Commission proposals will be implemented for many years yet and they may not ultimately follow the Commission's initial proposals outlined in the White Paper. No changes to the UK regime are therefore expected in the near future. Looking forward, however, there appears real merit in a system in which the OFT is able to receive a single notification and issue a decision which effectively covers both EU and UK competition rules. At the same time, concerns ave been expressed that such a system would heighten legal uncertainty and would impose a role on national courts for which they are not necessarily suited. A further concern is whether EU competition law would be applied uniformly throughout the Community.

7 - Procedure and Enforcement

Introduction [7.1]

The Act introduces sweeping new powers of investigation and enforcement. The new powers to enter premises and impose financial penalties on undertakings and individuals necessitate certain safeguards to ensure that the process operates fairly. This chapter considers the procedural framework which underpins the Act and, in particular:

O how to start the process – complaint or notification;
O powers of investigation of the OFT;
O offences;
O powers of enforcement;
O actions in national courts; and
O appeal and judicial review.

Some of the procedures for dealing with these aspects are dealt with in the Act itself, whilst others are found in the DGFT's Procedural Rules (the 'Rules').

Complaints [7.2]

One way in which to start the process is for a victim of an anti-competitive practice to complain and indeed the Government is hoping that the regime will be complaints driven. Anyone can make a complaint to the DGFT or a regulator about an anti-competitive agreement or abusive conduct including:

O parties to an agreement;
O any third party that has suffered from the effects of the alleged infringement or a body representing such persons e.g. a trade association.
O someone that has been refused the supply of a particular product for no apparent reason; or
O a supplier that is coming under pressure from a powerful customer to enter into a potentially anti-competitive agreement.

There is no formal procedure for making a complaint and no form to complete. It can be made, for example, by telephone or in writing.

Concurrent Jurisdiction [7.3]

Where a complaint made to the OFT falls under the concurrent jurisdiction of a regulator, it will be passed on to the appropriate regulator and the complainant will be informed of the transfer.

Information Required [7.4]

The complaint should contain as much information as possible to assist the DGFT in determining whether or not the complaint merits taking any further action. A complaint can also state what action it thinks the DGFT should take, e.g. interim measures if the alleged infringement is causing him serious and irreparable damage.

Before making a formal complaint, an undertaking could approach the OFT to discuss the matter informally. Having brought the alleged infringement to the attention of the OFT, the complainant could then withdraw and leave the DGFT to consider whether or not to launch an own-initiative investigation in which the complainant need not be involved. However, this may not be possible where the DGFT needs more information from the complainant to satisfy the test of having 'reasonable grounds for suspecting' that there has been an infringement.

Where a formal complaint is made, the OFT is likely to ask the complainant:

○ whether he is a competitor, customer or consumer;
○ the reasons for the complaint;
○ the details of the agreement or conduct complained about; and
○ for more detailed information such as details of the market concerned – e.g. its value, names of the main operators in the market and their respective market shares.

Complainant Protection [7.5]

Where the complainant provides the OFT with information, it must set out the part of the information which it considers to be confidential in a separate annex marked 'confidential information' and explain why it should be treated as such (*Rule 27*).

If the DGFT proposes to disclose any of the information contained in the annex, he will consult the complainant if it is practicable to do so. This means that he will give the complainant written notice that he proposes to disclose the information, giving the complainant the opportunity to make written representations, within a specified period of time, which the DGFT will consider (*Rule 29(1)(c)*).

If anonymity is a concern, the complainant should make it clear at the outset that it wants its identity to be concealed for as long as possible. There is no guarantee that the identity of the complainant will be concealed, particularly as it may be necessary to disclose its identity in order to verify the allegations of the infringement by presenting the undertaking complained of with the evidence against it. This may include copies of correspondence from the complainant to the OFT.

Rejecting Complaints [7.6]

The DGFT does not have to act on a complaint. Where he decides that it should be rejected, he will let the complainant know of its decision and either close the matter or redirect the complaint to another body if appropriate. Failure to act on a complaint may be subject to judicial review.

Where the DGFT decides to act on the complaint, he will tell the complainant of its decision and is likely to keep it informed of the investigation's progress.

Notification [7.7]

The Act provides a voluntary system for notification of agreements or conduct under the Chapter I and Chapter II Prohibitions for guidance or a decision. Prospective agreements and conduct cannot be notified.

Section	Description
12	Requests for DGFT to examine agreements.
13	Notification for guidance under the Chapter I Prohibition.
14	Notification for decision under the Chapter I Prohibition.
15	Effect of guidance.
16	Effect of a decision that the Chapter I Prohibition has not been infringed.
20	Requests for DGFT to consider conduct.
21	Notification for guidance under the Chapter II Prohibition.
22	Notification for a decision under the Chapter II Prohibition.
23	Effect of guidance.
24	Effect of a decision that the Chapter II Prohibition has not been infringed.
Sch 5	Notification under Chapter I: procedure.
Sch 6	Notification under Chapter II: procedure.

There is no obligation on undertakings to notify their agreements or conduct to the DGFT even if they infringe either of the prohibitions. However, in the case of the Chapter I Prohibition, notification is a prerequisite for obtaining an exemption. One major benefit to notifying an agreement under the Chapter I Prohibition is that it affords immunity from penalties from the date of notification. No such immunity exists under the Chapter II Prohibition.

The notification system is modelled on that which operates rather unsatisfactorily at the EU level. One of the major problems at EU level has been the sheer volume of precautionary notifications which have simply swamped the Commission. The DGFT has been at pains to deter precautionary notifications in the countdown to the Act.

Chapter I Prohibition (section 12) [7.8]

Before making a notification under the Chapter I Prohibition, the parties to the agreement should first consider whether the agreement falls within a domestic block exemption or an EC block exemption. In those cases the agreement is automatically exempt from the Chapter I Prohibition and does not need to be notified.

If the agreement is not exempt, the parties should consider whether the agreement falls under one of the exclusions in the Act. If the agreement is not excluded, the parties should only notify the agreement if they consider it has an appreciable effect on competition.

Chapter II Prohibition (section 20) [7.9]

Before making a notification under the Chapter II Prohibition, the undertaking notifying its conduct should first consider whether the conduct falls within an exclusion and, if not, whether it is dominant. If the undertaking is not dominant, it will not usually need to notify. Indeed, notifications under *sections 21* and *22* are likely to be very rare.

Form N [7.10]

Notifications under the Chapter I and Chapter II Prohibitions must be made to the DGFT on Form N, even where the notification relates to a market which is subject to sectoral regulation (*Rule 1*). Form N is available from the DGFT or a regulator. The form sets out a list of information to be provided, including:

○ a 250 word summary of the nature and objectives of the arrangement;
○ the identity of the undertakings submitting the notification or their representative;
○ the purpose of the notification, that is whether it is made under Chapter I or Chapter II and is for guidance or a decision;
○ matters relating to jurisdiction such as why the arrangement is not caught by Article 81(1), whether it has been notified to the European Commission and whether it relates to any of the utilities;
○ information on the parties and the groups to which they belong;
○ the relevant product and geographic markets;

○ market shares in the UK and the European Community of the parties and their five main competitors and customers;
○ market entry and potential competition in the relevant product and geographic markets;
○ reasons for seeking negative clearance or an exemption; and
○ any transitional periods.

Where a simultaneous notification is being made to the DGFT and the European Commission, parties may choose to send three copies of the completed Form A/B (the notification form for the European Commission) and supporting documents (and a further copy if there is concurrent jurisdiction both to the DGFT and the regulator) as well as the Form N. It will be unnecessary for the parties to repeat information given on Form A/B in the Form N, although cross-references to the relevant information on From A/B should be given. Information specific to the UK market will still need to be separately provided if it is not given on Form A/B.

The original, together with two extra copies of the Form N, must be sent to the DGFT by or on behalf of the applicants, together with one set of originals or true copies of the attached documents and two copies of them. The applicant must certify that each copy is a true copy of the original (*Rule 3(1)* and *(2)*).

Concurrent Jurisdiction [7.11]

If the applicant thinks that one or more of the regulators may have concurrent jurisdiction with the DGFT, it must submit one extra copy of the Form N and the attached documents for each of the regulators (*Rule 3(3)*). A copy of the Form N and attached documents should also be sent direct to the relevant regulator(s). If the DGFT considers that a regulator has concurrent jurisdiction to take action in relation to an agreement or conduct which has been notified, he will send a copy of the information submitted as Form N or the original to the regulator and inform the applicant that he has done so. This is to ensure that the appropriate regulator receives all the information as soon as possible, particularly where the applicant has not sent the information directly to the regulator.

Where there is a question as to who is going to deal with the application, the DGFT will write to the applicant telling him who is exercising jurisdiction in relation to the application, and the applicant will be kept informed of any subsequent transfer (*Rule 8*).

Information Supplied [7.12]

The information submitted must be correct and complete, and any information which is false or misleading will be treated as incorrect or incomplete (*Rule 4(2)*). The applicant can request that the DGFT dispense with the obligation to submit particular information, including any document forming part of Form N, if he considers that such information or document is unnecessary for the examination of the case (*Rule 4(4)*).

Any information that is confidential should be put in a separate annex marked 'confidential information' (*Rule 4(3)*). Information is confidential if it is either commercial information the disclosure of which would, or might, significantly harm the legitimate business interests of the undertaking to which it relates, or information relating to the private affairs of an individual the disclosure of which would, or might, significantly harm his interests (*Rule 29(1)(b)*).

Fees [7.13]

Different flat rate fees will be charged for notifications for guidance and decisions. A notification will not be duly made until the appropriate fee has been paid. The fee should therefore accompany the application when it is sent it.

Rules on fees may be made which include a rule to take into account an applicant's ability to pay, or where it would be appropriate to refund a fee in whole or in part. Any such rules would be the subject of consultation and, once approved, would be likely to be supplemental to the existing Rules.

Effective Date [7.14]

An application will become effective on the date on which it is received by the DGFT, and any fee payable in respect of the application has been paid. If an application is received after 6.00pm it will be treated as having been received on the next working day.

The applicant will be sent an acknowledgment of receipt (*Rule 5(1)(2)*). The date on which an application under the Chapter I Prohibition becomes effective is the date from which immunity from penalties runs.

However, if the Form N is incomplete, the DGFT will inform the applicant in writing of that fact and he will not treat the application as effective until he has received the complete information. If the DGFT does not inform the applicant that the Form N is incomplete within one month from the date of receipt, the application will be deemed to have become effective on the date of its receipt (*Rule 5(3)* and *(4)*).

Material Changes [7.15]

Once Form N has been sent, the applicant is under a continuing obligation to inform the DGFT of any material changes in the facts contained in the application without delay. Failure to do so may result in a finding that the application is, or has become, ineffective.

The DGFT will inform the applicant of this finding in writing as soon as it is practicable for him to do so and the application will not become effective until the material changes are communicated to him (*Rule 5(5)–(7)*).

Notifying Other Parties [7.16]

In the case of an application under the Chapter I Prohibition, an applicant must notify all the other parties to the agreement of whom he is aware that he has submitted an application and state whether it was for guidance or a decision. This notification should be in writing and be sent within seven working days of the date on which the applicant receives acknowledgment of receipt of its application.

The same obligation exists in respect of an application under the Chapter II Prohibition if the conduct in question is conduct of two or more persons.

A copy of this written notice must be sent to the DGFT without delay (*Rule 6*).

Choosing Guidance or Decision [7.17]

In respect of the Chapter I and the Chapter II Prohibitions, the Act allows for a notification to be made for 'guidance' or a 'decision'. The information required for each is the same but the parties will need to choose which route is more appropriate for them in the circumstances. There is currently no timetable indicating how long it will take for an application for guidance or a decision to be dealt with, but once the regime has bedded down, statutory timetables are likely to be introduced.

Guidance

Plus points:
- ○ favourable guidance gives immunity from penalties;
- ○ application is not published and whilst the DGFT is not prevented from seeking third party comments he is unlikely to do so;
- ○ cheaper;
- ○ possibly quicker as no need to seek public comment; and
- ○ guidance is not published.

Minus points:
- ○ can be reopened if a third party complains;
- ○ findings of fact are not binding on a court if proceedings are issued;
- ○ the DGFT cannot be compelled to give guidance; and
- ○ guidance cannot be appealed.

Decision

Plus points:
- ○ favourable decision gives immunity from penalties;
- ○ cannot be reopened if a third party complains, although a third party can apply to the DGFT to withdraw or vary a decision within one month from its date of issue;
- ○ findings of fact are binding on the courts;
- ○ the decision can be appealed; and
- ○ the DGFT may be given directions by a court to give a decision without further delay where a person applies to court because there has been undue delay.

Minus points:
- ○ the application and the decision will be made public so it is not confidential;
- ○ more expensive; and
- ○ may take longer because of public consultation.

Guidance (ss13 and 21) [7.18]

An application for guidance asks the DGFT to determine whether or not the agreement or conduct notified is likely to infringe the Chapter I or Chapter II Prohibition. In addition, in the case of the Chapter I Prohibition, where the DGFT considers that the agreement is likely to infringe if not exempt, whether the agreement is likely to be exempt from that Prohibition under a block or parallel exemption or whether he would be likely to grant the agreement an individual exemption if asked to do so by way of a decision.

If an agreement has been notified for guidance under the Chapter I Prohibition, the DGFT cannot impose a penalty in respect of an infringement by that agreement for the period from the date of notification until the date specified when the application is determined.

When the DGFT has determined an application for guidance he will give guidance to the applicant in writing without delay, stating the facts on which he bases the guidance and his reasons for it.

Effect of Favourable Guidance (ss 15 and 23) [7.19]

If the DGFT gives favourable guidance, he can take no further action unless:

○ he has reasonable grounds to believe that there has been a material change of circumstance since he gave the guidance;
○ he has a reasonable suspicion that the information on which he based his guidance was incomplete, false or misleading in a material particular; or
○ a third party makes a complaint about the agreement or conduct.

In the case of guidance under the Chapter I Prohibition, the DGFT can take further action on the additional ground that one of the parties to the agreement applies to him for a decision with respect to the agreement.

Where the DGFT proposes to take further action after giving favourable guidance, he will consult the undertaking to which he gave guidance (*Rule 11*). This involves the DGFT giving written notice, stating the action he proposes and his reasons for it, and informing the applicant that any written representations made to the DGFT, within a specified period of time, will be considered (*Rule 27(1)(c)*).

Removal of Immunity [7.20]

Favourable guidance protects the agreement or conduct concerned from the imposition of penalties. However, this immunity can be lost where the DGFT takes further action on the grounds set out in **7.19** above. The DGFT must also consider it likely that the Chapter I or Chapter II Prohibition will be infringed when taking such action.

The DGFT will give written notice informing the undertakings that he is removing the immunity as from the date specified in his notice. Where the DGFT withdraws the immunity because the information on which he based his guidance was incomplete, false or misleading, the date of withdrawal can be earlier than the date on which the notice is given.

Effect of Unfavourable Guidance [7.21]

Where the DGFT issues unfavourable guidance (i.e. that there is an infringement of either Prohibition and no exclusion or exemption applies), the enforcement procedure will apply (see **7.55** below).

Decision (*Section 14*) [7.22]

An application for a decision asks the DGFT to decide if the agreement or conduct concerned has infringed the Chapter I or Chapter II Prohibition. Additionally, in the case of the Chapter I Prohibition, whether it has not been infringed because of the effect of an exclusion or an exemption (i.e. a block, parallel or *section 11* exemption or an individual exemption).

The DGFT will maintain a register at the OFT which is open to the public between 10.00am and 4.30pm on each working day and on the Internet. The DGFT will enter on the register a summary of the nature and objectives of the agreement or conduct which is notified for a decision, and will give an indication of the outcome of the application (*Rule 7*). The DGFT will take into account any representations made to him by third parties in response to the publication (*Sch 5, para 5* and *Sch 6, para 5*).

The DGFT will also publish a weekly gazette containing summaries of notifications for decisions as well as the results of notifications for decisions.

Consultation [7.23]

The DGFT's rules of procedure (*Rule 12*) provide for varying levels of consultation depending on the type of decision to be taken, as follows, the DGFT:

○ *must* consult the applicant if he proposes to grant an exemption sunjectto conditions or obligations;
○ *must* consult the public if he proposes to grant an exemption with or without conditions or obligations; and
○ *may* consult the public if he proposes to decide there is no infringement.

Public consultation (*Rule 29(1)(d)*) involves the publication of the DGFT's proposal on the register and the OFT website and usually in the OFT's weekly gazette and relevant trade or national press, and subsequent discussions with any party that is not party to the agreement as appears to him likely to be interested.

Consultation on an Unfavourable Decision [7.24]

A decision that there has been an infringement which is prohibited and, in the case of the Chapter I Prohibition, a decision to grant an individual exemption subject to conditions or obligations are the only two decisions which require full consultation with the parties concerned. Where the DGFT proposes to make either of these decisions, he will send a written notice to the parties in which he will state:

○ the matters to which he has taken objection, the action he proposes and his reasons for it (including whether he proposes to make directions or impose a penalty);
○ that any oral and written representations made to the DGFT within the period specified in the notice will be considered, and that he will give all persons who he is aware are parties to the agreement or conduct, or their representatives, an opportunity to make such representations;
○ that he will give all persons who he is aware are parties to the agreement or conduct, or their authorised representatives, an opportunity to inspect the documents in the DGFT's file relating to the proposed decision; and
○ the period within which each person may indicate any part of the notice which he considers to be confidential.

The DGFT may have made a provisional decision or imposed interim measure directions. Where the DGFT has imposed the latter, he may replace them with directions in his final decision.

Effect of a Favourable Decision (ss16 and 24)   [7.25]

Where a favourable decision (i.e. a finding of no infringement or exemption) has been given, no penalty can be imposed in respect of an infringement by the agreement or conduct and the DGFT can take no further action unless:

○   he has reasonable grounds to believe that there has been a material change of circumstance since he gave the guidance;
○   he has a reasonable suspicion that the information on which he based his guidance was incomplete, false or misleading in a material particular;

Further Action   [7.26]

Where the DGFT proposes to take further action after giving a favourable decision (e.g. launch an own-initiative investigation), he will give written notice to the parties in question. This will state the action he proposes, his reasons for it, and inform that person that any written representations made to the DGFT within a specified period of time will be considered (*Rule 16*). He may also publish his proposal. If the DGFT then takes such further action he will publish a notice.

Where the DGFT takes further action, he may remove the immunity from penalties by giving written notice to the party or person on whose application the decision was made. Where the DGFT withdraws the immunity because the information on which based his decision was incomplete, false or misleading, the date of withdrawal can be earlier than the date on which the notice is given.

Effect of an Unfavourable Decision   [7.27]

Where the DGFT issues an unfavourable decision (i.e. that there is an infringement of either prohibition and no exclusion or exemption applies) the enforcement procedure will apply.

Other Decisions [7.28]

The DGFT may take a number of specific decisions under the Act according to the provisions of the rules, including:

○ extension of individual exemption (on application before the expiry of the existing exemption) (*s4(6)*);
○ extension of transitional period (on application before the expiry of the transitional period) (*s36*);
○ withdrawl of individual or parallel exemption (*s10(5)*)
○ withdrawl of exclusion (*s3(5)*)
○ termination of transitional period (*Schedule 13, para 37*).

Powers of Investigation [7.29]

The Act gives the DGFT wide powers of investigation which he can use to determine whether there has been an infringement of the Chapter I or Chapter II Prohibition. These powers can be used following a complaint, a notification or on the DGFT's own-initiative. In each case the powers available to the DGFT are the same. The DGFT can:

○ require the production of specified documents or specified information;
○ enter premises without a warrant; and
○ enter and search premises with a warrant.

Section	Description
25	DGFT's power to investigate.
26	Powers when conducting investigations.
27	Power to enter premises without a warrant.
28	Power to enter premises under a warrant.
29	Entry of premises under warrant: supplementary.
30	Privileged communications.
31	Decisions following an investigation.

Section	Power	Who exercises it?	How is it exercised	Documents involved	Scope of the Power
26	Power to request specified documents and information.	DGFT	By written notice	written notice	- Ask for specified documents and information. - Take copies or extracts. - Ask for explanations of any document produced. - Ask where a document is.
27	Power to enter premises without a warrant and ask for documents.	Any officer authorised in writing by the DGFT (an 'investigating officer').	By written notice where the premises are occupied by a third party.	- written notice - evidence of authorisation - evidence of identity - document setting out and notifying option to have legal adviser present.	- Enter premises without a warrant. - Use such equipment as is necessary. - Request the production of any document. - Requesting an explanation of any document produced. - Ask where document can be found. - Take copies of or extracts from documents produced. - Ask for information held on computer.
			Without notice where the premises are occupied by an undertaking being investigated or it has not been possible to give notice to the third party having taken all reasonably third party having practical steps to do so.	- evidence of authorisation - evidence of identity - document setting out same information as in written notice - document setting out powers and notifying option to have legal adviser present.	
28	Power to enter and search premises for documents with a warrant.	Authorised officer named in the warrant and any officers authorised to accompany the named officer.	By obtaining a warrant on one of three grounds	- a warrant - evidence of identity - document setting out powers and notifying option to have legal adviser present.	- Enter using force as is reasonably necessary. - Search premises and take copies or extracts from any document of the 'relevant kind'. - Take possession of documents to prevent interference or where it is not practicable to take copies. - Take any other necessary steps to preserve a document or prevent interference with it. - Require an explanation of a document of a relevant kind. - Ask where any document of the relevant kind can be found. - Require infromation held on computer.

Before using any of these powers, the DGFT must be satisfied that there are 'reasonable grounds for suspecting' that the Chapter I or Chapter II Prohibition has been infringed. In order to establish such grounds, the DGFT will consider the documents and information available to him at the time, in particular copies of agreements, statements from employees or ex-employees or a complaint.

Specified Documents and Information (s26) [7.30]

For the purposes of the investigation, the DGFT may require any person to produce a specified document or specified information which he considers relates to any matter relevant to the investigation. A request for a document or information which is unrelated to the application of the Chapter I or Chapter II Prohibition would be improper. The term 'document' includes information recorded in any form. This would cover information stored on a computer as well as hard copies.

This is the power that is most likely to be used, particularly as it can be used at any stage of the investigation.

The DGFT may require the undertakings under investigation to provide all the relevant documents and information that they have been asked for. This is particularly useful for the DGFT, as it puts the burden on the undertakings to sort out the documents and information asked for, without his officers having to attend the premises to request or search for the documents themselves. It is also the only power under which the DGFT can ask for information.

The DGFT is not restricted to asking for documents or information from the parties to the agreement or the undertakings carrying out the conduct, but may do so from any person he so chooses (including competitors, customers and consumers). The types of documents and information he can require is also wide, as it can relate to any matter relevant to the investigation. This would cover not only contracts and accounts but also, for example, personal diaries. The DGFT can also specify categories or types of documents or information rather than specific items (e.g. types of agreements, invoices and minutes of meetings).

Written Notice (section 26(2)) [7.31]

Each time the power is used, the DGFT will serve a written notice on the person required to produce the documents or information. This notice is likely to be sent by registered post.

The notice *must*:

○ state the subject matter and the purpose of the investigation;
○ specify or describe the documents or information, or categories of documents or information, required; and
○ set out the nature of the offences created by the Act by failing to comply with a requirement made under the powers of investigation.

The notice *may* also state:

○ the time and place at which a document or information must be produced; and
○ the manner and form in which it is to be produced.

Copies and Explanations (s26(6)) [7.32]

The DGFT can take copies or extracts of any documents he receives and he can ask the person required to produce it for an explanation of it. Where this is required, the person asked to give the explanation is entitled to be accompanied by a legal adviser (see **7.45** below on access to legal advice).

Failure to Produce (s26(6)) [7.33]

If a document that has been requested is not produced, the DGFT can require the person so required to state, to the best of their knowledge and belief, where the document can be found.

Entering Premises Without a Warrant [7.34]

Under *section 27*, any officer of the DGFT who is authorised in writing to do so (an 'investigating officer') can enter premises in connection with his investigation and ask for documents to be produced.

Entry *without notice* is permitted where the DGFT suspects that the premises are, or have been, occupied by a party to the agreement which he is investigating or whose conduct he is investigating. This could mean that the first time an undertaking becomes aware of an investigation is when the investigating officer turns up unannounced at his premises (a 'dawn-raid').

At least *two working days' written notice* prior to the date of entry is required where the premises are not occupied by a party to the agreement or whose conduct is not being investigated. However, the DGFT may enter these premises *without notice* if the investigating officer has been unable to give notice to the occupier despite taking all reasonably practicable steps to do so. This allows the DGFT to enter premises of third parties such as customers, competitors or employees with or without notice, depending on the circumstances. The investigating officer cannot use force to enter the premises and so will not be able to enter where the premises are unoccupied. This is in contrast to the power under *section 28* (see **7.37** below).

Where written notice is required, it must state:

❍ the subject matter and purpose of the investigation; and
❍ the nature of the offences created by failing to comply with a requirement made under the powers of investigation.

On arrival at the premises, whether with or without notice, the investigating officer will produce evidence of his identity, evidence of his authorisation and a separate document setting out his powers and stating that the occupier can request that his legal adviser is present. Where the DGFT has not given written notice, the investigating officer must also produce a document setting out the same information as the written notice.

The investigating officer should be asked to produce these documents before he is allowed to enter. The occupier should check that the investigating officer does have the authority to act, and to understand the scope of his powers.

The investigating officer can use such equipment that he deems necessary when entering any premises. This is likely to include computer equipment and tape recording equipment. However, the officer may not use equipment to force entry.

On Entry [7.35]

Once the investigating officer is on the premises he can require:

○ the production of documents which relate to the investigation;
○ copies or extracts from any document produced;
○ an explanation of a document from any person;
○ any person to state, to the best of his knowledge and belief, where any document can be found if not produced; and
○ any information which is held in a computer and is accessible from the premises and which the investigating officer considers relates to the investigating to be produced in a form in which it can be taken away and in which it is visible and legible.

The occupier, or his legal adviser, should keep a record of all the documents that were produced and of what copies and extracts were taken. Ideally the occupier should keep copies of anything taken by the investigating officer, to give to his legal adviser. In addition, the occupier should keep a minute of any explanations of documents given. It will be particularly important for an occupier to do this when his legal adviser is not present as, in order to give legal advice on the implications and consequences of the investigation, his/her lawyer will need to know what materials were seen and copied, and what questions were asked. The investigating officer must limit his/her questions to asking for an explanation of a document, or where it can be found.

Meaning of Premises   [7.36]

'Premises' will generally mean business premises, but can also include domestic premises if the home is used in connection with the business or if business documents are kept there. It also includes any vehicle used in connection with business.

Entering Premises with a Warrant   [7.37]

Under *section 28*, the DGFT can apply to a judge of the High Court or the Court of Session, for a warrant for a named officer to enter and search premises. This power can only be used if one of the three grounds on which a warrant can be applied for are satisfied, i.e:

○ there are reasonable grounds for suspecting that there are on any premises documents which the investigating officer has already asked for by using his other powers of investigation (*sections 26* and *27*) which have not been produced;
○ there are reasonable grounds for suspecting that there are on the

premises, documents which the DGFT could ask for under his power to request documents or information (*section 26*), but which, if asked for, would be concealed, removed, tampered with or destroyed; or

O   an investigating officer has attempted to enter premises without a warrant (*section 27*) but has been unable to do so and there are reasonable grounds for suspecting that there are on the premises documents, the production of which, could have been required on entering the premises without a warrant.

The warrant will authorise a named officer of the DGFT, and any other officers whom the DGFT has authorised in writing to accompany the named officer, to enter and search the premises.

The first and third grounds above require that the DGFT has already tried to obtain documents using one of his other powers of investigation. The second ground is the only one where prior action is not required. This power is most likely to be used where the DGFT suspects that documents or information would be concealed, removed, tampered with or destroyed although it will also be used where the fact that the premises are unoccupied has prevented the investigating officer from gaining entry.

On arrival at the premises, the authorised officer will produce: evidence of his identity; evidence of his authorisation; the warrant; and a separate document setting out the scope of his powers and the right for the occupier to request that his legal adviser be present.

The investigating officer should be asked to produce these documents before he is allowed to enter. The occupier should check that the investigating officer does have the authority to act, and to understand the scope of his powers.

Warrant Details [7.38]

The warrant must indicate:

O   the subject matter and purpose of the investigation; and
O   the nature of the offences created by failing to comply with a requirement made under the powers of investigation.

Unoccupied Premises [7.39]

If there is no-one at the premises when the named officer proposes to execute the warrant, he must, before executing it take such steps as are reasonable in all the circumstances to inform the occupier of the intended entry. If the named officer is unable to inform the occupier of his intended entry he must, when executing the warrant, leave a copy of it in a prominent place on the premises.

Equipment [7.40]

When entering the premises, the authorised officer can take with him such equipment as appears necessary. This is likely to include not only computer and tape recording equipment used to gather information, but other equipment to assist with entry to the premises such as drills and tools to break open locks. When the named officer leaves the premises he must leave them as effectively secured as he found them.

Powers Under the Warrant [7.41]

The named officer and other authorised officers have the power to:

O   enter the premises specified in the warrant, using such force as is reasonably necessary for the purpose;
O   search the premises and take copies of, or extracts from, any document for which the warrant was granted;
O   take possession of any document for which the warrant was granted if such action appears necessary to preserve the documents or prevent interference with them, or it is not reasonably practicable to take copies of the documents on the premises;
O   to take any other steps which appear to be necessary to preserve the documents or prevent interference with them;
O   require any person to provide an explanation of any document or to state to the best of their knowledge and belief where it may be found; and
O   require any information which is held on computer, is accessible from the premises and which the named officer considers relates to the investigation to be produced in a form in which it can be taken away and in which it is visible and legible.

Where documents have been taken, the occupier should check that they are returned within three months from the date on which they were taken.

As in the case of a 'dawn raid' without a warrant, the occupier or his legal adviser should keep a record of all documents produced, details of copies and extracts taken and what original documents are seized. In addition, the occupier should keep a minute of any explanations of documents given.

Period of Validity [7.42]

A warrant will last for one month during which time the named officer can enter the premises as many times as he needs. If an investigation has not been completed within a month, an application can be made to the court for the warrant to be extended or for a new warrant to be issued.

Constraints on the Use of the Powers [7.43]

The Act provides certain safeguards for undertakings that are being investigated. These are:

○ the protection of privileged communications;
○ access to legal advice;
○ privilege against self-incrimination;
○ the non-disclosure of confidential information; and
○ access to the file.

Privileged Communications [7.44]

Certain documents are protected because they enjoy legal professional privilege. The DGFT cannot require these documents to be produced under his powers of investigation, and if they are so required a person can refuse to produce them.

The Act refers to a 'privileged communication' as one which is:

○ between a professional legal adviser and their client; or

○ made in connection with, or in contemplation of, legal proceedings and for the purposes of those proceedings which would be protected from disclosure on grounds of legal professional privilege in the High Court on grounds of confidentiality of communications.

Communications between a client and his in-house lawyer as well as such communications between a client and his external lawyer are protected. The former may be harder to identify as privileged at first glance, and in-house lawyers should, therefore, adopt the practice of identifying privileged communications as such and keeping them seperate from non-privileged documents.

Access to Legal Advice   [7.45]

An occupier of premises that is subject to an on-site investigation will be entitled to contact his legal adviser and request that a reasonable time is allowed for his legal adviser to arrive at the premises before the investigation continues. A reasonable time will probably be not more than one to two hours so that the investigation is not impeded (*Rule 13(1)* and *(2)*).

The officer conducting the investigation will grant a request to wait if he considers it reasonable in the circumstances to do so and if he is satisfied that such conditions as he considers appropriate to impose in granting the occupier's request are, or will be, complied with.

Any conditions imposed would be to prevent the occupier from tampering with evidence or from warning others about the investigation. These conditions may include a ban on the use of external e-mail, or the use of the telephone, sealing of cabinets and allowing the investigating officer to wait in the office of his choice.

Where the occupier has been given notice of the investigation or the undertaking has an in-house legal adviser on the premises, the investigating officer will not wait for an external legal adviser to arrive. This will not prevent the occupier from contacting his external legal adviser as well, particularly where his in-house legal adviser is not an expert in handling competition matters.

If a person is required to provide an explanation of a document following a request for it under *section 26* his legal adviser may be present (*Rule 13(3)*).

Self-incrimination [7.46]

An undertaking that is being investigated has the right not to incriminate his or herself. This right does not appear in the Act, but is imported through *section 60* from EU principles. The boundaries of the right are unclear and the principle will develop in line with EU jurisprudence.

In principle, an undertaking does not have to answer questions that would amount to admissions of guilt, as this is something that the DGFT has to prove. During an on-site investigation, the officer carrying out the investigation can only ask two types of factual question: an explanation of a document, or where a document can be found. If, for example, a diary is produced, the officer could ask whether Mr X was at the meeting on a particular date but could not ask whether at that meeting Mr X discussed price-fixing.

Disclosure of Confidential Information (s55) [7.47]

An undertaking that is being investigated at its premises cannot refuse to hand over confidential information, but the fact that the information is confidential limits the extent to which it can be disclosed by the DGFT.

The DGFT cannot disclose confidential information obtained either through a complaint, a notification or through his powers of investigation which relates to the affairs of any individual or to any particular undertaking during the lifetime of an individual or while that undertaking continues to be carried on.

Disclosure with Consent [7.48]

Disclosure can be made if consent to the disclosure has been obtained from:

○ the person from whom the information was initially obtained, and if different:
  - the individual to whose affairs the information relates; or
  - the person for the time being carrying on the business to which the information relates.

Disclosure Without Consent [7.49]

In certain circumstances the DGFT can disclose the confidential information without consent. This is where disclosure is:

○ made for the purpose of:
- facilitating the performance of any relevant functions of a designated person (a relevant function includes any function under *Part I* of the Act and designated person includes the DGFT and the regulators (*Sch 11*);
- facilitating the performance of any functions of the Commission in respect of Community law about competition;
- facilitating the performance by the Comptroller and Auditor General of any of his functions;
- criminal proceedings in any part of the United Kingdom;

○ made with a view to the institution of, or otherwise for the purposes of, civil proceedings brought under or in connection with Part I of the Act;

○ made in connection with the investigation of any criminal offence triable in the United Kingdom or in any part of it; or

○ which is required to meet a Community obligation.

In addition, the restriction on disclosure does not apply to a disclosure of confidential information made for the purpose of facilitating the performance of specified functions of any specified person. Any such specified functions or persons would be set out in an order, but no such order has so far been made.

It is a criminal offence to disclose information without consent, unless the Act provides that the disclosure falls within an exception. This offence is punishable by a fine up to the statutory maximum (currently £5,000) and/or imprisonment of up to two years.

Criteria for Disclosure (s56) [7.50]

Where the DGFT is considering the disclosure of confidential information he must have regard to the need for excluding, so far as is practicable, information, the disclosure of which would in his opinion be contrary to the public interest. He must also consider the need to exclude, so far as is practicable:

○ commercial information the disclosure of which would or might,

in his opinion, significantly harm the legitimate business interests of the undertaking to which it relates; or
○ information relating to the private affairs of an individual the disclosure of which would, or might, significantly harm his interests, and
○ to the extent to which the disclosure is necessary for the purposes for which it is disclosed. This will involve a careful balancing exercise by the DGFT before any disclosure is made.

Human Rights Act 1998 [7.51]

The *Human Rights Act 1998* (*HRA 1998*) requires the courts to apply the Act in a way that is compatable with the European Convention on the Protection of Human Rights and Fundamental Freedoms ('the Convention') The *HRA 1998* will afford some additional safeguards as to the way in which the DGFT and the other relevant authorities use their powers under the Act.

The Convention confers a number of rights which may be relevant in the context of investigation and proceedings under the Act;

○ the right to a fair trial within a reasonable time by an independent and impartial tribunal established by law (Art 6(1));
○ the right to privacy (Art 8); and
○ the right against self–incrimination.

It is likely that objections based on *HRA 1998* will be raised in appeals under the Act or applications for judicial review.

Offences [7.52]

Where a person fails to co-operate with an investigation he may be guilty of committing a criminal offence. The offences and their sanctions are set out in the table opposite.

Defences [7.53]

A number of defences are provided for in the Act against the offences of failing to comply with a requirement imposed under the powers of investigation i.e:

Section	Offence	Sanction on summary conviction	Sanction on conviction on indictment
42	Failure to comply with a requirement imposed under the powers of investigation under ss26–28 (subject to certain defences (**see ?.??**)	Fine of up to the statutory maximum (currently £5,000).	Unlimited fine.
	Intentionally obstructing an officer carrying out an on-site investigation without a warrant under s27.	Fine of up to the statutory maximum.	Unlimited fine.
	Intentionally obstructing an officer carrying out an on-site investigation with a warrant under s28.	Fine of up to the statutory maximum.	Unlimited fine and/or up to two years imprisonment.
43	Intentionally or recklessly destroying, disposing of, falsifying or concealing a document the production of which has been required under ss 26, 27 or 28, or cause or permit its destruction etc.	Fine of up to the statutory maximum.	Unlimited fine and/or up to two years imprisonment.
44	Knowingly or recklessly providing information, that is false or misleading in a material particular, to the DGFT or another person such as a legal adviser, knowing that it will be used to provide information to the DGFT.	Fine of up to the statutory maximum.	Unlimited fine and/or up to two years imprisonment.

○ where a person is required to produce a document it is a defence for him to prove the document was not in his possession or under his control, and that it was not reasonably practicable from him to comply with the requirement;

○ if a person is charged with failing to provide information, or an explanation or a document or to state where a document is to be found, it is a defence for him to prove that he had a reasonable excuse for failing to comply with the requirement; and

○ it is not an offence to fail to comply with a requirement under *sections 26* or *27* if the person imposing the requirement has failed to act within his powers.

Who is Guilty?   [7.54]

If a body corporate, such as a company, commits any of the offences described above and the offence is proved to have been committed with the consent or connivance of an officer or to be attributable to his neglect, the officer as well as the body corporate, is guilty of the offence. An officer means a director, manager, secretary or other similar officer of the company or a person purporting to act in any such capacity.

If the offence is committed by a body corporate which is managed by its members, a member may be similarly guilty, as well as the body concerned, if the offence was committed with his consent or connivance or attributable to his neglect.

Enforcement   [7.55]

The Act gives the DGFT powers to enforce the Chapter I and Chapter II Prohibitions using the powers set out in Chapter III of the Act. Two of these powers can be used while the investigation is still ongoing (namely interim measures directions and provisional decisions), and the others can only be used when an infringement decision is made (namely giving directions and imposing financial penalties). The powers of enforcement are set out in the table below.

Section	Description
32	Directions in relation to agreements
33	Directions in relation to conduct
34	Enforcement of directions
35	Interim measures
36	Penalty for infringing the Chapter I or Chapter II Prohibition
37	Recovery of penalties
38	The appropriate level of a penalty
39	Limited immunity for small agreements
40	Limited immunity in relation to the Chapter II Prohibition
41	Agreements notified to the Commission

Interim Measures [7.56]

Where the DGFT has 'a reasonable suspicion' that the Chapter I or Chapter II Prohibition has been infringed but he has not completed his investigation, he can make interim measures directions if he thinks that it is necessary for him to act as a matter of urgency in order to:

○ prevent serious, irreparable damage to a particular person or category of person (e.g. someone is being driven out of business by a competitor); or
○ protect the public interest (e.g. to prevent damage to a particular industry).

This is a very useful power as it enables the DGFT to act at an early stage of the investigation to prevent further harm from occurring as a result of an infringement.

Before giving an interim measures direction, the DGFT, under *section 35*, must give written notice to the person to whom he proposes to give the direction and give that person an opportunity to make representations. The notice must indicate the nature of the direction and the reasons for it. The DGFT must also give the person to whom the directions are to be given, or his authorised representative, access to the file under *Rule 18*.

The types of interim measure the DGFT may give include requiring the termination of the agreement in question or ceasing the anti-competitive conduct. Alternatively he may require the agreement or conduct to be modified.

An interim measures direction will not affect the final decision, so the DGFT could go on to make a decision that there has not been an infringement. Where a favourable decision is given, the party to whom the interim measures direction was addressed has no course of redress so that it cannot recover any loss suffered as a result of the direction before the final decision was made. It is therefore important that if parties object to an interim measures direction they make their representations at the time. An interim measures direction can be appealed, but an appeal will not suspend the effect of the direction.

If a person fails, without reasonable excuse, to comply with an interim measures direction, the DGFT may apply to the court for an order:

○ requiring the defaulter to make good his default within a time specified in the order; or
○ if the interim measures direction related to anything to be done in the management or administration of an undertaking requiring the undertaking or any of its officers to do it.

Provisional Decision [7.57]

The other interim power available to the DGFT is the making of a provisional decision (*s12(2), s20(2); Sch 5, para 3; Sch 6, para 3* and *Rule 9*). It is likely that this power will be used less than the power to impose interim measures directions. It can only be used where an application has been made, and not following a complaint or an own-initiative investigation.

If after a preliminary investigation of an application, the DGFT considers that it is likely that the agreement or conduct notified will infringe the

Chapter I or Chapter II Prohibition, and in the case of the agreement it would not be appropriate to grant it an individual exemption, he may make a provisional decision.

If the DGFT proposes to make a provisional decision, he will consult the applicant. This means that he will give written notice to the applicant stating the action he proposes and his reasons for it, and inform the applicant that any written representations made to the DGFT within a specified period of time will be considered (*Rule 27(1)(c)*).

If the DGFT goes on to make a provisional decision he will give a written notification of the decision to the applicant in which he will give an account of the facts on which he bases the decision and his reasons for it. However, this decision cannot be appealed as it is only an interim step and it has no immediate consequences. To a certain extent, a provisional decision serves as an early warning to the applicant that the DGFT is likely to find that the agreement or conduct is unlawful. It will then be up to the applicant to modify its practices so as to avoid a subsequent infringement decision or unfavourable guidance.

In the case of an application under the Chapter I Prohibition, a provisional decision has the effect of removing the immunity from penalties afforded from the date of notification as if it had never applied. No such immunity exists under the Chapter II Prohibition.

Directions (s32) [7.58]

Where the DGFT has made a decision that an agreement or conduct infringes the Chapter I or Chapter II prohibition, he may give directions to such person or persons as he considers appropriate. This means that directions can be given to individuals and undertakings whether or not they are the infringing parties, e.g. a direction may be addressed to a parent company of one of the parties to the offending agreement.

A direction may require the parties or the person concerned to modify the agreement or conduct in question or terminate the agreement or cease the conduct. Directions may also require positive action such as informing third parties that an infringement has been brought to an end and reporting back periodically to the DGFT on certain matters such as prices charged. Most such directions will have immediate effect, although in some cases a period of time will be allowed in which the undertaking can comply with the direction.

The directions must be given in writing and they are likely to form part of the infringement decision where the directions and the decision are addressed to the same person. Where the DGFT gives a direction to a person he shall inform that person in writing of the facts on which he bases the direction and his reasons for giving it (*Rule 17*). Where the directions form part of the infringement decision, the person to whom the directions are addressed will have an opportunity to make written and oral representations, and have access to the file.

The DGFT will publish any directions he gives on the register at the OFT and on a website on the Internet. Directions can be appealed to the appeal tribunal of the Competition Commission.

If a person fails without reasonable excuse to comply with a direction the DGFT may apply to the court for an order requiring the defaulter to make good his default within a time specified in the order or if the direction related to anything to be done in the management or administration of an undertaking requiring the undertaking or any of its officers to do it.

An order of the court may make provision for all the costs of the application of the order to be paid by the person in default or any officer of an undertaking who is responsible for the default.

Penalties [7.59]

The Act allows the DGFT to impose a financial penalty on an undertaking that has intentionally or negligently infringed the Chapter I or Chapter II Prohibition. The amount of the penalty can be up to 10 per cent of the undertaking's turnover in the UK. Turnover will be defined in a statutory instrument yet to be issued.

The DGFT will make a finding of intention where, for example:

O the agreement or conduct has as its object the restriction of competition, e.g. a price fixing restriction;
O the undertaking is aware that its actions will be, or are reasonably likely to be, restrictive of competition but still decides to go ahead; or
O the undertaking could not have been unaware that its agreement or conduct had as it object the restriction of competition, even if it did not know that it would infringe a prohibition.

Where an undertaking knew or ought to have know that its actions would result in an infringement it is likely to have negligently infringed one of the prohibitions.

Immunity from Penalties [7.60]

In certain circumstances an undertaking is immune from the imposition of a penalty. These are where:

○ it is a small agreement or conduct of minor significance;
○ the agreement has been notified under Article 81 to the European Commission;
○ the agreement has been notified to the DGFT under the Chapter I Prohibition; or
○ favourable guidance or a favourable decision has been given.

Conduct of Minor Significance [7.61]

In order to reduce burdens on small undertakings, the Act provides that 'small agreements' and 'conduct of minor significance' are immune from penalties. Both these terms will be defined in orders, and are likely to be based on turnover thresholds of the undertakings concerned in the region of £20–50 million. An undertaking will also be protected by the immunity if it acted on the reasonable assumption that it fell below the specified threshold.

However, the immunity can be withdrawn by the DGFT if, as a result of this investigation, he considers the agreement or conduct is likely to infringe the Chapter I or Chapter II Prohibition. The DGFT will give written notice to the person or persons from whom the immunity has been withdrawn. The date on which the withdrawal of immunity has effect cannot be earlier than the date on which it is given. When deciding on the date for withdrawl, the DGFT will consider how much time the person or persons affected are likely to need to make sure that there is no further infringement.

EU Notification [7.62]

An undertaking will also be immune from penalties under the Chapter

I Prohibition where it has notified the agreement to the European Commission under Article 81(1) of the EC Treaty. The period of immunity will run from the date of notification to the European Commission to the date on which it determines the matter, unless it has withdrawn the benefit of immunity from fines under Article 81(1), in which case the immunity under the Chapter I Prohibition will automatically cease.

UK Notification [7.63]

An undertaking will be immune from penalties under the Chapter I Prohibition where it has notified the agreement to the DGFT. The period of immunity will run from the date of notification until the date specified in a written notice given on determination of the application. This immunity can only be removed if the DGFT makes a provisional decision. No such immunity exists under the Chapter II Prohibition.

Amount [7.64]

Section 38 requires the DGFT to prepare and publish guidance as to the appropriate amount of any penalty. Guidance will set out the main steps the DGFT will follow when calculating the amount of any penalty, and shows what factors he is likely to consider. A consultation document on guidance on penalties was published in March 1999 (OFT 423). The steps are likely to be as follows.

O calaculation of the starting point by applying a percentage determined by the nature of the infringement to the relevant turnover of the undertaking;
O adjustment for duration;
O adjustment for other factors;
O adjustment for further aggravting or mitigating factors; and
O adjustment if the maximum penalty of 10% of the turnover of the undertaking is exceeded.

Co-operation by an undertaking during an investigation will be considered as a mitigating factor, whereas the obstruction of an investigation or failure to co-operate may lead to an increase in the penalty.

The DGFT will also offer favourable treatment to undertakings that 'blow the whistle' on secret cartels. This policy of leniency may lead to a total or substantial reduction in the amount of a penalty which would otherwise be imposed for the first undertaking to come forward or provide evidence of a cartel before written notice of decision is given.

Where the DGFT requires an undertaking to pay a penalty he will inform that person in writing of the facts on which he bases the penalty and his reasons for requiring that person to pay it (*Rule 17(1)(b)*).

Actual payment will be requested by way of a written notice which will state the date within which payment must be made. Failure to pay may result in enforcement proceedings being issued by the DGFT to recover the amount as a civil debt.

An undertaking can appeal the decision to impose a penalty and the amount of the penalty. The appeal will suspend the payment of the penalty, but will not affect the enforcement of the rest of the decision.

Third Party Claims [7.65]

Third parties that have suffered loss as a result of an infringement of the Chapter I or Chapter II Prohibition may wish to consider whether they can exercise any other rights or remedies other than the possibility of complaining to the DGFT. The Act itself does not state that third parties have a right to claim damages or seek an injunction against an undertaking that has breached the Chapter I of Chapter II Prohibition. However, such rights have been confirmed by Ministers and can be inferred in the Act.

Lord Haskel said:

> 'third parties have a right of private action. Our clear intention in framing this Bill is that third parties may seek injunctions or damages in the courts if they have been adversely affected by the action of undertakings in breach of the prohibitions. This is an important element of the regime. There is no need to make explicit provision in the Bill to achieve that result'.
>
> (Lords, 25.11.97, col 955-6)

Inferences can be drawn from various provisions in the Act, for example that:

○   a decision of the appeal tribunal can be 'enforced' in the same manner as a decision of the DGFT (*Sch 8, para 3(3)*) ;

○   information may be disclosed 'with a view to the institution of, or otherwise for the purposes of, civil proceedings brought under or in connection with Part I of the Act' (*section 55(3)(b)*) ; and

○   findings of fact by the DGFT are binding on the parties once the time for appealing against the DGFT's decision has expired or the appeal tribunal upheld the finding in proceedings in respect of an alleged infringement of the Chapter I or Chapter II Prohibition but which are brought otherwise than by the DGFT (furthermore, rules of court may make provision in respect of assistance to be given by the DGFT to the court where proceedings are brought (*section 58*);

○   a decision by the European Court includes a decision as to the 'civil liability of an undertaking for harm caused by its infringement of Community law' (section *60(6)(b)*) .

The absence of any clear right to third party actions on the face of the Act, suggests that such action is not intended to form a central role in the Act notwithstanding ministerial statements in parliament. Whilst section 58, for example, will offer some practical encouragement for third parties, it remains to be seen whether private actions will become a feature of competition law enforcement in the UK as they are in the US.

Appeals [7.66]

Section	Description
46	Appealable decisions
47	Third party appeals
48	Appeals tribunal
49	Appeals on point of law etc.
Sch 8	Appeals

The Act allows parties to appeal certain decisions of the DGFT to the appeal tribunal of the Competition Commission. The appeal tribunal will put itself in the position of the DGFT and reconsider the same information. The appeal tribunal will serve an adjudicatory rather than an investigatory function. Where further investigation is required, the appeal tribunal will hand the matter back to the DGFT.

The government has stated that the tribunal should be primarily concerned with the correctness or otherwise of the conclusions contained in the appealed decision, and not with how the decision was reached or the reasoning expressed in it. The government has also stated that, wherever possible, they want the tribunal to decide a case on the facts before it, even where there has been a procedural error, and to avoid remitting the case to the DGFT. The rules of the tribunal are likely to reflect this approach.

This approach will apply unless defects in how the decision was reached or the reasoning make it impracticable for the tribunal fairly to determine the correctness or otherwise of the conclusions or of any directions contained in the decision. Undertakings will therefore be able to appeal those cases where they believe that failure on the part of the DGFT to follow proper procedure has led him to reach an incorrect conclusion. This will allow the tribunal to remedy the consequences of any procedural defects. However, appeals on points of procedure which had no effect on the outcome of the case will not be allowed.

Appealable Decisions [7.67]

Appeals can be made against decisions concerning:

❍ infringement of the Chapter I Prohibition (*s14(2)*);
❍ infringement of the Chapter II Prohibition (*s20(2)*);
❍ the granting of an individual exemption (*s4(1)*) including:
  ● whether to impose any condition or obligation (*s4(3)(a)*);
  ● the terms of such condition or obligation;
  ● the period fixed for an individual exemption – including whether to extend it and the period of such an extension;
  ● the date from when an individual exemption has effect (*s4(6)*);
  ● cancelling an exemption (*ss5(1)(a), 6(6), 10(5)*);
❍ withdrawing or varying any of those decisions following a third party application under *s47(1)*;
❍ the imposition or amount of a penalty (*s36*);
❍ an interim measures direction (*s35*); or
❍ a direction (*ss32* and *33*).

An appeal will only suspend the effect of the decision where the decision is in respect of the imposition or the amount of a penalty. In all other cases the decision will continue to have effect until the appeal is determined.

An order could be made to allow other decisions to be appealable, although there is no current proposal to do so. This means that some decisions cannot be appealed, for example, a decision to start an investigation under *s25*; require documents to be produced under *s26*; and enter premises under *ss27* and *28*. This appears to be a clear and intentional departure from the position under EU law.

Who May Appeal ? [7.68]

Appeals may be made by:

○ any party to an agreement who is the subject of a decision (*s46(1)*);
○ any person whose conduct is the subject of a decision (*s46(2)*);
○ a third party applicant under *s47(1)* in relation to any rejection by the DGFT of his application (*s47(6)*).

A third party must satisfy the DGFT that it has a sufficient interest to justify withdrawing or varying the relevant decision. *Section 47* also provides that applications may be made by representative bodies.

Procedure [7.69]

A notice of appeal must be sent to the Competition Commission within a specified period. The notice of appeal must set out the grounds of appeal in sufficient detail and indicate:

○ under which provision of the Act the appeal is brought;
○ to what extent the appellant contends that the decision was based on an error of fact or was wrong in law; and
○ to what extent the appellant is appealing against the DGFT's exercise of his discretion in making the disputed decision.

The appeal tribunal may confirm or set aside the decision which is the subject of the appeal, or a part of it and can:

○ send the matter back to the DGFT for further investigation;
○ impose or revoke, or vary the amount of a penalty;
○ grant or cancel an individual exemption or vary any conditions or obligations imposed in relation to the exemption;

- give directions or take such others steps as the DGFT could have taken; or
- make any other decision which the DGFT could have made.

If the appeal tribunal confirms the decision which is the subject of the appeal it can still set aside a finding of fact on which the decision was based.

The appeal tribunal will produce rules governing its procedure. These will cover matters such as the time within which an appeal must be brought, the form of the notice of appeal and the information which must be given in it, the power to reject an appeal if it reveals no valid ground of appeal, rules for pre-hearing review and preliminary matters, general conduct of the hearing, the charging of interest for example on a penalty, fees, rules to withdraw an appeal and interim orders.

Appeal to the Court of Appeal [7.70]

A decision of the appeal tribunal can be appealed on a point of law or as to the amount of a penalty to the Court of Appeal, the Court of Session or the Court of Appeal in Northern Ireland with leave by a party to the proceedings in which the decision was made, or on behalf of a person who has a sufficient interest in the matter.

Judicial Review [7.71]

In addition to the appeal route discussed above, the actions of the DGFT can be judicially reviewed by the High Court. Judicial review is a means by which the improper exercise of a statutory power can be remedied, for example, an abuse of the powers of investigation.

Before embarking on judicial review, undertakings should exhaust their remedies in the appeal tribunal, as it is only in exceptional circumstances that a court will grant leave to bring judicial review proceedings if a statutory right of appeal exists. A detailed discussion of judicial review is outside the scope of this book.

8 – Compliance

Introduction

The new Act brings with it considerably strengthened powers to detect and punish anti-competitive behaviour. The competition authorities will have increased powers of investigation, including the right to conduct 'dawn raids'. Interim measures such as ordering companies to cease offending behaviour immediately will be brought in. However, more significantly, infringement of the Chapter I and II Prohibitions could well lead to a fine of up to 10% of a company's UK turnover and this may be imposed for the duration of the infringement, subject to a maximum of three years. It is clear, therefore, that the implications of non-compliance will be far more serious than they have been under previous legislation.

Consequently, the DGFT has strongly advised undertakings to think carefully about what they can do to ensure that they will comply with the new Act. In fact, the main reasons for the transitional arrangements is to allow undertakings a reasonable time to modify agreements and practices in order to bring them into line with the new legislation.

There will be a period of about 15 months from Royal Assent, which took place in November 1998, before the Prohibitions contained in the new law come into effect. In this interim period undertakings are expected to ensure that key personnel are at least aware of the new provisions and their implications.

An OFT survey in April 1999 showed that 77% of key business managers were then unaware of the new Act. This means that for the majority of undertakings a considerable amount of work will almost certainly need to be done between now and the Start Date in order to introduce an effective compliance programme. Even for those which operate an existing programme covering EU Law and the existing UK legislation, some work will have to be undertaken in order to adapt those programmes to cover the new law. This Chapter therefore aims to help with that preparation.

Benefits of a Compliance Programme [8.2]

Developing and implementing a compliance programme costs time and money. It is not surprising that senior management should ask the question 'Why should we bother?'. The short answer is that it is highly likely, on the basis of their public statements to date, that the OFT will use its new powers to the full.

Section 36(3) of the Act provides for the imposition of fines only if the DGFT is satisfied that the infringement was intentional or negligent. A compliance programme which is well supported by senior management should deter intentional infringements and minimise negligent ones.

Risk Management [8.3]

Such programmes will involve a system of vetting existing agreements and practices in order to weed out any possible competition issues which could be avoided or at least adjusted in order to comply with the new law. This type of audit might also alert the business to possible infringements by trading partners or competitors which could be exploited to the undertaking's advantage.

An effective programme will also minimise the risk of infringing the law in the future as relevant employees should be sufficiently knowledgeable about the provisions of the law to avoid any inadvertent infringement. Also, where infringements do occur they will be identified at an early stage and the appropriate remedial action taken.

Mitigation of Fines [8.4]

A compliance programme is not a fail-safe means of ensuring that competition rules are never infringed. Other than in very small undertakings, commercial agreements and practices are frequently entered into by employees on behalf of their employers in instances where senior management are unaware of the arrangements. It is therefore very easy for employees to act outside the scope of their authority and in doing so breach competition law.

Both the EU Competition Authorities and the UK courts have taken a very stringent line in regard to disobedient employees. For example, the European Commission had investigated a complaint about Parker Pen Ltd in its decision (*92/426/EEC*) of 19 May 1988 in *Vito/Parker Pen (OJ (1992) L233, p27)* where it found that distributors in Italy and Germany were prohibited from exporting outside their respective countries. Parker Pen argued that the Marketing Director, who had inserted the infringing clauses in both Distribution Agreements, had no authority to do so. This argument did not serve to remove the company's responsibility and it incurred a considerable fine.

In the UK, the House of Lords in *DGFT v Pioneer Concrete* overruled the Court of Appeal to find that a company could only act through its agent and therefore acts done by its directors or employees in the scope of their employment bound the company. It was not open for a company to escape liability on the basis that it did not know about and did not intend to breach the law. There is therefore an onus on every business to ensure effective compliance procedures so that it does not find itself infringing competition law through disobedient or ignorant acts of its employees.

In view of these cases, businesses might be forgiven for taking the stance that as they could well end up incurring hefty fines anyway, there is little point pouring valuable resources into a compliance programme at the outset. With this in mind and in order to incentivise compliance, a system for mitigating fines has been introduced. In the OFT's guideline: *Enforcement*, it is stated that the Director General can take into account the existence of a compliance programme as a mitigating circumstance to reduce a penalty. However, the infringing undertaking will need to show that:

O   the programme has been actively implemented;
O   the programme has the visible and continuing support of and is observed by senior management;
O   there are appropriate compliance policies and procedures in place;
O   there is active and on-going training for all employees who encounter competition law in their work;
O   the programme is evaluated and formal audits carried out at regular intervals to ensure that it is delivering its objectives.

(Paragraph 4.35 of the *Enforcement* guideline.)

Cost Benefits   [8.5]

If the costs of a compliance programme were weighed against the cost of infringement, the latter would be far greater. On the assumption that investigations by the OFT will be similar to those carried out by the European Commission, they will detailed, lengthy and disruptive. Costs will be incurred in terms of both legal fees and loss of management time in dealing with investigations. Certain business activities might be suspended pending a full enquiry, and important provisions in agreements might be void. Fines can be considerable and the loss of business reputation serious. Other undertakings might be deterred from doing business with one which is non-compliant and adverse publicity could well result in customers defecting to competitors.

There is also the danger of private litigation being brought by third parties who have suffered loss as a result of anti-competitive conduct, for example, by being prevented from entering a particular market.

Market Shares [8.6]

It is essential to understnad where a business stands in its market place, and inorder to do this it must make an assessment in accordance with the Act and guidelines of its own and its competitors' market shares. The Chapter I Prohibition will only apply to agreements or arrangements which have an appreciale effect on competition. The guideline *Market Definition* states that an arrangement will generally not have an appreciable effect on compettioin where the parties' combined market shares do not exceed 25%. Even this is only a rule of thumb, it may still be that on looking at the structure of a particular market higher shares will still not result in an appreciable effect on competition. However, agreements which:

O   directly or indirectly fix prices or share markets;
O   impose minimum resale prices;
O   are part of a network of similar agreements which together restrict competition;

will be prohibited, even if the combined market share of the parties is *less* than 25%. Similarly, the guideline on the Chapter II Prohibition indicates that a business is unlikely to be dominant with a market share below 40%.

Particular attention must be paid in the context of the Act to local markets in the United Kingdom. It is clear from *Market Definition* guide-line that the narrowest potential market definition will be taken and in the context of the geographic market, the DGFT will start by looking at the area supplied by the parties to an agreement or the subject of a complaint.

Adopting a Compliance Procedure [8.7]

There are a number of different methods by which undertakings can adopt a compliance procedure.

External Programmes [8.8]

The Government has launched its own education programme in order to advise undertakings on how to comply with the new law. The programme includes:

❍ the publication of a series of pamphlets which summarise the new legislation in plain English;
❍ the production of a video to assist with in-house training;
❍ seminars organised by the CBI, the Institute of Directors, Chambers of Commerce and other independent bodies; and
❍ presentations by the OFT at trade fairs for the benefit of smaller undertakings.

It must be stressed that the competition authorities will not consider it sufficient to merely take advantage of external education; this is meant to supplement programmes operated by businesses themselves.

Internal Programmes [8.9]

The fundamental requirement of a compliance programme is that it is tailored to suit the needs of the individual undertaking. This is not only to mitigate fines in the event of infringement, but also to ensure that resources allocated to such a programme are used efficiently.

As a minimum, there should be four basic elements:

❍ support of senior management;
❍ appropriate compliance policy and procedures;
❍ training; and
❍ evaluation.

Each of these elements provides scope for a variety of activities, which are examined below. First, however an effective compliance team must be established. Then an audit must be carried out in order to ascertain the current position on compliance and what is needed in the future.

Establishing a Compliance Team [8.10]

Depending on the size of the undertaking, the team should consist of a compliance officer appointed by the Board and with the Board's authority to implement the programme assisted by an in-house legal team and, if appropriate, outside lawyers.

The team should ultimately report to, and be overseen by the Board, or a committee of the Board. A series of dates should be set at the outset for future reports onprogress.

Audit [8.11]

Before an audit can be carried out effectively, the relevant head of each business unit should send a memo to all staff informing them of the audit and giving instructions to co-operate fully with the compliance team.

Business Practices [8.12]

Those areas of the business most likely to produce competition problems should be identified and key personnel within those departments should be interviewed to determine the existing policies and practices taking place there. Typically, key personnel are involved in:

- Sales;
- Marketing and Advertising;
- Distribution;
- Customer relations;
- Market Research;
- Intellectual Property; and
- Corporate Planning.

From the response given at these interviews, the compliance team can then consider whether the undertaking is involved in any anti-competitive activities. The undertaking should guarantee a moratorium in relation to past infringements for employees in order to flush these out and get as full an understanding of business practices as possible.

Document Review [8.13]

During the interview a list of files to be reviewed should be compiled. These should include all files and documents relating to:

○ marketing;
○ competitors;
○ customers;
○ distributors or joint ventures; and
○ Trade Associations.

Documents to be examined should include:

○ formal agreements;
○ internal memoranda/letters/faxes (particularly those prepared by sales personnel and senior managers);
○ minutes of meeting/telephone conversations (relating to competitors and customers including customer visits).

Agreements [8.14]

With regard to agreements, the following exercises should be undertaken as soon as possible.

✓ Obtain an up-to-date listing of agreements on the RTPA Register and compile a list of agreements which have received *section 21(2)* directions. This would save you changing existing agreement needlessly.
✓ Identify any agreements which benefit from a parallel exemption under *section 10* by having received individual exemption from the European Commission or benefit from a European Block Exemption.
✓ Identify any agreements that have been notified to the Commission and where the Commission has either terminated proceedings by means of a comfort letter or has not yet determined the matter. (It is thought that the OFT will not generally investigate agreements benefitting from a *reasoned* EC comfort letter, or a comfort letter preceded by an Article 19(3) regulation 17/62 OJ Notice. In the event of pending EC investigations, penalties cannot be imposed until the Commission determines the matter).
✓ If existing agreements potentially infringe the Chapter I Prohibition, either renegotiate them prior to the start date or consider notifying them to the OFT for early guidance or a decision.

Reports [8.15]

The results of the key personnel interviews and the document review should be used to prepare a report to senior management. This should:

○ identify any problems which have been discovered;
○ suggest solutions; and
○ recommend policies and procedures which should be introduced as part of the compliance programme.

Where the report may show infringements of EU competition law, it should be prepared by outside lawyers for the Board. If prepared internally, it will not be legally privileged under EU rules and could be considered by the European Commission. It is unlikely that infringements of the new Act will not also involve infringements of EU competition law.

Support of Board and Senior Management [8.16]

The support of the Board and senior management should be properly minuted.

Once the Board has approved the scope and content of the compliance programme, the head of the organisation should prepare a letter emphasising their commitment and that of the undertaking to comply with competition law. The letter could also briefly outline the penalties for failing to observe the competition rules and contain a message to all staff to observe the compliance programme. This letter should be sent to all staff individually and could also be incorporated into the compliance manual.

The head of the undertaking, together with directors and senior management must then be involved in the compliance programme to show an example to junior members of the staff.

Example letter **[8.17]**

Dear Member of Staff

[**Name of company**] is a progressive and vigorously competitive organisation. In order to build on our present success, it is imperative that we continue to operate within the law at all times. This includes compliance with competition law.

If we fail to comply, [**Name of company**] would be exposed to fines of up to 10% of the Group's annual turnover. There is also a danger of serious damage to our valuable reputation and relationships with our business partners. Additionally, we might find ourselves facing a private claim from third parties who believe that they have suffered loss from our business practices. [If appropriate: the consequences for the individual at fault could also be severe; the Board has decided that infringing the company's policy on compliance with competition law will be a disciplinary matter.]

In order to minimise the risk of such liability, [**Name of company**] has implemented a compliance programme to educate us all on how to avoid infringing competition law. The programme will be run by our compliance team, led by [**Name of individual**], our compliance officer. The team will be conducting training sessions and putting appropriate procedures in place. These will broadly consist of seminars, document reviews, written guidelines and feedback sessions. We have used our best efforts to ensure that the programme will complement and enhance your current practices. [**Name of compliance officer**] is on hand to answer any queries that may arise, now or in the future.

Your co-operation is very much appreciated. Together we can create a compliance culture which will form an integral part of our commercial activities to ensure that [**Name of company**] continues to thrive into the 21st Century.

Yours faithfully

Chief Executive

Policy Statement [8.18]

The policy statement might be:

○ in the board's resolution to set up the compliance programme;
○ a letter from the head of the organisation to all staff; or
○ an additional statement which could form part of the mission statement of the business.

Whichever form it takes, it will essentially set out the business' aim to comply fully with the relevant legislation by not engaging in anti-competitive behaviour itself or actively condoning such behaviour by joining in illegal activities initiated by another party. Procedures must then be put in place to implement that policy.

Employment Contracts [8.19]

It is advisable to amend existing employment contracts to place an obligation on those employees whose duties are most likely to involve the need to comply with competition law. A contractual undertaking may only be appropriate for a limited number of senior people. Senior employees could also be asked to sign a separate undertaking to the same effect in order to bring the importance of compliance to their attention. In order to deter negligent or intentional infringements of the Prohibitions by employees, managers are strongly advised to consider making it possible to take disciplinary action against such an employee. The contract clause should refer to such action and the disciplinary procedures should be clearly set out in a handbook.

Example Contract Clause [8.20]

You must comply at all times with the Company's rules and policies and procedures relating to competition law compliance. Copies of all such rules, policies and procedures can be obtained from the Personnel Department and are set out in the Compliance Programme Manual. For the avoidance of doubt such rules, policies and procedures are not incorporated by reference into this Contract and they can be changed, replaced or withdrawn at any time at the discretion of the Company. Breach of such rules, policies or procedures may result in disciplinary action.

Compliance Officer/Help Desk [8.21]

It is essential that each undertaking has at least one compliance officer. In larger businesses with substantial market shares, it may be sensible for each department to have a compliance officer who then reports to the central compliance officer. Their job is to keep a record of training and ensure that all staff have been given the appropriate training on a sufficiently regular basis. The nature of the training might vary according to the type of work undertaken by the employee in question.

The compliance officer should also be a port of call for employees who need to check that an arrangement which they are entering into or a business practice does not fall foul of the new law. In larger organisations such supervision might take the form of a centrally located compliance 'help desk'.

The central compliance officer would typically be the company secretary or a senior member of the in-house legal department. The greater the risk of competition law infringements, the more senior the person needs to be. Employees may need to consult the compliance officer in confidence about competition law problems and the compliance officer needs to be someone who can if necessary act independently and take responsibility.

Manual [8.22]

The Compliance Manual must provide an 'alarm bell' awareness for any employee who feels that a certain course of action will bring the undertaking into conflict with competition law. A typical manual would contain:

○   a compliance policy statement;
○   an explanation of the main provisions of the legislation in plain English;
○   investigative powers of competition authorities and penalties for infringement;
○   a 'Do's and Don'ts' list tailored to the needs and activities of the organisation which, in particular, sets out the activities which should not be engaged in without the prior approval of the compliance office;
○   annual training requirements;
○   the undertaking's procedures, including:

- the reporting of suspected wrongdoing;
- sanctions for infringement of the programme;
- agreements to be reviewed by the in-house legal department/compliance officer; and
- dawn raid rapid response procedure, if appropriate; and
○ the undertaking's document retention policy.

Employees should have to sign an annual acknowledgement form stating that they have received the latest version of the manual and read and understood its contents.

Example Do's and Don'ts List   [8.23]

Note: the list **MUST** be tailored to the particular business in question, but this is an example of the type of list you might see.

Don't:

○ tell our customers what to charge when they resell our products;
○ set minimum or maximum profit margins on customers;
○ penalise customers for discounting from recommended resale prices;
○ discriminate between customers;
○ discuss or exchange information about our prices or our trading terms with our competitors;
○ refuse to supply customers other than on the grounds referred to in paragraphs [   ] of the Manual;
○ enter into any agreements or arrangements with restrictions; or
○ write correspondence which, because of ambiguity or exaggeration, conveys an erroneous impression that there has been anti-competitive behaviour, e.g. 'industry agreement' or 'industry policy', this will 'drive out the competition', 'dominant position'; 'fixed price' or 'a special deal just for you'.

Do:

○ leave meetings with competitors, trading partners or trade association meetings if any 'forbidden' topics are discussed such as:
  - prices and discounts;

- profit or profit margins;
- sharing customers or territories; or
- terms and conditions of sale;
○ keep a written record of all meetings, and telephone conversations;
○ contact the compliance office/in-house legal team if you have any queries about compliance of the competition law or are in any doubt as to what you should do; and
○ contact your head of department/compliance officer if you suspect that an infringement has occurred.

Annual Certificate [8.24]

Once the compliance programme has been operating for long enough each member of staff should sign an Annual Certificate, to certify that they have had the appropriate training. Employees would certify that they are unaware of any breaches of the undertaking's policy or procedures and are unaware of any infringements of the law. Department Managers should also sign on behalf of their team. The reason for certification is that it is a useful mechanism for demonstrating the seriousness of compliance and concentrating minds on the issue.

Handling Infringements [8.25]

If an infringement of the competition rules is discovered, the undertaking must decide what action to take. This may involve notification to the competition authorities or termination of the infringement.

The undertaking should also consider what steps it should take with a view to defending any possible proceedings relating to the infringement. For example, preparing file notes explaining how the document was generated or why the course of action was taken, the remedial action taken to prevent a recurrence and the disciplinary action taken against the employees involved in the infringement. This should obviously be done whilst the matter is still fresh in people's minds.

Dawn Raid Rapid Response Team [8.26]

Undertakings should ensure that all employees know what to do in the event of a dawn raid. It would be sensible to obtain legal assistance as soon as possible either in-house or from external solicitors. Ideally, an undertaking should be able to call upon a rapid response team to handle the investigation. The team would usually consist of specialist solicitors who would be contactable at all times. The OFT has said that its officials will be prepared to wait for about an hour, where there is no in-house lawyer, for outside lawyers to arrive, before starting their investigation. Therefore, it is important that in addition to an external rapid response team, the relevant personnel in the business are familiar with dawn raid procedures. In particular, the relevant members of staff should know to do the following.

Dawn Raid Checklist [8.27]

✓ Check officials' identity and mandate, particularly its scope.
✓ Contact the internal and external rapid response team.
✓ Ensure that each official is shadowed by a member of the team at all times.
✓ Arrange an appropriate system for the control of, collation and photocopying of documents.
✓ Check all files for privileged documents before handing over. Any correspondence with *external* lawyers are protected against disclosure. In-house legal advisers enjoy the same protection under the UK regime only.
✓ Obtain a signed inventory of copied documents from the officials.
✓ Answer as far as possible any specific questions relating to a particular document. Note that the authorities are not permitted to go on a fishing expedition by asking free ranging, general questions or those which do not relate to the documents in question.
✓ Ask to be shown any minutes of questions asked by the officials and the responses given. Make a note of any disagreement with the content of minutes and retain a copy of an annotated version.
✓ Request that answers be put in writing where a verbal answer cannot readily be provided.
✓ Note that no relevant documents should be destroyed or concealed.

Training [8.28]

An essential part of the compliance programme involves training for all employees. The compliance manual alone is not sufficient to ensure that all employees have understood the message. People understand and retain information more easily when it has been conveyed to them in person.

Training should be tailored to the undertaking in question taking into account its particular activities and resources available. For instance, smaller undertakings might take advantage of commercially produced videos together with a basic presentation. Others might opt for a law firm to design a programme for their specific needs.

Training also needs to be tailored to the group of people addressed. Receptionists will need a different seminar from the sales staff for example.

In order to create a 'culture of compliance', training should take place on an ongoing basis at regular intervals. This not only reinforces the compliance message to employees, but also significantly helps to demonstrate a 'mitigating circumstance' in the event of a fine by the authorities.

It will be the responsibility of the compliance officer to maintain the training register.

Audit Evaluation and Development [8.29]

The final essential ingredient in a compliance programme is evaluation. The effectiveness of the programme should be evaluated at regular intervals in order to ensure that it is delivering its objective. Evaluation would typically include some if not all of the following.

✓ Individual feed back sessions with employees in order to test the knowledge of the law and the compliance policy and procedure.
✓ Appraising employees on their observance of the compliance policy.
✓ Taking compliance into account when awarding bonuses.
✓ Auditing groups on an ad hoc basis and without notice to check for actual/potential infringement.
✓ Where appropriate, a mock dawn raid.

Evaluation must be carried out openly if it is to be effective. It will serve to minimise the occurrence of complacency where employees know that their activities always carry the prospect of a review.

Conclusion [8.30]

The time to start implementing a compliance programme is now. The authors summarise that the OFT will take advantage of finally having real weapons with which to fight anti-competitive behaviour. Businesses are therefore strongly advised to put their houses in order before the prohibitions become effective. This means taking time to develop the right programme for the particular business. A token effort will not be acceptable. And finally, that programme must be implemented on a continuing basis to reinforce the compliance message and keep employees informed of any developments in the law.

Appendix

Exclusions from the Chapter I and the Chapter II Prohibition.

Relvant Provision	Exclusion	Exclusion from Chapter I?	Exclusion from Chapter II?
Sch 1, Part I, paras 1–3	UK mergers under *FTA 1976*	Yes	Yes
Sch 1, Part II	EC Mergers under EC Merger Regulation	Yes	Yes
Sch 2, Part I	Investment business	Yes	No
Sch 2, Part II	Supervision of auitors	Yes	No
Sch 2, Part III	Broadcasting: networking arrangements	Yes	No
Sch 2, Part IV	Environmental exemption schemes	Yes	No
Sch 3, para 1	Planning obligations	Yes	No
Sch 3, para 2	RTPA 1976, s21(2)	Yes	No
Sch 3, para 3	EEA regulated markets	Yes	No
Sch 3, para 4	Services of general economic interest	Yes	Yes
Sch 3, para 5	Compliance with legal requirements	Yes	Yes
Sch 3, para 6	Avoidance of conflict with international obligations	Yes	Yes
Sch 3, para 7	Public policy	Yes	Yes
Sch 3, para 8	Coal and Steel	Yes	Yes
Sch 3, para 9	Agriculture products	Yes	Yes
Sch 4, Parts I and II	Professional rules	Yes	No
Section 50	Vertical agreements	Yes*	No
Section 50	Land agreements	Yes*	No

*Draft exclusion Order circulated for consultation

Competition Act 1998

1998 Chapter 41

An Act to make provision about competition and the abuse of a dominant position in the market; to confer powers in relation to investigations conducted in connection with Article 85 or 86 of the treaty establishing the European Community; to amend the Fair Trading Act 1973 in relation to information which may be required in connection with investigations under that Act; to make provision with respect to the meaning of "supply of services" in the Fair Trading Act 1973; and for connected purposes.

[9th November 1998]

BE IT ENACTED by the Queen's most Excellent Majesty, by and with the advice and consent of the Lords Spiritual and Temporal, and Commons, in this present Parliament assembled, and by the authority of the same, as follows: –

PART I
COMPETITION
CHAPTER I
AGREEMENTS

Introduction

1. The following shall cease to have effect –
    (a) the Restrictive Practices Court Act 1976 (c 33),
    (b) the Restrictive Trade Practices Act 1976 (c 34),
    (c) the Resale Prices Act 1976 (c 53), and
    (d) the Restrictive Trade Practices Act 1977 (c 19).

The prohibition

2. – (1) Subject to section 3, agreements between undertakings, decisions by associations of undertakings or concerted practices which –
    (a) may affect trade within the United Kingdom, and
    (b) have as their object or effect the prevention, restriction or distortion of competition within the United Kingdom,
are prohibited unless they are exempt in accordance with the provisions of this Part.

(2) Subsection (1) applies, in particular, to agreements, decisions or practices which –
    (a) directly or indirectly fix purchase or selling prices or any other trading conditions;

(b) limit or control production, markets, technical development or investment;

(c) share markets or sources of supply;

(d) apply dissimilar conditions to equivalent transactions with other trading parties, thereby placing them at a competitive disadvantage;

(e) make the conclusion of contracts subject to acceptance by the other parties of supplementary obligations which, by their nature or according to commercial usage, have no connection with the subject of such contracts.

(3) Subsection (1) applies only if the agreement, decision or practice is, or is intended to be, implemented in the United Kingdom.

(4) Any agreement or decision which is prohibited by subsection (1) is void.

(5) A provision of this Part which is expressed to apply to, or in relation to, an agreement is to be read as applying equally to, or in relation to, a decision by an association of undertakings or a concerted practice (but with any necessary modifications).

(6) Subsection (5) does not apply where the context otherwise requires.

(7) In this section "the United Kingdom" means, in relation to an agreement which operates or is intended to operate only in a part of the United Kingdom, that part.

(8) The prohibition imposed by subsection (1) is referred to in this Act as "the Chapter I prohibition".

Excluded agreements

3. – (1) The Chapter I prohibition does not apply in any of the cases in which it is excluded by or as a result of –

(a) Schedule 1 (mergers and concentrations);

(b) Schedule 2 (competition scrutiny under other enactments);

(c) Schedule 3 (planning obligations and other general exclusions); or

(d) Schedule 4 (professional rules).

(2) The Secretary of State may at any time by order amend Schedule 1, with respect to the Chapter I prohibition, by –

(a) providing for one or more additional exclusions; or

(b) amending or removing any provision (whether or not it has been added by an order under this subsection).

(3) The Secretary of State may at any time by order amend Schedule 3, with respect to the Chapter I prohibition, by –
>   (a) providing for one or more additional exclusions; or
>   (b) amending or removing any provision –
>>   (i) added by an order under this subsection; or
>>   (ii) included in paragraph 1, 2, 8 or 9 of Schedule 3.

(4) The power under subsection (3) to provide for an additional exclusion may be exercised only if it appears to the Secretary of State that agreements which fall within the additional exclusion –
>   (a) do not in general have an adverse effect on competition, or
>   (b) are, in general, best considered under Chapter II or the Fair Trading Act 1973.

(5) An order under subsection (2)(a) or (3)(a) may include provision (similar to that made with respect to any other exclusion provided by the relevant Schedule) for the exclusion concerned to cease to apply to a particular agreement.

(6) Schedule 3 also gives the Secretary of State power to exclude agreements from the Chapter I prohibition in certain circumstances.

Exemptions

4. – (1) The Director may grant an exemption from the Chapter I prohibition with respect to a particular agreement if –
>   (a) a request for an exemption has been made to him under section 14 by a party to the agreement; and
>   (b) the agreement is one to which section 9 applies.

(2) An exemption granted under this section is referred to in this Part as an individual exemption.

(3) The exemption –
>   (a) may be granted subject to such conditions or obligations as the Director considers it appropriate to impose; and
>   (b) has effect for such period as the Director considers appropriate.

(4) That period must be specified in the grant of the exemption.

(5) An individual exemption may be granted so as to have effect from a date earlier than that on which it is granted.

(6) On an application made in such way as may be specified by rules under section 51, the Director may extend the period for which an

exemption has effect; but, if the rules so provide, he may do so only in specified circumstances.

5. – (1) If the Director has reasonable grounds for believing that there has been a material change of circumstance since he granted an individual exemption, he may by notice in writing –
    (a) cancel the exemption;
    (b) vary or remove any condition or obligation; or
    (c) impose one or more additional conditions or obligations.

(2) If the Director has a reasonable suspicion that the information on which he based his decision to grant an individual exemption was incomplete, false or misleading in a material particular, he may by notice in writing take any of the steps mentioned in subsection (1).

(3) Breach of a condition has the effect of cancelling the exemption.

(4) Failure to comply with an obligation allows the Director, by notice in writing, to take any of the steps mentioned in subsection (1).

(5) Any step taken by the Director under subsection (1), (2) or (4) has effect from such time as may be specified in the notice.

(6) If an exemption is cancelled under subsection (2) or (4), the date specified in the notice cancelling it may be earlier than the date on which the notice is given.

(7) The Director may act under subsection (1), (2) or (4) on his own initiative or on a complaint made by any person.

6. – (1) If agreements which fall within a particular category of agreement are, in the opinion of the Director, likely to be agreements to which section 9 applies, the Director may recommend that the Secretary of State make an order specifying that category for the purposes of this section.

(2) The Secretary of State may make an order ("a block exemption order") giving effect to such a recommendation –
    (a) in the form in which the recommendation is made; or
    (b) subject to such modifications as he considers appropriate.

(3) An agreement which falls within a category specified in a block exemption order is exempt from the Chapter I prohibition.

(4) An exemption under this section is referred to in this Part as a block exemption.

(5) A block exemption order may impose conditions or obligations subject to which a block exemption is to have effect.

(6) A block exemption order may provide –

(a) that breach of a condition imposed by the order has the effect of cancelling the block exemption in respect of an agreement;

(b) that if there is a failure to comply with an obligation imposed by the order, the Director may, by notice in writing, cancel the block exemption in respect of the agreement;

(c) that if the Director considers that a particular agreement is not one to which section 9 applies, he may cancel the block exemption in respect of that agreement.

(7) A block exemption order may provide that the order is to cease to have effect at the end of a specified period.

(8) In this section and section 7 "specified" means specified in a block exemption order.

7. – (1) A block exemption order may provide that a party to an agreement which –

(a) does not qualify for the block exemption created by the order, but

(b) satisfies specified criteria,

may notify the Director of the agreement for the purposes of subsection (2).

(2) An agreement which is notified under any provision included in a block exemption order by virtue of subsection (1) is to be treated, as from the end of the notice period, as falling within a category specified in a block exemption order unless the Director –

(a) is opposed to its being so treated; and

(b) gives notice in writing to the party concerned of his opposition before the end of that period.

(3) If the Director gives notice of his opposition under subsection (2), the notification under subsection (1) is to be treated as both notification under section 14 and as a request for an individual exemption made under subsection (3) of that section.

(4) In this section "notice period" means such period as may be specified with a view to giving the Director sufficient time to consider whether to oppose under subsection (2).

8. – (1) Before making a recommendation under section 6(1), the Director must –

    (a) publish details of his proposed recommendation in such a way as he thinks most suitable for bringing it to the attention of those likely to be affected; and

    (b) consider any representations about it which are made to him.

(2) If the Secretary of State proposes to give effect to such a recommendation subject to modifications, he must inform the Director of the proposed modifications and take into account any comments made by the Director.

(3) If, in the opinion of the Director, it is appropriate to vary or revoke a block exemption order he may make a recommendation to that effect to the Secretary of State.

(4) Subsection (1) also applies to any proposed recommendation under subsection (3).

(5) Before exercising his power to vary or revoke a block exemption order (in a case where there has been no recommendation under subsection (3)), the Secretary of State must—

    (a) inform the Director of the proposed variation or revocation; and

    (b) take into account any comments made by the Director.

(6) A block exemption order may provide for a block exemption to have effect from a date earlier than that on which the order is made.

9. This section applies to any agreement which –

    (a) contributes to –

        (i) improving production or distribution, or

        (ii) promoting technical or economic progress,

    while allowing consumers a fair share of the resulting benefit; but

    (b) does not –

        (i) impose on the undertakings concerned restrictions which are not indispensable to the attainment of those objectives; or

        (ii) afford the undertakings concerned the possibility of eliminating competition in respect of a substantial part of the products in question.

10. – (1) An agreement is exempt from the Chapter I prohibition if it

is exempt from the Community prohibition –
(a) by virtue of a Regulation,
(b) because it has been given exemption by the Commission, or
(c) because it has been notified to the Commission under the appropriate opposition or objection procedure and –
    (i) the time for opposing, or objecting to, the agreement has expired and the Commission has not opposed it; or
    (ii) the Commission has opposed, or objected to, the agreement but has withdrawn its opposition or objection.

(2) An agreement is exempt from the Chapter I prohibition if it does not affect trade between Member States but otherwise falls within a category of agreement which is exempt from the Community prohibition by virtue of a Regulation.

(3) An exemption from the Chapter I prohibition under this section is referred to in this Part as a parallel exemption.

(4) A parallel exemption –
(a) takes effect on the date on which the relevant exemption from the Community prohibition takes effect or, in the case of a parallel exemption under subsection (2), would take effect if the agreement in question affected trade between Member States; and
(b) ceases to have effect –
    (i) if the relevant exemption from the Community prohibition ceases to have effect; or
    (ii) on being cancelled by virtue of subsection (5) or (7).

(5) In such circumstances and manner as may be specified in rules made under section 51, the Director may –
(a) impose conditions or obligations subject to which a parallel exemption is to have effect;
(b) vary or remove any such condition or obligation;
(c) impose one or more additional conditions or obligations;
(d) cancel the exemption.

(6) In such circumstances as may be specified in rules made under section 51, the date from which cancellation of an exemption is to take effect may be earlier than the date on which notice of cancellation is given.

(7) Breach of a condition imposed by the Director has the effect of cancelling the exemption.

(8)   In exercising his powers under this section, the Director may require any person who is a party to the agreement in question to give him such information as he may require.

(9)   For the purpose of this section references to an agreement being exempt from the Community prohibition are to be read as including references to the prohibition being inapplicable to the agreement by virtue of a Regulation or a decision by the Commission.

(10) In this section –
"the Community prohibition" means the prohibition contained in –
      (a) paragraph 1 of Article 85;
      (b) any corresponding provision replacing, or otherwise derived from, that provision;
      (c) such other Regulation as the Secretary of State may by order specify; and
"Regulation" means a Regulation adopted by the Commission or by the Council.

(11) This section has effect in relation to the prohibition contained in paragraph 1 of Article 53 of the EEA Agreement (and the EFTA Surveillance Authority) as it has effect in relation to the Community prohibition (and the Commission) subject to any modifications which the Secretary of State may by order prescribe.

11. – (1) The fact that a ruling may be given by virtue of Article 88 of the Treaty on the question whether or not agreements of a particular kind are prohibited by Article 85 does not prevent such agreements from being subject to the Chapter I prohibition.

(2)   But the Secretary of State may by regulations make such provision as he considers appropriate for the purpose of granting an exemption from the Chapter I prohibition, in prescribed circumstances, in respect of such agreements.

(3)   An exemption from the Chapter I prohibition by virtue of regulations under this section is referred to in this Part as a section 11 exemption.

12. – (1) Sections 13 and 14 provide for an agreement to be examined by the Director on the application of a party to the agreement who thinks that it may infringe the Chapter I prohibition.

(2)   Schedule 5 provides for the procedure to be followed –
      (a) by any person making such an application; and
      (b) by the Director, in considering such an application.

(3) The Secretary of State may by regulations make provision as to the application of sections 13 to 16 and Schedule 5, with such modifications (if any) as may be prescribed, in cases where the Director –
    (a) has given a direction withdrawing an exclusion; or
    (b) is considering whether to give such a direction.

13. – (1) A party to an agreement who applies for the agreement to be examined under this section must –
    (a) notify the Director of the agreement; and
    (b) apply to him for guidance.

(2) On an application under this section, the Director may give the applicant guidance as to whether or not, in his view, the agreement is likely to infringe the Chapter I prohibition.

(3) If the Director considers that the agreement is likely to infringe the prohibition if it is not exempt, his guidance may indicate –
    (a) whether the agreement is likely to be exempt from the prohibition under—
        (i) a block exemption;
        (ii) a parallel exemption; or
        (iii) a section 11 exemption; or
    (b) whether he would be likely to grant the agreement an individual exemption if asked to do so.

(4) If an agreement to which the prohibition applies has been notified to the Director under this section, no penalty is to be imposed under this Part in respect of any infringement of the prohibition by the agreement which occurs during the period –
    (a) beginning with the date on which notification was given; and
    (b) ending with such date as may be specified in a notice in writing given to the applicant by the Director when the application has been determined.

(5) The date specified in a notice under subsection (4)(b) may not be earlier than the date on which the notice is given.

14. – (1) A party to an agreement who applies for the agreement to be examined under this section must –
    (a) notify the Director of the agreement; and
    (b) apply to him for a decision.

(2) On an application under this section, the Director may make a decision as to –

(a) whether the Chapter I prohibition has been infringed; and

(b) if it has not been infringed, whether that is because of the effect of an exclusion or because the agreement is exempt from the prohibition.

(3)   If an agreement is notified to the Director under this section, the application may include a request for the agreement to which it relates to be granted an individual exemption.

(4)   If an agreement to which the prohibition applies has been notified to the Director under this section, no penalty is to be imposed under this Part in respect of any infringement of the prohibition by the agreement which occurs during the period –

(a) beginning with the date on which notification was given; and

(b) ending with such date as may be specified in a notice in writing given to the applicant by the Director when the application has been determined.

(5)   The date specified in a notice under subsection (4)(b) may not be earlier than the date on which the notice is given.

15. – (1) This section applies to an agreement if the Director has determined an application under section 13 by giving guidance that–

(a) the agreement is unlikely to infringe the Chapter I prohibition, regardless of whether or not it is exempt;

(b) the agreement is likely to be exempt under –

(i)   a block exemption;

(ii) a parallel exemption; or

(iii) a section 11 exemption; or

(c) he would be likely to grant the agreement an individual exemption if asked to do so.

(2)   The Director is to take no further action under this Part with respect to an agreement to which this section applies, unless –

(a) he has reasonable grounds for believing that there has been a material change of circumstance since he gave his guidance;

(b) he has a reasonable suspicion that the information on which he based his guidance was incomplete, false or misleading in a material particular;

(c) one of the parties to the agreement applies to him for a decision under section 14 with respect to the agreement; or

(d) a complaint about the agreement has been made to him by a person who is not a party to the agreement.

(3) No penalty may be imposed under this Part in respect of any infringement of the Chapter I prohibition by an agreement to which this section applies.

(4) But the Director may remove the immunity given by subsection (3) if –
> (a) he takes action under this Part with respect to the agreement in one of the circumstances mentioned in subsection (2);
>
> (b) he considers it likely that the agreement will infringe the prohibition; and
>
> (c) he gives notice in writing to the party on whose application the guidance was given that he is removing the immunity as from the date specified in his notice.

(5) If the Director has a reasonable suspicion that information –
> (a) on which he based his guidance, and
>
> (b) which was provided to him by a party to the agreement,

was incomplete, false or misleading in a material particular, the date specified in a notice under subsection (4)(c) may be earlier than the date on which the notice is given.

16. – (1) This section applies to an agreement if the Director has determined an application under section 14 by making a decision that the agreement has not infringed the Chapter I prohibition.

(2) The Director is to take no further action under this Part with respect to the agreement unless –
> (a) he has reasonable grounds for believing that there has been a material change of circumstance since he gave his decision; or
>
> (b) he has a reasonable suspicion that the information on which he based his decision was incomplete, false or misleading in a material particular.

(3) No penalty may be imposed under this Part in respect of any infringement of the Chapter I prohibition by an agreement to which this section applies.

(4) But the Director may remove the immunity given by subsection (3) if –
> (a) he takes action under this Part with respect to the agreement in one of the circumstances mentioned in subsection (2);
>
> (b) he considers that it is likely that the agreement will infringe the prohibition; and
>
> (c) he gives notice in writing to the party on whose application

the decision was made that he is removing the immunity as from the date specified in his notice.

(5)   If the Director has a reasonable suspicion that information –
    (a) on which he based his decision, and
    (b) which was provided to him by a party to the agreement,
was incomplete, false or misleading in a material particular, the date specified in a notice under subsection (4)(c) may be earlier than the date on which the notice is given.

CHAPTER II
ABUSE OF DOMINANT POSITION

Introduction

17. Sections 2 to 10 of the Competition Act 1980 (control of anti-competitive practices) shall cease to have effect.

18. – (1) Subject to section 19, any conduct on the part of one or more undertakings which amounts to the abuse of a dominant position in a market is prohibited if it may affect trade within the United Kingdom.

(2)   Conduct may, in particular, constitute such an abuse if it consists in –
    (a) directly or indirectly imposing unfair purchase or selling prices or other unfair trading conditions;
    (b) limiting production, markets or technical development to the prejudice of consumers;
    (c) applying dissimilar conditions to equivalent transactions with other trading parties, thereby placing them at a competitive disadvantage;
    (d) making the conclusion of contracts subject to acceptance by the other parties of supplementary obligations which, by their nature or according to commercial usage, have no connection with the subject of the contracts.

(3)   In this section –

"dominant position" means a dominant position within the United Kingdom; and
"the United Kingdom" means the United Kingdom or any part of it.

(4)   The prohibition imposed by subsection (1) is referred to in this Act as "the Chapter II prohibition".

19. – (1) The Chapter II prohibition does not apply in any of the cases

in which it is excluded by or as a result of –
    (a) Schedule 1 (mergers and concentrations); or
    (b) Schedule 3 (general exclusions).

(2) The Secretary of State may at any time by order amend Schedule 1, with respect to the Chapter II prohibition, by –
    (a) providing for one or more additional exclusions; or
    (b) amending or removing any provision (whether or not it has been added by an order under this subsection).

(3) The Secretary of State may at any time by order amend paragraph 8 of Schedule 3 with respect to the Chapter II prohibition.

(4) Schedule 3 also gives the Secretary of State power to provide that the Chapter II prohibition is not to apply in certain circumstances.

20. – (1) Sections 21 and 22 provide for conduct of a person which that person thinks may infringe the Chapter II prohibition to be considered by the Director on the application of that person.

(2) Schedule 6 provides for the procedure to be followed –
    (a) by any person making an application, and
    (b) by the Director, in considering an application.

21. – (1) A person who applies for conduct to be considered under this section must –
    (a) notify the Director of it; and
    (b) apply to him for guidance.

(2) On an application under this section, the Director may give the applicant guidance as to whether or not, in his view, the conduct is likely to infringe the Chapter II prohibition.

22. – (1) A person who applies for conduct to be considered under this section must –
    (a) notify the Director of it; and
    (b) apply to him for a decision.

(2) On an application under this section, the Director may make a decision as to –
    (a) whether the Chapter II prohibition has been infringed; and
    (b) if it has not been infringed, whether that is because of the effect of an exclusion.

23. – (1) This section applies to conduct if the Director has determined an application under section 21 by giving guidance that the conduct is unlikely to infringe the Chapter II prohibition.

(2)   The Director is to take no further action under this Part with respect to the conduct to which this section applies, unless –
>   (a) he has reasonable grounds for believing that there has been a material change of circumstance since he gave his guidance;
>   (b) he has a reasonable suspicion that the information on which he based his guidance was incomplete, false or misleading in a material particular; or
>   (c) a complaint about the conduct has been made to him.

(3)   No penalty may be imposed under this Part in respect of any infringement of the Chapter II prohibition by conduct to which this section applies.

(4)   But the Director may remove the immunity given by subsection (3) if –
>   (a) he takes action under this Part with respect to the conduct in one of the circumstances mentioned in subsection (2);
>   (b) he considers that it is likely that the conduct will infringe the prohibition; and
>   (c) he gives notice in writing to the undertaking on whose application the guidance was given that he is removing the immunity as from the date specified in his notice.

(5)   If the Director has a reasonable suspicion that information –
>   (a) on which he based his guidance, and
>   (b) which was provided to him by an undertaking engaging in the conduct,
was incomplete, false or misleading in a material particular, the date specified in a notice under subsection (4)(c) may be earlier than the date on which the notice is given.

24. – (1) This section applies to conduct if the Director has determined an application under section 22 by making a decision that the conduct has not infringed the Chapter II prohibition.

(2)   The Director is to take no further action under this Part with respect to the conduct unless –
>   (a) he has reasonable grounds for believing that there has been a material change of circumstance since he gave his decision; or
>   (b) he has a reasonable suspicion that the information on which he based his decision was incomplete, false or misleading in a material particular.

(3) No penalty may be imposed under this Part in respect of any infringement of the Chapter II prohibition by conduct to which this section applies.

(4) But the Director may remove the immunity given by subsection (3) if –

> (a) he takes action under this Part with respect to the conduct in one of the circumstances mentioned in subsection (2);
>
> (b) he considers that it is likely that the conduct will infringe the prohibition; and
>
> (c) he gives notice in writing to the undertaking on whose application the decision was made that he is removing the immunity as from the date specified in his notice.

(5) If the Director has a reasonable suspicion that information –

> (a) on which he based his decision, and
>
> (b) which was provided to him by an undertaking engaging in the conduct,

was incomplete, false or misleading in a material particular, the date specified in a notice under subsection (4)(c) may be earlier than the date on which the notice is given.

CHAPTER III
INVESTIGATION AND ENFORCEMENT

Investigations

25. – The Director may conduct an investigation if there are reasonable grounds for suspecting –

> (a) that the Chapter I prohibition has been infringed; or
>
> (b) that the Chapter II prohibition has been infringed.

26. – (1) For the purposes of an investigation under section 25, the Director may require any person to produce to him a specified document, or to provide him with specified information, which he considers relates to any matter relevant to the investigation.

(2) The power conferred by subsection (1) is to be exercised by a notice in writing.

(3) A notice under subsection (2) must indicate –

> (a) the subject matter and purpose of the investigation; and
>
> (b) the nature of the offences created by sections 42 to 44.

(4) In subsection (1) "specified" means –

> (a) specified, or described, in the notice; or

(b) falling within a category which is specified, or described, in the notice.

(5) The Director may also specify in the notice –
(a) the time and place at which any document is to be produced or any information is to be provided;
(b) the manner and form in which it is to be produced or provided.

(6) The power under this section to require a person to produce a document includes power –
(a) if the document is produced –
(i) to take copies of it or extracts from it;
(ii) to require him, or any person who is a present or past officer of his, or is or was at any time employed by him, to provide an explanation of the document;
(b) if the document is not produced, to require him to state, to the best of his knowledge and belief, where it is.

27. – (1) Any officer of the Director who is authorised in writing by the Director to do so ("an investigating officer") may enter any premises in connection with an investigation under section 25.

(2) No investigating officer is to enter any premises in the exercise of his powers under this section unless he has given to the occupier of the premises a written notice which –
(a) gives at least two working days' notice of the intended entry;
(b) indicates the subject matter and purpose of the investigation; and
(c) indicates the nature of the offences created by sections 42 to 44.

(3) Subsection (2) does not apply –
(a) if the Director has a reasonable suspicion that the premises are, or have been, occupied by –
(i) a party to an agreement which he is investigating under section 25(a); or
(ii) an undertaking the conduct of which he is investigating under section 25(b); or
(b) if the investigating officer has taken all such steps as are reasonably practicable to give notice but has not been able to do so.

(4) In a case falling within subsection (3), the power of entry conferred by subsection (1) is to be exercised by the investigating officer on production of –

(a) evidence of his authorisation; and

(b) a document containing the information referred to in subsection (2)(b) and (c).

(5) An investigating officer entering any premises under this section may –

(a) take with him such equipment as appears to him to be necessary;

(b) require any person on the premises –

(i) to produce any document which he considers relates to any matter relevant to the investigation; and

(ii) if the document is produced, to provide an explanation of it;

(c) require any person to state, to the best of his knowledge and belief, where any such document is to be found;

(d) take copies of, or extracts from, any document which is produced;

(e) require any information which is held in a computer and is accessible from the premises and which the investigating officer considers relates to any matter relevant to the investigation, to be produced in a form –

(i) in which it can be taken away, and

(ii) in which it is visible and legible.

28. – (1) On an application made by the Director to the court in accordance with rules of court, a judge may issue a warrant if he is satisfied that –

(a) there are reasonable grounds for suspecting that there are on any premises documents –

(i) the production of which has been required under section 26 or 27; and

(ii) which have not been produced as required;

(b) there are reasonable grounds for suspecting that –

(i) there are on any premises documents which the Director has power under section 26 to require to be produced; and

(ii) if the documents were required to be produced, they would not be produced but would be concealed, removed, tampered with or destroyed; or

(c) an investigating officer has attempted to enter premises in the exercise of his powers under section 27 but has been unable to do so and that there are reasonable grounds for suspecting that there are on the premises documents the production of which could have been required under that section.

(2) A warrant under this section shall authorise a named officer of the

Director, and any other of his officers whom he has authorised in writing to accompany the named officer –

    (a) to enter the premises specified in the warrant, using such force as is reasonably necessary for the purpose;

    (b) to search the premises and take copies of, or extracts from, any document appearing to be of a kind in respect of which the application under subsection (1) was granted ("the relevant kind");

    (c) to take possession of any documents appearing to be of the relevant kind if –

        (i) such action appears to be necessary for preserving the documents or preventing interference with them; or

        (ii) it is not reasonably practicable to take copies of the documents on the premises;

    (d) to take any other steps which appear to be necessary for the purpose mentioned in paragraph (c)(i);

    (e) to require any person to provide an explanation of any document appearing to be of the relevant kind or to state, to the best of his knowledge and belief, where it may be found;

    (f) to require any information which is held in a computer and is accessible from the premises and which the named officer considers relates to any matter relevant to the investigation, to be produced in a form –

        (i) in which it can be taken away, and

        (ii) in which it is visible and legible.

(3) If, in the case of a warrant under subsection (1)(b), the judge is satisfied that it is reasonable to suspect that there are also on the premises other documents relating to the investigation concerned, the warrant shall also authorise action mentioned in subsection (2) to be taken in relation to any such document.

(4) Any person entering premises by virtue of a warrant under this section may take with him such equipment as appears to him to be necessary.

(5) On leaving any premises which he has entered by virtue of a warrant under this section, the named officer must, if the premises are unoccupied or the occupier is temporarily absent, leave them as effectively secured as he found them.

(6) A warrant under this section continues in force until the end of the period of one month beginning with the day on which it is issued.

(7) Any document of which possession is taken under subsection (2)(c) may be retained for a period of three months.

29. – (1) A warrant issued under section 28 must indicate –
(a) the subject matter and purpose of the investigation;
(b) the nature of the offences created by sections 42 to 44.

(2) The powers conferred by section 28 are to be exercised on production of a warrant issued under that section.

(3) If there is no one at the premises when the named officer proposes to execute such a warrant he must, before executing it –
(a) take such steps as are reasonable in all the circumstances to inform the occupier of the intended entry; and
(b) if the occupier is informed, afford him or his legal or other representative a reasonable opportunity to be present when the warrant is executed.

(4) If the named officer is unable to inform the occupier of the intended entry he must, when executing the warrant, leave a copy of it in a prominent place on the premises.

(5) In this section –

"named officer" means the officer named in the warrant; and
"occupier", in relation to any premises, means a person whom the named officer reasonably believes is the occupier of those premises.

30. – (1) A person shall not be required, under any provision of this Part, to produce or disclose a privileged communication.

(2) "Privileged communication" means a communication –
(a) between a professional legal adviser and his client, or
(b) made in connection with, or in contemplation of, legal proceedings and for the purposes of those proceedings,
which in proceedings in the High Court would be protected from disclosure on grounds of legal professional privilege.

(3) In the application of this section to Scotland –
(a) references to the High Court are to be read as references to the Court of Session; and
(b) the reference to legal professional privilege is to be read as a reference to confidentiality of communications.

31. – (1) Subsection (2) applies if, as the result of an investigation conducted under section 25, the Director proposes to make –
(a) a decision that the Chapter I prohibition has been infringed, or
(b) a decision that the Chapter II prohibition has been infringed.

(2) Before making the decision, the Director must –
    (a) give written notice to the person (or persons) likely to be affected by the proposed decision; and
    (b) give that person (or those persons) an opportunity to make representations.

32. – (1) If the Director has made a decision that an agreement infringes the Chapter I prohibition, he may give to such person or persons as he considers appropriate such directions as he considers appropriate to bring the infringement to an end.

(2) Subsection (1) applies whether the Director's decision is made on his own initiative or on an application made to him under this Part.

(3) A direction under this section may, in particular, include provision –
    (a) requiring the parties to the agreement to modify the agreement; or
    (b) requiring them to terminate the agreement.

(4) A direction under this section must be given in writing.

33. – (1) If the Director has made a decision that conduct infringes the Chapter II prohibition, he may give to such person or persons as he considers appropriate such directions as he considers appropriate to bring the infringement to an end.

(2) Subsection (1) applies whether the Director's decision is made on his own initiative or on an application made to him under this Part.

(3) A direction under this section may, in particular, include provision –
    (a) requiring the person concerned to modify the conduct in question; or
    (b) requiring him to cease that conduct.
(4) A direction under this section must be given in writing.

34. – (1) If a person fails, without reasonable excuse, to comply with a direction under section 32 or 33, the Director may apply to the court for an order –
    (a) requiring the defaulter to make good his default within a time specified in the order; or
    (b) if the direction related to anything to be done in the management or administration of an undertaking, requiring the undertaking or any of its officers to do it.

(2) An order of the court under subsection (1) may provide for all of

the costs of, or incidental to, the application for the order to be borne by –

    (a) the person in default; or

    (b) any officer of an undertaking who is responsible for the default.

(3) In the application of subsection (2) to Scotland, the reference to "costs" is to be read as a reference to "expenses".

35. – (1) This section applies if the Director –

    (a) has a reasonable suspicion that the Chapter I prohibition has been infringed, or

    (b) has a reasonable suspicion that the Chapter II prohibition has been infringed,

but has not completed his investigation into the matter.

(2) If the Director considers that it is necessary for him to act under this section as a matter of urgency for the purpose –

    (a) of preventing serious, irreparable damage to a particular person or category of person, or

    (b) of protecting the public interest,

he may give such directions as he considers appropriate for that purpose.

(3) Before giving a direction under this section, the Director must –

    (a) give written notice to the person (or persons) to whom he proposes to give the direction; and

    (b) give that person (or each of them) an opportunity to make representations.

(4) A notice under subsection (3) must indicate the nature of the direction which the Director is proposing to give and his reasons for wishing to give it.

(5) A direction given under this section has effect while subsection (1) applies, but may be replaced if the circumstances permit by a direction under section 32 or (as appropriate) section 33.

(6) In the case of a suspected infringement of the Chapter I prohibition, sections 32(3) and 34 also apply to directions given under this section.

(7) In the case of a suspected infringement of the Chapter II prohibition, sections 33(3) and 34 also apply to directions given under this section.

36. – (1) On making a decision that an agreement has infringed the

Chapter I prohibition, the Director may require an undertaking which is a party to the agreement to pay him a penalty in respect of the infringement.

(2) On making a decision that conduct has infringed the Chapter II prohibition, the Director may require the undertaking concerned to pay him a penalty in respect of the infringement.

(3) The Director may impose a penalty on an undertaking under subsection (1) or (2) only if he is satisfied that the infringement has been committed intentionally or negligently by the undertaking.

(4) Subsection (1) is subject to section 39 and does not apply if the Director is satisfied that the undertaking acted on the reasonable assumption that that section gave it immunity in respect of the agreement.

(5) Subsection (2) is subject to section 40 and does not apply if the Director is satisfied that the undertaking acted on the reasonable assumption that that section gave it immunity in respect of the conduct.

(6) Notice of a penalty under this section must –
    (a) be in writing; and
    (b) specify the date before which the penalty is required to be paid.

(7) The date specified must not be earlier than the end of the period within which an appeal against the notice may be brought under section 46.

(8) No penalty fixed by the Director under this section may exceed 10% of the turnover of the undertaking (determined in accordance with such provisions as may be specified in an order made by the Secretary of State).

(9) Any sums received by the Director under this section are to be paid into the Consolidated Fund.

37. – (1) If the specified date in a penalty notice has passed and –
    (a) the period during which an appeal against the imposition, or amount, of the penalty may be made has expired without an appeal having been made, or
    (b) such an appeal has been made and determined,
the Director may recover from the undertaking, as a civil debt due to him, any amount payable under the penalty notice which remains outstanding.

(2)   In this section –
"penalty notice" means a notice given under section 36; and
"specified date" means the date specified in the penalty notice.

38. – (1) The Director must prepare and publish guidance as to the appropriate amount of any penalty under this Part.

(2)   The Director may at any time alter the guidance.

(3)   If the guidance is altered, the Director must publish it as altered.

(4)   No guidance is to be published under this section without the approval of the Secretary of State.

(5)   The Director may, after consulting the Secretary of State, choose how he publishes his guidance.

(6)   If the Director is preparing or altering guidance under this section he must consult such persons as he considers appropriate.

(7)   If the proposed guidance or alteration relates to a matter in respect of which a regulator exercises concurrent jurisdiction, those consulted must include that regulator.

(8)   When setting the amount of a penalty under this Part, the Director must have regard to the guidance for the time being in force under this section.

(9)   If a penalty or a fine has been imposed by the Commission, or by a court or other body in another Member State, in respect of an agreement or conduct, the Director, an appeal tribunal or the appropriate court must take that penalty or fine into account when setting the amount of a penalty under this Part in relation to that agreement or conduct.

(10) In subsection (9) "the appropriate court" means –
    (a) in relation to England and Wales, the Court of Appeal;
    (b) in relation to Scotland, the Court of Session;
    (c) in relation to Northern Ireland, the Court of Appeal in Northern Ireland;
    (d) the House of Lords.

39. – (1) In this section "small agreement" means an agreement –
    (a) which falls within a category prescribed for the purposes of this section; but
    (b) is not a price fixing agreement.

(2) The criteria by reference to which a category of agreement is prescribed may, in particular, include –
> (a) the combined turnover of the parties to the agreement (determined in accordance with prescribed provisions);
> (b) the share of the market affected by the agreement (determined in that way).

(3) A party to a small agreement is immune from the effect of section 36(1); but the Director may withdraw that immunity under subsection (4).

(4) If the Director has investigated a small agreement, he may make a decision withdrawing the immunity given by subsection (3) if, as a result of his investigation, he considers that the agreement is likely to infringe the Chapter I prohibition.

(5) The Director must give each of the parties in respect of which immunity is withdrawn written notice of his decision to withdraw the immunity.

(6) A decision under subsection (4) takes effect on such date ("the withdrawal date") as may be specified in the decision.

(7) The withdrawal date must be a date after the date on which the decision is made.

(8) In determining the withdrawal date, the Director must have regard to the amount of time which the parties are likely to require in order to secure that there is no further infringement of the Chapter I prohibition with respect to the agreement.

(9) In subsection (1) "price fixing agreement" means an agreement which has as its object or effect, or one of its objects or effects, restricting the freedom of a party to the agreement to determine the price to be charged (otherwise than as between that party and another party to the agreement) for the product, service or other matter to which the agreement relates.

40. – (1) In this section "conduct of minor significance" means conduct which falls within a category prescribed for the purposes of this section.

(2) The criteria by reference to which a category is prescribed may, in particular, include –
> (a) the turnover of the person whose conduct it is (determined in accordance with prescribed provisions);

(b) the share of the market affected by the conduct (determined in that way).

(3) A person is immune from the effect of section 36(2) if his conduct is conduct of minor significance; but the Director may withdraw that immunity under subsection (4).

(4) If the Director has investigated conduct of minor significance, he may make a decision withdrawing the immunity given by subsection (3) if, as a result of his investigation, he considers that the conduct is likely to infringe the Chapter II prohibition.

(5) The Director must give the person, or persons, whose immunity has been withdrawn written notice of his decision to withdraw the immunity.

(6) A decision under subsection (4) takes effect on such date ("the withdrawal date") as may be specified in the decision.

(7) The withdrawal date must be a date after the date on which the decision is made.

(8) In determining the withdrawal date, the Director must have regard to the amount of time which the person or persons affected are likely to require in order to secure that there is no further infringement of the Chapter II prohibition.

41. – (1) This section applies if a party to an agreement which may infringe the Chapter I prohibition has notified the agreement to the Commission for a decision as to whether an exemption will be granted under Article 85 with respect to the agreement.

(2) A penalty may not be required to be paid under this Part in respect of any infringement of the Chapter I prohibition after notification but before the Commission determines the matter.

(3) If the Commission withdraws the benefit of provisional immunity from penalties with respect to the agreement, subsection (2) ceases to apply as from the date on which that benefit is withdrawn.

(4) The fact that an agreement has been notified to the Commission does not prevent the Director from investigating it under this Part.

(5) In this section "provisional immunity from penalties" has such meaning as may be prescribed.

Offences

42. – (1) A person is guilty of an offence if he fails to comply with a requirement imposed on him under section 26, 27 or 28.

(2) If a person is charged with an offence under subsection (1) in respect of a requirement to produce a document, it is a defence for him to prove –
>   (a) that the document was not in his possession or under his control; and
>   (b) that it was not reasonably practicable for him to comply with the requirement.

(3) If a person is charged with an offence under subsection (1) in respect of a requirement –
>   (a) to provide information,
>   (b) to provide an explanation of a document, or
>   (c) to state where a document is to be found,
it is a defence for him to prove that he had a reasonable excuse for failing to comply with the requirement.

(4) Failure to comply with a requirement imposed under section 26 or 27 is not an offence if the person imposing the requirement has failed to act in accordance with that section.

(5) A person is guilty of an offence if he intentionally obstructs an officer acting in the exercise of his powers under section 27.

(6) A person guilty of an offence under subsection (1) or (5) is liable –
>   (a) on summary conviction, to a fine not exceeding the statutory maximum;
>   (b) on conviction on indictment, to a fine.

(7) A person who intentionally obstructs an officer in the exercise of his powers under a warrant issued under section 28 is guilty of an offence and liable –
>   (a) on summary conviction, to a fine not exceeding the statutory maximum;
>   (b) on conviction on indictment, to imprisonment for a term not exceeding two years or to a fine or to both.

43. – (1) A person is guilty of an offence if, having been required to produce a document under section 26, 27 or 28 –
>   (a) he intentionally or recklessly destroys or otherwise disposes of it, falsifies it or conceals it, or

(b) he causes or permits its destruction, disposal, falsification or concealment.

(2)   A person guilty of an offence under subsection (1) is liable –
(a) on summary conviction, to a fine not exceeding the statutory maximum;
(b) on conviction on indictment, to imprisonment for a term not exceeding two years or to a fine or to both.

44. – (1) If information is provided by a person to the Director in connection with any function of the Director under this Part, that person is guilty of an offence if –
(a) the information is false or misleading in a material particular, and
(b) he knows that it is or is reckless as to whether it is.

(2)   A person who –
(a) provides any information to another person, knowing the information to be false or misleading in a material particular, or
(b) recklessly provides any information to another person which is false or misleading in a material particular,
knowing that the information is to be used for the purpose of providing information to the Director in connection with any of his functions under this Part, is guilty of an offence.

(3)   A person guilty of an offence under this section is liable –
(a) on summary conviction, to a fine not exceeding the statutory maximum;
(b) on conviction on indictment, to imprisonment for a term not exceeding two years or to a fine or to both.

CHAPTER IV
THE COMPETITION COMMISSION AND APPEALS

The Commission

45. – (1) There is to be a body corporate known as the Competition Commission.

(2)   The Commission is to have such functions as are conferred on it by or as a result of this Act.

(3)   The Monopolies and Mergers Commission is dissolved and its functions are transferred to the Competition Commission.

(4)   In any enactment, instrument or other document, any reference

to the Monopolies and Mergers Commission which has continuing effect is to be read as a reference to the Competition Commission.

(5) The Secretary of State may by order make such consequential, supplemental and incidental provision as he considers appropriate in connection with –

(a) the dissolution of the Monopolies and Mergers Commission; and

(b) the transfer of functions effected by subsection (3).

(6) An order made under subsection (5) may, in particular, include provision –

(a) for the transfer of property, rights, obligations and liabilities and the continuation of proceedings, investigations and other matters; or

(b) amending any enactment which makes provision with respect to the Monopolies and Mergers Commission or any of its functions.

(7) Schedule 7 makes further provision about the Competition Commission.

46. – (1) Any party to an agreement in respect of which the Director has made a decision may appeal to the Competition Commission against, or with respect to, the decision.

(2) Any person in respect of whose conduct the Director has made a decision may appeal to the Competition Commission against, or with respect to, the decision.

(3) In this section "decision" means a decision of the Director –

(a) as to whether the Chapter I prohibition has been infringed,

(b) as to whether the Chapter II prohibition has been infringed,

(c) as to whether to grant an individual exemption,

(d) in respect of an individual exemption –

(i) as to whether to impose any condition or obligation under section 4(3)(a) or 5(1)(c),

(ii) where such a condition or obligation has been imposed, as to the condition or obligation,

(iii) as to the period fixed under section 4(3)(b), or

(iv) as to the date fixed under section 4(5),

(e) as to –

(i) whether to extend the period for which an individual exemption has effect, or

(ii) the period of any such extension,

(f) cancelling an exemption,

(g) as to the imposition of any penalty under section 36 or as to the amount of any such penalty,

(h) withdrawing or varying any of the decisions in paragraphs (a) to (f) following an application under section 47(1),

and includes a direction given under section 32, 33 or 35 and such other decision as may be prescribed.

(4) Except in the case of an appeal against the imposition, or the amount, of a penalty, the making of an appeal under this section does not suspend the effect of the decision to which the appeal relates.

(5) Part I of Schedule 8 makes further provision about appeals.

47. – (1) A person who does not fall within section 46(1) or (2) may apply to the Director asking him to withdraw or vary a decision ("the relevant decision") falling within paragraphs (a) to (f) of section 46(3) or such other decision as may be prescribed.

(2) The application must –

(a) be made in writing, within such period as the Director may specify in rules under section 51; and

(b) give the applicant's reasons for considering that the relevant decision should be withdrawn or (as the case may be) varied.

(3) If the Director decides –

(a) that the applicant does not have a sufficient interest in the relevant decision,

(b) that, in the case of an applicant claiming to represent persons who have such an interest, the applicant does not represent such persons, or

(c) that the persons represented by the applicant do not have such an interest,

he must notify the applicant of his decision.

(4) If the Director, having considered the application, decides that it does not show sufficient reason why he should withdraw or vary the relevant decision, he must notify the applicant of his decision.

(5) Otherwise, the Director must deal with the application in accordance with such procedure as may be specified in rules under section 51.

(6) The applicant may appeal to the Competition Commission against a decision of the Director notified under subsection (3) or (4).

(7)   The making of an application does not suspend the effect of the relevant decision.

48. – (1) Any appeal made to the Competition Commission under section 46 or 47 is to be determined by an appeal tribunal.

(2)   The Secretary of State may, after consulting the President of the Competition Commission Appeal Tribunals and such other persons as he considers appropriate, make rules with respect to appeals and appeal tribunals.

(3)   The rules may confer functions on the President.

(4)   Part II of Schedule 8 makes further provision about rules made under this section but is not to be taken as restricting the Secretary of State's powers under this section.

49. – (1) An appeal lies –
>   (a) on a point of law arising from a decision of an appeal tribunal, or
>   (b) from any decision of an appeal tribunal as to the amount of a penalty.

(2)   An appeal under this section may be made only –
>   (a) to the appropriate court;
>   (b) with leave; and
>   (c) at the instance of a party or at the instance of a person who has a sufficient interest in the matter.

(3)   Rules under section 48 may make provision for regulating or prescribing any matters incidental to or consequential upon an appeal under this section.

(4)   In subsection (2) –
"the appropriate court" means –
>   (a) in relation to proceedings before a tribunal in England and Wales, the Court of Appeal;
>   (b) in relation to proceedings before a tribunal in Scotland, the Court of Session;
>   (c) in relation to proceedings before a tribunal in Northern Ireland, the Court of Appeal in Northern Ireland;
"leave" means leave of the tribunal in question or of the appropriate court; and
"party", in relation to a decision, means a person who was a party to the proceedings in which the decision was made.

CHAPTER V
MISCELLANEOUS

Vertical agreements and land agreements

50. – (1) The Secretary of State may by order provide for any provision of this Part to apply in relation to –

(a)   vertical agreements, or

(b)   land agreements,

with such modifications as may be prescribed.

(2)   An order may, in particular, provide for exclusions or exemptions, or otherwise provide for prescribed provisions not to apply, in relation to –

(a) vertical agreements, or land agreements, in general; or

(b) vertical agreements, or land agreements, of any prescribed description.

(3)   An order may empower the Director to give directions to the effect that in prescribed circumstances an exclusion, exemption or modification is not to apply (or is to apply in a particular way) in relation to an individual agreement.

(4)   Subsections (2) and (3) are not to be read as limiting the powers conferred by section 71.

(5)   In this section –

"land agreement" and "vertical agreement" have such meaning as may be prescribed; and

"prescribed" means prescribed by an order.

51. – (1) The Director may make such rules about procedural and other matters in connection with the carrying into effect of the provisions of this Part as he considers appropriate.

(2)   Schedule 9 makes further provision about rules made under this section but is not to be taken as restricting the Director's powers under this section.

(3)   If the Director is preparing rules under this section he must consult such persons as he considers appropriate.

(4)   If the proposed rules relate to a matter in respect of which a regulator exercises concurrent jurisdiction, those consulted must include that regulator.

(5)   No rule made by the Director is to come into operation until it has been approved by an order made by the Secretary of State.

(6)   The Secretary of State may approve any rule made by the Director –
   (a) in the form in which it is submitted; or
   (b) subject to such modifications as he considers appropriate.

(7)   If the Secretary of State proposes to approve a rule subject to modifications he must inform the Director of the proposed modifications and take into account any comments made by the Director.

(8)   Subsections (5) to (7) apply also to any alteration of the rules made by the Director.

(9)   The Secretary of State may, after consulting the Director, by order vary or revoke any rules made under this section.

(10) If the Secretary of State considers that rules should be made under this section with respect to a particular matter he may direct the Director to exercise his powers under this section and make rules about that matter.

52. – (1) As soon as is reasonably practicable after the passing of this Act, the Director must prepare and publish general advice and information about –
   (a) the application of the Chapter I prohibition and the Chapter II prohibition, and
   (b) the enforcement of those prohibitions.

(2)   The Director may at any time publish revised, or new, advice or information.

(3)   Advice and information published under this section must be prepared with a view to –
   (a) explaining provisions of this Part to persons who are likely to be affected by them; and
   (b) indicating how the Director expects such provisions to operate.

(4)   Advice (or information) published by virtue of subsection (3)(b) may include advice (or information) about the factors which the Director may take into account in considering whether, and if so how, to exercise a power conferred on him by Chapter I, II or III.

(5)   Any advice or information published by the Director under this

section is to be published in such form and in such manner as he considers appropriate.

(6) If the Director is preparing any advice or information under this section he must consult such persons as he considers appropriate.

(7) If the proposed advice or information relates to a matter in respect of which a regulator exercises concurrent jurisdiction, those consulted must include that regulator.

(8) In preparing any advice or information under this section about a matter in respect of which he may exercise functions under this Part, a regulator must consult –
  (a) the Director;
  (b) the other regulators; and
  (c) such other persons as he considers appropriate.

53. – (1) The Director may charge fees, of specified amounts, in connection with the exercise by him of specified functions under this Part.

(2) Rules may, in particular, provide –
  (a) for the amount of any fee to be calculated by reference to matters which may include –
    (i) the turnover of any party to an agreement (determined in such manner as may be specified);
    (ii) the turnover of a person whose conduct the Director is to consider (determined in that way);
  (b) for different amounts to be specified in connection with different functions;
  (c) for the repayment by the Director of the whole or part of a fee in specified circumstances;
  (d) that an application or notice is not to be regarded as duly made or given unless the appropriate fee is paid.

(3) In this section –
  (a) "rules" means rules made by the Director under section 51; and
  (b) "specified" means specified in rules.

54. – (1) In this Part "regulator" means any person mentioned in paragraphs (a) to (g) of paragraph 1 of Schedule 10.

(2) Parts II and III of Schedule 10 provide for functions of the Director under this Part to be exercisable concurrently by regulators.

(3) Parts IV and V of Schedule 10 make minor and consequential amendments in connection with the regulators' competition functions.

(4) The Secretary of State may make regulations for the purpose of co-ordinating the performance of functions under this Part ("Part I functions") which are exercisable concurrently by two or more competent persons as a result of any provision made by Part II or III of Schedule 10.

(5) The regulations may, in particular, make provision –
    (a) as to the procedure to be followed by competent persons when determining who is to exercise Part I functions in a particular case;
    (b) as to the steps which must be taken before a competent person exercises, in a particular case, such Part I functions as may be prescribed;
    (c) as to the procedure for determining, in a particular case, questions arising as to which competent person is to exercise Part I functions in respect of the case;
    (d) for Part I functions in a particular case to be exercised jointly –
        (i) by the Director and one or more regulators, or
        (ii) by two or more regulators,
    and as to the procedure to be followed in such cases;
    (e) as to the circumstances in which the exercise by a competent person of such Part I functions as may be prescribed is to preclude the exercise of such functions by another such person;
    (f) for cases in respect of which Part I functions are being, or have been, exercised by a competent person to be transferred to another such person;
    (g) for the person ("A") exercising Part I functions in a particular case –
        (i) to appoint another competent person ("B") to exercise Part I functions on A's behalf in relation to the case; or
        (ii) to appoint officers of B (with B's consent) to act as officers of A in relation to the case;
    (h) for notification as to who is exercising Part I functions in respect of a particular case.

(6) Provision made by virtue of subsection (5)(c) may provide for questions to be referred to and determined by the Secretary of State or by such other person as may be prescribed.

(7) "Competent person" means the Director or any of the regulators.

55. – (1) No information which –

(a) has been obtained under or as a result of any provision of this Part, and

(b) relates to the affairs of any individual or to any particular business of an undertaking,

is to be disclosed during the lifetime of that individual or while that business continues to be carried on, unless the condition mentioned in subsection (2) is satisfied.

(2) The condition is that consent to the disclosure has been obtained from −

(a) the person from whom the information was initially obtained under or as a result of any provision of this Part (if the identity of that person is known); and

(b) if different −

(i) the individual to whose affairs the information relates, or

(ii) the person for the time being carrying on the business to which the information relates.

(3) Subsection (1) does not apply to a disclosure of information −

(a) made for the purpose of −

(i) facilitating the performance of any relevant functions of a designated person;

(ii) facilitating the performance of any functions of the Commission in respect of Community law about competition;

(iii) facilitating the performance by the Comptroller and Auditor General of any of his functions;

(iv) criminal proceedings in any part of the United Kingdom;

(b) made with a view to the institution of, or otherwise for the purposes of, civil proceedings brought under or in connection with this Part;

(c) made in connection with the investigation of any criminal offence triable in the United Kingdom or in any part of the United Kingdom; or

(d) which is required to meet a Community obligation.

(4) In subsection (3) "relevant functions" and "designated person" have the meaning given in Schedule 11.

(5) Subsection (1) also does not apply to a disclosure of information made for the purpose of facilitating the performance of specified functions of any specified person.

(6) In subsection (5) "specified" means specified in an order made by the Secretary of State.

(7) If information is disclosed to the public in circumstances in which the disclosure does not contravene subsection (1), that subsection does not prevent its further disclosure by any person.

(8) A person who contravenes this section is guilty of an offence and liable –

    (a) on summary conviction, to a fine not exceeding the statutory maximum; or

    (b) on conviction on indictment, to imprisonment for a term not exceeding two years or to a fine or to both.

56. – (1) This section applies if the Secretary of State or the Director is considering whether to disclose any information acquired by him under, or as a result of, any provision of this Part.

(2) He must have regard to the need for excluding, so far as is practicable, information the disclosure of which would in his opinion be contrary to the public interest.

(3) He must also have regard to –

    (a) the need for excluding, so far as is practicable –

        (i) commercial information the disclosure of which would, or might, in his opinion, significantly harm the legitimate business interests of the undertaking to which it relates, or

        (ii) information relating to the private affairs of an individual the disclosure of which would, or might, in his opinion, significantly harm his interests; and

    (b) the extent to which the disclosure is necessary for the purposes for which the Secretary of State or the Director is proposing to make the disclosure.

57. For the purposes of the law relating to defamation, absolute privilege attaches to any advice, guidance, notice or direction given, or decision made, by the Director in the exercise of any of his functions under this Part.

58. – (1) Unless the court directs otherwise or the Director has decided to take further action in accordance with section 16(2) or 24(2), a Director's finding which is relevant to an issue arising in Part I proceedings is binding on the parties if –

    (a) the time for bringing an appeal in respect of the finding has expired and the relevant party has not brought such an appeal; or

    (b) the decision of an appeal tribunal on such an appeal has confirmed the finding.

(2) In this section –

"a Director's finding" means a finding of fact made by the Director in the course of –

(a) determining an application for a decision under section 14 or 22, or

(b) conducting an investigation under section 25;

"Part I proceedings" means proceedings –

(a) in respect of an alleged infringement of the Chapter I prohibition or of the Chapter II prohibition; but

(b) which are brought otherwise than by the Director;

"relevant party" means –

(a) in relation to the Chapter I prohibition, a party to the agreement which is alleged to have infringed the prohibition; and

(b) in relation to the Chapter II prohibition, the undertaking whose conduct is alleged to have infringed the prohibition.

(3) Rules of court may make provision in respect of assistance to be given by the Director to the court in Part I proceedings.

Interpretation and governing principles
59. – (1) In this Part –

"appeal tribunal" means an appeal tribunal established in accordance with the provisions of Part III of Schedule 7 for the purpose of hearing an appeal under section 46 or 47;

"Article 85" means Article 85 of the Treaty;

"Article 86" means Article 86 of the Treaty;

"block exemption" has the meaning given in section 6(4);

"block exemption order" has the meaning given in section 6(2);

"the Chapter I prohibition" has the meaning given in section 2(8);

"the Chapter II prohibition" has the meaning given in section 18(4);

"the Commission" (except in relation to the Competition Commission) means the European Commission;

"the Council" means the Council of the European Union;

"the court", except in sections 58 and 60 and the expression "European Court", means –

(a) in England and Wales, the High Court;

(b) in Scotland, the Court of Session; and

(c) in Northern Ireland, the High Court;

"the Director" means the Director General of Fair Trading;

"document" includes information recorded in any form;

"the EEA Agreement" means the Agreement on the European Economic Area signed at Oporto on 2nd May 1992 as it has effect for the time being;

"the European Court" means the Court of Justice of the European Communities and includes the Court of First Instance;

"individual exemption" has the meaning given in section 4(2);

"information" includes estimates and forecasts;

"investigating officer" has the meaning given in section 27(1);

"Minister of the Crown" has the same meaning as in the Ministers of the Crown Act 1975;

"officer", in relation to a body corporate, includes a director, manager or secretary and, in relation to a partnership in Scotland, includes a partner;

"parallel exemption" has the meaning given in section 10(3);

"person", in addition to the meaning given by the Interpretation Act 1978, includes any undertaking;

"premises" does not include domestic premises unless—

> (a) they are also used in connection with the affairs of an undertaking, or
>
> (b) documents relating to the affairs of an undertaking are kept there,

but does include any vehicle;

"prescribed" means prescribed by regulations made by the Secretary of State;

"regulator" has the meaning given by section 54;

"section 11 exemption" has the meaning given in section 11(3); and

"the Treaty" means the treaty establishing the European Community.

(2) The fact that to a limited extent the Chapter I prohibition does not apply to an agreement, because of an exclusion provided by or under this Part or any other enactment, does not require those provisions of the agreement to which the exclusion relates to be disregarded when considering whether the agreement infringes the prohibition for other reasons.

(3) For the purposes of this Part, the power to require information, in relation to information recorded otherwise than in a legible form, includes power to require a copy of it in a legible form.

(4) Any power conferred on the Director by this Part to require information includes power to require any document which he believes may contain that information.

60. – (1) The purpose of this section is to ensure that so far as is possible (having regard to any relevant differences between the provisions concerned), questions arising under this Part in relation to competition within the United Kingdom are dealt with in a manner which is consistent with the treatment of corresponding questions arising in Community law in relation to competition within the Community.

(2)　At any time when the court determines a question arising under this Part, it must act (so far as is compatible with the provisions of this Part and whether or not it would otherwise be required to do so) with a view to securing that there is no inconsistency between –
> (a) the principles applied, and decision reached, by the court in determining that question; and
> (b) the principles laid down by the Treaty and the European Court, and any relevant decision of that Court, as applicable at that time in determining any corresponding question arising in Community law.

(3)　The court must, in addition, have regard to any relevant decision or statement of the Commission.

(4)　Subsections (2) and (3) also apply to –
> (a) the Director; and
> (b) any person acting on behalf of the Director, in connection with any matter arising under this Part.

(5)　In subsections (2) and (3), "court" means any court or tribunal.

(6)　In subsections (2)(b) and (3), "decision" includes a decision as to –
> (a) the interpretation of any provision of Community law;
> (b) the civil liability of an undertaking for harm caused by its infringement of Community law.

Part II

Investigations in Relation to Articles 85 and 86

61. – (1) In this Part –
"Article 85" and "Article 86" have the same meaning as in Part I;
"authorised officer", in relation to the Director, means an officer to whom an authorisation has been given under subsection (2);
"the Commission" means the European Commission;
"the Director" means the Director General of Fair Trading;
"Commission investigation" means an investigation ordered by a decision of the Commission under a prescribed provision of Community law relating to Article 85 or 86;
"Director's investigation" means an investigation conducted by the Director at the request of the Commission under a prescribed provision of Community law relating to Article 85 or 86;
"Director's special investigation" means a Director's investigation conducted at the request of the Commission in connection with a Commission investigation;
"prescribed" means prescribed by order made by the Secretary of State;

"premises" means –

(a) in relation to a Commission investigation, any premises, land or means of transport which an official of the Commission has power to enter in the course of the investigation; and

(b) in relation to a Director's investigation, any premises, land or means of transport which an official of the Commission would have power to enter if the investigation were being conducted by the Commission.

(2) For the purposes of a Director's investigation, an officer of the Director to whom an authorisation has been given has the powers of an official authorised by the Commission in connection with a Commission investigation under the relevant provision.

(3) "Authorisation" means an authorisation given in writing by the Director which –

(a) identifies the officer;

(b) specifies the subject matter and purpose of the investigation; and

(c) draws attention to any penalties which a person may incur in connection with the investigation under the relevant provision of Community law.

62. – (1) A judge of the High Court may issue a warrant if satisfied, on an application made to the High Court in accordance with rules of court by the Director, that a Commission investigation is being, or is likely to be, obstructed.

(2) A Commission investigation is being obstructed if –

(a) an official of the Commission ("the Commission official"), exercising his power in accordance with the provision under which the investigation is being conducted, has attempted to enter premises but has been unable to do so; and

(b) there are reasonable grounds for suspecting that there are books or records on the premises which the Commission official has power to examine.

(3) A Commission investigation is also being obstructed if there are reasonable grounds for suspecting that there are books or records on the premises –

(a) the production of which has been required by an official of the Commission exercising his power in accordance with the provision under which the investigation is being conducted; and

(b) which have not been produced as required.

(4)   A Commission investigation is likely to be obstructed if –
    (a) an official of the Commission ("the Commission official") is authorised for the purpose of the investigation;
    (b) there are reasonable grounds for suspecting that there are books or records on the premises which the Commission official has power to examine; and
    (c) there are also reasonable grounds for suspecting that, if the Commission official attempted to exercise his power to examine any of the books or records, they would not be produced but would be concealed, removed, tampered with or destroyed.

(5)   A warrant under this section shall authorise –
    (a) a named officer of the Director,
    (b) any other of his officers whom he has authorised in writing to accompany the named officer, and
    (c) any official of the Commission authorised for the purpose of the Commission investigation,
to enter the premises specified in the warrant, and search for books and records which the official has power to examine, using such force as is reasonably necessary for the purpose.

(6)   Any person entering any premises by virtue of a warrant under this section may take with him such equipment as appears to him to be necessary.

(7)   On leaving any premises entered by virtue of the warrant the named officer must, if the premises are unoccupied or the occupier is temporarily absent, leave them as effectively secured as he found them.

(8)   A warrant under this section continues in force until the end of the period of one month beginning with the day on which it is issued.

(9)   In the application of this section to Scotland, references to the High Court are to be read as references to the Court of Session.

63. – (1) A judge of the High Court may issue a warrant if satisfied, on an application made to the High Court in accordance with rules of court by the Director, that a Director's special investigation is being, or is likely to be, obstructed.

(2)   A Director's special investigation is being obstructed if –
    (a) an authorised officer of the Director has attempted to enter premises but has been unable to do so;
    (b) the officer has produced his authorisation to the undertaking, or association of undertakings, concerned; and

(c) there are reasonable grounds for suspecting that there are books or records on the premises which the officer has power to examine.

(3) A Director's special investigation is also being obstructed if –

(a) there are reasonable grounds for suspecting that there are books or records on the premises which an authorised officer of the Director has power to examine;

(b) the officer has produced his authorisation to the undertaking, or association of undertakings, and has required production of the books or records; and

(c) the books and records have not been produced as required.

(4) A Director's special investigation is likely to be obstructed if –

(a) there are reasonable grounds for suspecting that there are books or records on the premises which an authorised officer of the Director has power to examine; and

(b) there are also reasonable grounds for suspecting that, if the officer attempted to exercise his power to examine any of the books or records, they would not be produced but would be concealed, removed, tampered with or destroyed.

(5) A warrant under this section shall authorise –

(a) a named authorised officer of the Director,

(b) any other authorised officer accompanying the named officer, and

(c) any named official of the Commission,

to enter the premises specified in the warrant, and search for books and records which the authorised officer has power to examine, using such force as is reasonably necessary for the purpose.

(6) Any person entering any premises by virtue of a warrant under this section may take with him such equipment as appears to him to be necessary.

(7) On leaving any premises which he has entered by virtue of the warrant the named officer must, if the premises are unoccupied or the occupier is temporarily absent, leave them as effectively secured as he found them.

(8) A warrant under this section continues in force until the end of the period of one month beginning with the day on which it is issued.

(9) In the application of this section to Scotland, references to the High Court are to be read as references to the Court of Session.

64. – (1) A warrant issued under section 62 or 63 must indicate –
  (a) the subject matter and purpose of the investigation;
  (b) the nature of the offence created by section 65.

(2) The powers conferred by section 62 or 63 are to be exercised on production of a warrant issued under that section.

(3) If there is no one at the premises when the named officer proposes to execute such a warrant he must, before executing it –
  (a) take such steps as are reasonable in all the circumstances to inform the occupier of the intended entry; and
  (b) if the occupier is informed, afford him or his legal or other representative a reasonable opportunity to be present when the warrant is executed.

(4) If the named officer is unable to inform the occupier of the intended entry he must, when executing the warrant, leave a copy of it in a prominent place on the premises.

(5) In this section –
"named officer" means the officer named in the warrant; and
"occupier", in relation to any premises, means a person whom the named officer reasonably believes is the occupier of those premises.

65. – (1) A person is guilty of an offence if he intentionally obstructs any person in the exercise of his powers under a warrant issued under section 62 or 63.

(2) A person guilty of an offence under subsection (1) is liable –
  (a) on summary conviction, to a fine not exceeding the statutory maximum;
  (b) on conviction on indictment, to imprisonment for a term not exceeding two years or to a fine or to both.

PART III

Monopolies

66. – (1) Section 44 of the Fair Trading Act 1973 (power of the Director to require information about monopoly situations) is amended as follows.

(2) In subsection (1), for the words after paragraph (b) substitute –
"the Director may exercise the powers conferred by subsection (2) below for the purpose of assisting him in determining whether to take either of the following decisions with regard to that situation."

(3) After subsection (1) insert –

"(1A) Those decisions are –

(a) whether to make a monopoly reference with respect to the existence or possible existence of the situation;

(b) whether, instead, to make a proposal under section 56A below for the Secretary of State to accept undertakings."

(4) For subsection (2) substitute –

"(2) In the circumstances and for the purpose mentioned in subsection (1) above, the Director may –

(a) require any person within subsection (3) below to produce to the Director, at a specified time and place –

(i) any specified documents, or

(ii) any document which falls within a specified category, which are in his custody or under his control and which are relevant;

(b) require any person within subsection (3) below who is carrying on a business to give the Director specified estimates, forecasts, returns, or other information, and specify the time at which and the form and manner in which the estimates, forecasts, returns or information are to be given;

(c) enter any premises used by a person within subsection (3) below for business purposes, and –

(i) require any person on the premises to produce any documents on the premises which are in his custody or under his control and which are relevant;

(ii) require any person on the premises to give the Director such explanation of the documents as he may require.

(3) A person is within this subsection if –

(a) he produces goods of the description in question in the United Kingdom;

(b) he supplies goods or (as the case may be) services of the description in question in the United Kingdom; or

(c) such goods (or services) are supplied to him in the United Kingdom.

(4) The power to impose a requirement under subsection (2)(a) or (b) above is to be exercised by notice in writing served on the person on whom the requirement is imposed; and "specified" in those provisions means specified or otherwise described in the notice, and "specify" is to be read accordingly.

(5) The power under subsection (2)(a) above to require a person ("the person notified") to produce a document includes power –

(a) if the document is produced –

(i) to take copies of it or extracts from it;

(ii) to require the person notified, or any person who is a present or past officer of his, or is or was at any time employed by him, to provide an explanation of the document;

(b) if the document is not produced, to require the person notified to state, to the best of his knowledge and belief, where it is.

(6) Nothing in this section confers power to compel any person –

(a) to produce any document which he could not be compelled to produce in civil proceedings before the High Court or, in Scotland, the Court of Session; or

(b) in complying with any requirement for the giving of information, to give any information which he could not be compelled to give in evidence in such proceedings.

(7) No person has to comply with a requirement imposed under subsection (2) above by a person acting under an authorisation under paragraph 7 of Schedule 1 to this Act unless evidence of the authorisation has, if required, been produced.

(8) For the purposes of subsection (2) above –

(a) a document is relevant if –

(i) it is relevant to a decision mentioned in subsection (1A) above; and

(ii) the powers conferred by this section are exercised in relation to the document for the purpose of assisting the Director in determining whether to take that decision;

(b) "document" includes information recorded in any form; and

(c) in relation to information recorded otherwise than in legible form, the power to require its production includes power to require production of it in legible form, so far as the means to do so are within the custody or under the control of the person on whom the requirement is imposed."

(5) The amendments made by this section and section 67 have effect in relation to sectoral regulators in accordance with paragraph 1 of Schedule 10.

67. – (1) Section 46 of the Fair Trading Act 1973 is amended as follows.

(2) Omit subsections (1) and (2).

(3) At the end insert –

"(4) Any person who refuses or wilfully neglects to comply

with a requirement imposed under section 44(2) above is guilty of an offence and liable –

(a) on summary conviction, to a fine not exceeding the prescribed sum, or

(b) on conviction on indictment, to imprisonment for a term not exceeding two years or to a fine or to both.

(5) If a person is charged with an offence under subsection (4) in respect of a requirement to produce a document, it is a defence for him to prove –

(a) that the document was not in his possession or under his control; and

(b) that it was not reasonably practicable for him to comply with the requirement.

(6) If a person is charged with an offence under subsection (4) in respect of a requirement –

(a) to provide an explanation of a document, or

(b) to state where a document is to be found,

it is a defence for him to prove that he had a reasonable excuse for failing to comply with the requirement.

(7) A person who intentionally obstructs the Director in the exercise of his powers under section 44 is guilty of an offence and liable –

(a) on summary conviction, to a fine not exceeding the prescribed sum;

(b) on conviction on indictment, to a fine.

(8) A person who wilfully alters, suppresses or destroys any document which he has been required to produce under section 44(2) is guilty of an offence and liable –

(a) on summary conviction, to a fine not exceeding the prescribed sum;

(b) on conviction on indictment, to imprisonment for a term not exceeding two years or to a fine or to both."

68. – In section 137 of the Fair Trading Act 1973, after subsection (3) insert –

"(3A) The Secretary of State may by order made by statutory instrument –

(a) provide that "the supply of services" in the provisions of this Act is to include, or to cease to include, any activity specified in the order which consists in, or in making arrangements in connection with, permitting the use of land; and

(b) for that purpose, amend or repeal any of paragraphs (c), (d), (e) or (g) of subsection (3) above.

(3B) No order under subsection (3A) above is to be made unless a draft of the order has been laid before Parliament and approved by a resolution of each House of Parliament.

(3C) The provisions of Schedule 9 to this Act apply in the case of a draft of any such order as they apply in the case of a draft of an order to which section 91(1) above applies."

69. In section 83 of the Fair Trading Act 1973 –

(a) in subsection (1), omit "Subject to subsection (1A) below"; and

(b) omit subsection (1A) (reports on monopoly references to be transmitted to certain persons at least twenty-four hours before laying before Parliament).

PART IV
SUPPLEMENTAL AND TRANSITIONAL

70. Sections 44 and 45 of the Patents Act 1977 shall cease to have effect.

71. – (1) Any power to make regulations or orders which is conferred by this Act is exercisable by statutory instrument.

(2) The power to make rules which is conferred by section 48 is exercisable by statutory instrument.

(3) Any statutory instrument made under this Act may –

(a) contain such incidental, supplemental, consequential and transitional provision as the Secretary of State considers appropriate; and

(b) make different provision for different cases.

(4) No order is to be made under –

(a) section 3,

(b) section 19,

(c) section 36(8),

(d) section 50, or

(e) paragraph 6(3) of Schedule 4,

unless a draft of the order has been laid before Parliament and approved by a resolution of each House.

(5) Any statutory instrument made under this Act, apart from one made –

(a) under any of the provisions mentioned in subsection (4), or

(b) under section 76(3),

shall be subject to annulment by a resolution of either House of Parliament.

72. – (1) This section applies to an offence under any of sections 42 to 44, 55(8) or 65.

(2) If an offence committed by a body corporate is proved –
    (a) to have been committed with the consent or connivance of an officer, or
    (b) to be attributable to any neglect on his part,
the officer as well as the body corporate is guilty of the offence and liable to be proceeded against and punished accordingly.

(3) In subsection (2) "officer", in relation to a body corporate, means a director, manager, secretary or other similar officer of the body, or a person purporting to act in any such capacity.

(4) If the affairs of a body corporate are managed by its members, subsection (2) applies in relation to the acts and defaults of a member in connection with his functions of management as if he were a director of the body corporate.

(5) If an offence committed by a partnership in Scotland is proved –
    (a) to have been committed with the consent or connivance of a partner, or
    (b) to be attributable to any neglect on his part,
the partner as well as the partnership is guilty of the offence and liable to be proceeded against and punished accordingly.

(6) In subsection (5) "partner" includes a person purporting to act as a partner.

73. – (1) Any provision made by or under this Act binds the Crown except that –
    (a) the Crown is not criminally liable as a result of any such provision;
    (b) the Crown is not liable for any penalty under any such provision; and
    (c) nothing in this Act affects Her Majesty in her private capacity.

(2) Subsection (1)(a) does not affect the application of any provision of this Act in relation to persons in the public service of the Crown.

(3) Subsection (1)(c) is to be interpreted as if section 38(3) of the Crown Proceedings Act 1947 (interpretation of references in that Act

to Her Majesty in her private capacity) were contained in this Act.

(4) If, in respect of a suspected infringement of the Chapter I prohibition or of the Chapter II prohibition otherwise than by the Crown or a person in the public service of the Crown, an investigation is conducted under section 25 –
> (a) the power conferred by section 27 may not be exercised in relation to land which is occupied by a government department, or otherwise for purposes of the Crown, without the written consent of the appropriate person; and
> (b) section 28 does not apply in relation to land so occupied.

(5) In any case in which consent is required under subsection (4), the person who is the appropriate person in relation to that case is to be determined in accordance with regulations made by the Secretary of State.

(6) Sections 62 and 63 do not apply in relation to land which is occupied by a government department, or otherwise for purposes of the Crown, unless the matter being investigated is a suspected infringement by the Crown or by a person in the public service of the Crown.

(7) In subsection (6) "infringement" means an infringement of Community law relating to Article 85 or 86 of the Treaty establishing the European Community.

(8) If the Secretary of State certifies that it appears to him to be in the interests of national security that the powers of entry –
> (a) conferred by section 27, or
> (b) that may be conferred by a warrant under section 28, 62 or 63,

should not be exercisable in relation to premises held or used by or on behalf of the Crown and which are specified in the certificate, those powers are not exercisable in relation to those premises.

(9) Any amendment, repeal or revocation made by this Act binds the Crown to the extent that the enactment amended, repealed or revoked binds the Crown.

74. – (1) The minor and consequential amendments set out in Schedule 12 are to have effect.

(2) The transitional provisions and savings set out in Schedule 13 are to have effect.

(3) The enactments set out in Schedule 14 are repealed.

75. – (1) The Secretary of State may by order make such incidental, consequential, transitional or supplemental provision as he thinks necessary or expedient for the general purposes, or any particular purpose, of this Act or in consequence of any of its provisions or for giving full effect to it.

(2) An order under subsection (1) may, in particular, make provision –
    (a) for enabling any person by whom any powers will become exercisable, on a date specified by or under this Act, by virtue of any provision made by or under this Act to take before that date any steps which are necessary as a preliminary to the exercise of those powers;
    (b) for making savings, or additional savings, from the effect of any repeal made by or under this Act.

(3) Amendments made under this section shall be in addition, and without prejudice, to those made by or under any other provision of this Act.

(4) No other provision of this Act restricts the powers conferred by this section.

76. – (1) This Act may be cited as the Competition Act 1998.

(2) Sections 71 and 75 and this section and paragraphs 1 to 7 and 35 of Schedule 13 come into force on the passing of this Act.

(3) The other provisions of this Act come into force on such day as the Secretary of State may by order appoint; and different days may be appointed for different purposes.

(4) This Act extends to Northern Ireland.

SCHEDULES

Schedule 1
Exclusions: Mergers and Concentrations
Sections 3(1)(a) and 19(1)(a)
PART I
MERGERS
Enterprises ceasing to be distinct: the Chapter I prohibition

1. – (1) To the extent to which an agreement (either on its own or when taken together with another agreement) results, or if carried out

would result, in any two enterprises ceasing to be distinct enterprises for the purposes of Part V of the Fair Trading Act 1973 ("the 1973 Act"), the Chapter I prohibition does not apply to the agreement.

(2) The exclusion provided by sub-paragraph (1) extends to any provision directly related and necessary to the implementation of the merger provisions.

(3) In sub-paragraph (2) "merger provisions" means the provisions of the agreement which cause, or if carried out would cause, the agreement to have the result mentioned in sub-paragraph (1).

(4) Section 65 of the 1973 Act applies for the purposes of this paragraph as if –
      (a) in subsection (3) (circumstances in which a person or group of persons may be treated as having control of an enterprise), and
      (b) in subsection (4) (circumstances in which a person or group of persons may be treated as bringing an enterprise under their control),
for "may" there were substituted "must".

Enterprises ceasing to be distinct: the Chapter II prohibition
2. – (1) To the extent to which conduct (either on its own or when taken together with other conduct) –
      (a) results in any two enterprises ceasing to be distinct enterprises for the purposes of Part V of the 1973 Act), or
      (b) is directly related and necessary to the attainment of the result mentioned in paragraph (a),
the Chapter II prohibition does not apply to that conduct.

(2) Section 65 of the 1973 Act applies for the purposes of this paragraph as it applies for the purposes of paragraph 1.

Transfer of a newspaper or of newspaper assets
3. – (1) The Chapter I prohibition does not apply to an agreement to the extent to which it constitutes, or would if carried out constitute, a transfer of a newspaper or of newspaper assets for the purposes of section 57 of the 1973 Act.

(2) The Chapter II prohibition does not apply to conduct (either on its own or when taken together with other conduct) to the extent to which –
      (a) it constitutes such a transfer, or
      (b) it is directly related and necessary to the implementation of the transfer.

(3) The exclusion provided by sub-paragraph (1) extends to any provision directly related and necessary to the implementation of the transfer.

Withdrawal of the paragraph 1 exclusion
4. – (1) The exclusion provided by paragraph 1 does not apply to a particular agreement if the Director gives a direction under this paragraph to that effect.

(2) If the Director is considering whether to give a direction under this paragraph, he may by notice in writing require any party to the agreement in question to give him such information in connection with the agreement as he may require.

(3) The Director may give a direction under this paragraph only as provided in sub-paragraph (4) or (5).

(4) If at the end of such period as may be specified in rules under section 51 a person has failed, without reasonable excuse, to comply with a requirement imposed under sub-paragraph (2), the Director may give a direction under this paragraph.

(5) The Director may also give a direction under this paragraph if –
  (a) he considers –
    (i) that the agreement will, if not excluded, infringe the Chapter I prohibition; and
    (ii) that he is not likely to grant it an unconditional individual exemption; and
  (b) the agreement is not a protected agreement.

(6) For the purposes of sub-paragraph (5), an individual exemption is unconditional if no conditions or obligations are imposed in respect of it under section 4(3)(a).

(7) A direction under this paragraph –
  (a) must be in writing;
  (b) may be made so as to have effect from a date specified in the direction (which may not be earlier than the date on which it is given).

Protected agreements
5. An agreement is a protected agreement for the purposes of paragraph 4 if –
    (a) the Secretary of State has announced his decision not to make a merger reference to the Competition Commission under section 64 of the 1973 Act in connection with the agreement;

(b) the Secretary of State has made a merger reference to the Competition Commission under section 64 of the 1973 Act in connection with the agreement and the Commission has found that the agreement has given rise to, or would if carried out give rise to, a merger situation qualifying for investigation;

(c) the agreement does not fall within sub-paragraph (a) or (b) but has given rise to, or would if carried out give rise to, enterprises to which it relates being regarded under section 65 of the 1973 Act as ceasing to be distinct enterprises (otherwise than as the result of subsection (3) or (4)(b) of that section); or

(d) the Secretary of State has made a merger reference to the Competition Commission under section 32 of the Water Industry Act 1991 in connection with the agreement and the Commission has found that the agreement has given rise to, or would if carried out give rise to, a merger of the kind to which that section applies.

PART II
CONCENTRATIONS SUBJECT TO EC CONTROLS

6. – (1) To the extent to which an agreement (either on its own or when taken together with another agreement) gives rise to, or would if carried out give rise to, a concentration, the Chapter I prohibition does not apply to the agreement if the Merger Regulation gives the Commission exclusive jurisdiction in the matter.

(2)   To the extent to which conduct (either on its own or when taken together with other conduct) gives rise to, or would if pursued give rise to, a concentration, the Chapter II prohibition does not apply to the conduct if the Merger Regulation gives the Commission exclusive jurisdiction in the matter.

(3)   In this paragraph –
"concentration" means a concentration with a Community dimension within the meaning of Articles 1 and 3 of the Merger Regulation; and
"Merger Regulation" means Council Regulation (EEC) No 4064/89 of 21st December 1989 on the control of concentrations between undertakings as amended by Council Regulation (EC) No 1310/97 of 30th June 1997.

Schedule 2
Exclusions: Other Competition Scrutiny
Section 3(1)(b)
PART I
FINANCIAL SERVICES

The Financial Services Act 1986 (c. 60)
1. – (1) The Financial Services Act 1986 is amended as follows.

(2) For section 125 (effect of the Restrictive Trade Practices Act 1976), substitute –

"125. – (1) The Chapter I prohibition does not apply to an agreement for the constitution of –
  (a) a recognised self-regulating organisation,
  (b) a recognised investment exchange, or
  (c) a recognised clearing house,
to the extent to which the agreement relates to the regulating provisions of the body concerned.
(2) Subject to subsection (3) below, the Chapter I prohibition does not apply to an agreement for the constitution of –
  (a) a self-regulating organisation,
  (b) an investment exchange, or
  (c) a clearing house,
to the extent to which the agreement relates to the regulating provisions of the body concerned.
(3) The exclusion provided by subsection (2) above applies only if –
  (a) the body has applied for a recognition order in accordance with the provisions of this Act; and
  (b) the application has not been determined.
(4) The Chapter I prohibition does not apply to a decision made by –
  (a) a recognised self-regulating organisation,
  (b) a recognised investment exchange, or
  (c) a recognised clearing house,
to the extent to which the decision relates to any of that body's regulating provisions or specified practices.
(5) The Chapter I prohibition does not apply to the specified practices of –
  (a) a recognised self-regulating organisation, a recognised investment exchange or a recognised clearing house; or
  (b) a person who is subject to –
    (i) the rules of one of those bodies, or
    (ii) the statements of principle, rules, regulations or

codes of practice made by a designated agency in the exercise of functions transferred to it by a delegation order.

(6) The Chapter I prohibition does not apply to any agreement the parties to which consist of or include –

(a) a recognised self-regulating organisation, a recognised investment exchange or a recognised clearing house; or

(b) a person who is subject to –

(i) the rules of one of those bodies, or

(ii) the statements of principle, rules, regulations or codes of practice made by a designated agency in the exercise of functions transferred to it by a delegation order,

to the extent to which the agreement consists of provisions the inclusion of which is required or contemplated by any of the body's regulating provisions or specified practices or by the statements of principle, rules, regulations or codes of practice of the agency.

(7) The Chapter I prohibition does not apply to –

(a) any clearing arrangements; or

(b) any agreement between a recognised investment exchange and a recognised clearing house, to the extent to which the agreement consists of provisions the inclusion of which in the agreement is required or contemplated by any clearing arrangements.

(8) If the recognition order in respect of a body of the kind mentioned in subsection (1)(a), (b) or (c) above is revoked, subsections (1) and (4) to (7) above are to have effect as if that body had continued to be recognised until the end of the period of six months beginning with the day on which the revocation took effect.

(9) In this section –

"the Chapter I prohibition" means the prohibition imposed by section 2(1) of the Competition Act 1998;

"regulating provisions" means –

(a) in relation to a self-regulating organisation, any rules made, or guidance issued, by the organisation;

(b) in relation to an investment exchange, any rules made, or guidance issued, by the exchange;

(c) in relation to a clearing house, any rules made, or guidance issued, by the clearing house;

"specified practices" means –

(a) in the case of a recognised self-regulating organisation, the practices mentioned in section 119(2)(a)(ii) and (iii) above (read with section 119(5) and (6)(a));

(b) in the case of a recognised investment exchange, the practices mentioned in section 119(2)(b)(ii) and (iii) above (read with section 119(5) and (6)(b));

(c) in the case of a recognised clearing house, the practices mentioned in section 119(2)(c)(ii) and (iii) above (read with section 119(5) and (6)(b));

(d) in the case of a person who is subject to the statements of principle, rules, regulations or codes of practice issued or made by a designated agency in the exercise of functions transferred to it by a delegation order, the practices mentioned in section 121(2)(c) above (read with section 121(4));

and expressions used in this section which are also used in Part I of the Competition Act 1998 are to be interpreted in the same way as for the purposes of that Part of that Act."

(3)   Omit section 126 (certain practices not to constitute anti-competitive practices for the purposes of the Competition Act 1980).

(4)   For section 127 (modification of statutory provisions in relation to recognised professional bodies), substitute –

"127. – (1) This section applies to –

(a) any agreement for the constitution of a recognised professional body to the extent to which it relates to the rules or guidance of that body relating to the carrying on of investment business by persons certified by it ("investment business rules"); and

(b) any other agreement, the parties to which consist of or include—

(i) a recognised professional body,

(ii) a person certified by such a body, or

(iii) a member of such a body,

and which contains a provision required or contemplated by that body's investment business rules.

(2) If it appears to the Treasury, in relation to some or all of the provisions of an agreement to which this section applies –

(a) that the provisions in question do not have, and are not intended or likely to have, to any significant extent the effect of restricting, distorting or preventing competition; or

(b) that the effect of restricting, distorting or preventing competition which the provisions in question do have, or are intended or are likely to have, is not greater than is necessary for the protection of investors,

the Treasury may make a declaration to that effect.

(3) If the Treasury make a declaration under this section, the Chapter I prohibition does not apply to the agreement to the extent to which the agreement consists of provisions to which the declaration relates.

(4) If the Treasury are satisfied that there has been a material change of circumstances, they may –

(a) revoke a declaration made under this section, if they consider that the grounds on which it was made no longer exist;

(b) vary such a declaration, if they consider that there are grounds for making a different declaration; or

(c) make a declaration even though they have notified the Director of their intention not to do so.

(5) If the Treasury make, vary or revoke a declaration under this section they must notify the Director of their decision.

(6) If the Director proposes to exercise any Chapter III powers in respect of any provisions of an agreement to which this section applies, he must –

(a) notify the Treasury of his intention to do so; and

(b) give the Treasury particulars of the agreement and such other information –

(i) as he considers will assist the Treasury to decide whether to exercise their powers under this section; or

(ii) as the Treasury may request.

(7) The Director may not exercise his Chapter III powers in respect of any provisions of an agreement to which this section applies, unless the Treasury –

(a) have notified him that they have not made a declaration in respect of those provisions under this section and that they do not intend to make such a declaration; or

(b) have revoked a declaration under this section and a period of six months beginning with the date on which the revocation took effect has expired.

(8) A declaration under this section ceases to have effect if the agreement to which it relates ceases to be one to which this section applies.

(9) In this section –

"the Chapter I prohibition" means the prohibition imposed by section 2(1) of the Competition Act 1998,

"Chapter III powers" means the powers given to the Director by Chapter III of Part I of that Act so far as they relate to the Chapter I prohibition, and

expressions used in this section which are also used in Part I of the Competition Act 1998 are to be interpreted in the same way as for the purposes of that Part of that Act.

(10) In this section references to an agreement are to be read as applying equally to, or in relation to, a decision or concerted practice.
(11) In the application of this section to decisions and concerted practices, references to provisions of an agreement are to be read as references to elements of a decision or concerted practice."

PART II
COMPANIES

The Companies Act 1989 (c 40)
2. – (1) The Companies Act 1989 is amended as follows.

(2) In Schedule 14, for paragraph 9 (exclusion of certain agreements from the Restrictive Trade Practices Act 1976), substitute –

"The Competition Act 1998
9. – (1) The Chapter I prohibition does not apply to an agreement for the constitution of a recognised supervisory or qualifying body to the extent to which it relates to –
    (a) rules of, or guidance issued by, the body; and
    (b) incidental matters connected with the rules or guidance.
(2) The Chapter I prohibition does not apply to an agreement the parties to which consist of or include –
    (a) a recognised supervisory or qualifying body, or
    (b) any person mentioned in paragraph 3(5) or (6) above,
to the extent to which the agreement consists of provisions the inclusion of which in the agreement is required or contemplated by the rules or guidance of that body.
(3) The Chapter I prohibition does not apply to the practices mentioned in paragraph 3(4)(a) and (b) above.
(4) Where a recognition order is revoked, sub-paragraphs (1) to (3) above are to continue to apply for a period of six months beginning with the day on which the revocation takes effect, as if the order were still in force.
(5) In this paragraph –
    (a) "the Chapter I prohibition" means the prohibition imposed by section 2(1) of the Competition Act 1998,
    (b) references to an agreement are to be read as applying equally to, or in relation to, a decision or concerted practice,
and expressions used in this paragraph which are also used in Part I of the Competition Act 1998 are to be interpreted in the same way as for the purposes of that Part of that Act.
(6) In the application of this paragraph to decisions and concerted practices, references to provisions of an agreement are to be read as references to elements of a decision or concerted practice."

The Companies (Northern Ireland) Order 1990 (SI 1990/593 (NI 5))
3. – (1) The Companies (Northern Ireland) Order 1990 is amended as follows.

(2) In Schedule 14, for paragraph 9 (exclusion of certain agreements from the Restrictive Trade Practices Act 1976), substitute –

"The Competition Act 1998
9. –(1) The Chapter I prohibition does not apply to an agreement for the constitution of a recognised supervisory or qualifying body to the extent to which it relates to –
(a) rules of, or guidance issued by, the body; and
(b) incidental matters connected with the rules or guidance.
(2) The Chapter I prohibition does not apply to an agreement the parties to which consist of or include –
(a) a recognised supervisory or qualifying body, or
(b) any person mentioned in paragraph 3(5) or (6),
to the extent to which the agreement consists of provisions the inclusion of which in the agreement is required or contemplated by the rules or guidance of that body.
(3) The Chapter I prohibition does not apply to the practices mentioned in paragraph 3(4)(a) and (b).
(4) Where a recognition order is revoked, sub-paragraphs (1) to (3) are to continue to apply for a period of 6 months beginning with the day on which the revocation takes effect, as if the order were still in force.
(5) In this paragraph –
(a) "the Chapter I prohibition" means the prohibition imposed by section 2(1) of the Competition Act 1998,
(b) references to an agreement are to be read as applying equally to, or in relation to, a decision or concerted practice,
and expressions used in this paragraph which are also used in Part I of the Competition Act 1998 are to be interpreted in the same way as for the purposes of that Part of that Act.
(6) In the application of this paragraph to decisions and concerted practices, references to provisions of an agreement are to be read as references to elements of a decision or concerted practice."

PART III
BROADCASTING

The Broadcasting Act 1990 (c 42)
4. – (1) The Broadcasting Act 1990 is amended as follows.

(2) In section 194A (which modifies the Restrictive Trade Practices

Act 1976 in its application to agreements relating to Channel 3 news provision), for subsections (2) to (6), substitute –

"(2) If, having sought the advice of the Director, it appears to the Secretary of State, in relation to some or all of the provisions of a relevant agreement, that the conditions mentioned in subsection (3) are satisfied, he may make a declaration to that effect.

(3) The conditions are that –

(a) the provisions in question do not have, and are not intended or likely to have, to any significant extent the effect of restricting, distorting or preventing competition; or

(b) the effect of restricting, distorting or preventing competition which the provisions in question do have or are intended or are likely to have, is not greater than is necessary –

(i) in the case of a relevant agreement falling within subsection (1)(a), for securing the appointment by holders of regional Channel 3 licences of a single body corporate to be the appointed news provider for the purposes of section 31(2), or

(ii) in the case of a relevant agreement falling within subsection (1)(b), for compliance by them with conditions included in their licences by virtue of section 31(1) and (2).

(4) If the Secretary of State makes a declaration under this section, the Chapter I prohibition does not apply to the agreement to the extent to which the agreement consists of provisions to which the declaration relates.

(5) If the Secretary of State is satisfied that there has been a material change of circumstances, he may –

(a) revoke a declaration made under this section, if he considers that the grounds on which it was made no longer exist;

(b) vary such a declaration, if he considers that there are grounds for making a different declaration; or

(c) make a declaration, even though he has notified the Director of his intention not to do so.

(6) If the Secretary of State makes, varies or revokes a declaration under this section, he must notify the Director of his decision.

(7) The Director may not exercise any Chapter III powers in respect of a relevant agreement, unless –

(a) he has notified the Secretary of State of his intention to do so; and

(b) the Secretary of State –

(i) has notified the Director that he has not made a declaration in respect of the agreement, or provisions of the agreement, under this section and that he does not intend to make such a declaration; or

(ii) has revoked a declaration under this section and a period of six months beginning with the date on which the revocation took effect has expired.

(8) If the Director proposes to exercise any Chapter III powers in respect of a relevant agreement, he must give the Secretary of State particulars of the agreement and such other information –

(a) as he considers will assist the Secretary of State to decide whether to exercise his powers under this section; or

(b) as the Secretary of State may request.

(9) In this section –

"the Chapter I prohibition" means the prohibition imposed by section 2(1) of the Competition Act 1998;

"Chapter III powers" means the powers given to the Director by Chapter III of Part I of that Act so far as they relate to the Chapter I prohibition;

"Director" means the Director General of Fair Trading;

"regional Channel 3 licence" has the same meaning as in Part I;

and expressions used in this section which are also used in Part I of the Competition Act 1998 are to be interpreted in the same way as for the purposes of that Part of that Act.

(10) In this section references to an agreement are to be read as applying equally to, or in relation to, a decision or concerted practice.

(11) In the application of this section to decisions and concerted practices, references to provisions of an agreement are to be read as references to elements of a decision or concerted practice."

Networking arrangements under the Broadcasting Act 1990 (c. 42)
5. – (1) The Chapter I prohibition does not apply in respect of any networking arrangements to the extent to which they –

(a) are subject to Schedule 4 to the Broadcasting Act 1990 (competition references with respect to networking arrangements); or

(b) contain provisions which have been considered under that Schedule.

(2) The Independent Television Commission ("ITC") must publish a list of the networking arrangements which in their opinion are excluded from the Chapter I prohibition by virtue of sub-paragraph (1).

(3) The ITC must –
    (a) consult the Director before publishing the list, and
    (b) publish the list in such a way as they think most suitable for bringing it to the attention of persons who, in their opinion, would be affected by, or likely to have an interest in, it.

(4) In this paragraph "networking arrangements" means –
    (a) any arrangements entered into as mentioned in section 39(4) or (7)(b) of the Broadcasting Act 1990, or
    (b) any agreements –
        (i) which do not constitute arrangements of the kind mentioned in paragraph (a), but
        (ii) which are made for the purpose mentioned in section 39(1) of that Act, or
    (c) any modification of the arrangements or agreements mentioned in paragraph (a) or (b).

PART IV
ENVIRONMENTAL PROTECTION

Producer responsibility obligations

6. – (1) The Environment Act 1995 is amended as follows.

(2) In section 94(1) (supplementary provisions about regulations imposing producer responsibility obligations on prescribed persons), after paragraph (o), insert –
    "(oa) the exclusion or modification of any provision of Part I of the Competition Act 1998 in relation to exemption schemes or in relation to any agreement, decision or concerted practice at least one of the parties to which is an operator of an exemption scheme;".

(3) After section 94(6), insert –
    "(6A) Expressions used in paragraph (oa) of subsection (1) above which are also used in Part I of the Competition Act 1998 are to be interpreted in the same way as for the purposes of that Part of that Act."

(4) After section 94, insert –
    "94A. – (1) For the purposes of this section, the relevant paragraphs are paragraphs (n), (o), (oa) and (ya) of section 94(1) above.
    (2) Regulations made by the virtue of any of the relevant paragraphs may include transitional provision in respect of agreements or exemption schemes –

(a) in respect of which information has been required for the purposes of competition scrutiny under any regulation made by virtue of paragraph (ya);

(b) which are being, or have been, considered for the purposes of competition scrutiny under any regulation made by virtue of paragraph (n) or (ya); or

(c) in respect of which provisions of the Restrictive Trade Practices Acts 1976 and 1977 have been modified or excluded in accordance with any regulation made by virtue of paragraph (o).

(3) Subsections (2), (3), (5) to (7) and (10) of section 93 above do not apply to a statutory instrument which contains only regulations made by virtue of any of the relevant paragraphs or subsection (2) above.

(4) Such a statutory instrument shall be subject to annulment in pursuance of a resolution of either House of Parliament."

Schedule 3
GENERAL EXCLUSIONS

Planning obligations

1. – (1) The Chapter I prohibition does not apply to an agreement –

(a) to the extent to which it is a planning obligation;

(b) which is made under section 75 (agreements regulating development or use of land) or 246 (agreements relating to Crown land) of the Town and Country Planning (Scotland) Act 1997; or

(c) which is made under Article 40 of the Planning (Northern Ireland) Order 1991.

(2) In sub-paragraph (1)(a), "planning obligation" means –

(a) a planning obligation for the purposes of section 106 of the Town and Country Planning Act 1990; or

(b) a planning obligation for the purposes of section 299A of that Act.

Section 21(2) agreements

2. – (1) The Chapter I prohibition does not apply to an agreement in respect of which a direction under section 21(2) of the Restrictive Trade Practices Act 1976 is in force immediately before the coming into force of section 2 ("a section 21(2) agreement").

(2) If a material variation is made to a section 21(2) agreement, sub-paragraph (1) ceases to apply to the agreement on the coming into force of the variation.

(3) Sub-paragraph (1) does not apply to a particular section 21(2) agreement if the Director gives a direction under this paragraph to that effect.

(4) If the Director is considering whether to give a direction under this paragraph, he may by notice in writing require any party to the agreement in question to give him such information in connection with the agreement as he may require.

(5) The Director may give a direction under this paragraph only as provided in sub-paragraph (6) or (7).

(6) If at the end of such period as may be specified in rules under section 51 a person has failed, without reasonable excuse, to comply with a requirement imposed under sub-paragraph (4), the Director may give a direction under this paragraph.

(7) The Director may also give a direction under this paragraph if he considers –
> (a) that the agreement will, if not excluded, infringe the Chapter I prohibition; and
> (b) that he is not likely to grant it an unconditional individual exemption.

(8) For the purposes of sub-paragraph (7) an individual exemption is unconditional if no conditions or obligations are imposed in respect of it under section 4(3)(a).

(9) A direction under this paragraph –
> (a) must be in writing;
> (b) may be made so as to have effect from a date specified in the direction (which may not be earlier than the date on which it is given).

EEA Regulated Markets

3. – (1) The Chapter I prohibition does not apply to an agreement for the constitution of an EEA regulated market to the extent to which the agreement relates to any of the rules made, or guidance issued, by that market.

(2) The Chapter I prohibition does not apply to a decision made by an EEA regulated market, to the extent to which the decision relates to any of the market's regulating provisions.

(3) The Chapter I prohibition does not apply to –

(a) any practices of an EEA regulated market; or

(b) any practices which are trading practices in relation to an EEA regulated market.

(4) The Chapter I prohibition does not apply to an agreement the parties to which are or include –

(a) an EEA regulated market, or

(b) a person who is subject to the rules of that market,

to the extent to which the agreement consists of provisions the inclusion of which is required or contemplated by the regulating provisions of that market.

(5) In this paragraph –

"EEA regulated market" is a market which –

(a) is listed by an EEA State other than the United Kingdom pursuant to article 16 of Council Directive No 93/22/EEC of 10th May 1993 on investment services in the securities field; and

(b) operates without any requirement that a person dealing on the market should have a physical presence in the EEA State from which any trading facilities are provided or on any trading floor that the market may have;

"EEA State" means a State which is a contracting party to the EEA Agreement;

"regulating provisions", in relation to an EEA regulated market, means –

(a) rules made, or guidance issued, by that market,

(b) practices of that market, or

(c) practices which, in relation to that market, are trading practices;

"trading practices", in relation to an EEA regulated market, means practices of persons who are subject to the rules made by that market, and –

(a) which relate to business in respect of which those persons are subject to the rules of that market, and which are required or contemplated by those rules or by guidance issued by that market; or

(b) which are otherwise attributable to the conduct of that market as such.

Services of general economic interest etc

4.   Neither the Chapter I prohibition nor the Chapter II prohibition applies to an undertaking entrusted with the operation of services of general economic interest or having the character of a revenue-producing monopoly in so far as the prohibition would obstruct the performance,

in law or in fact, of the particular tasks assigned to that undertaking.

Compliance with legal requirements

5. – (1) The Chapter I prohibition does not apply to an agreement to the extent to which it is made in order to comply with a legal requirement.

(2)   The Chapter II prohibition does not apply to conduct to the extent to which it is engaged in an order to comply with a legal requirement.

(3)   In this paragraph "legal requirement" means a requirement –
(a) imposed by or under any enactment in force in the United Kingdom;
(b) imposed by or under the Treaty or the EEA Agreement and having legal effect in the United Kingdom without further enactment; or
(c) imposed by or under the law in force in another Member State and having legal effect in the United Kingdom.

Avoidance of conflict with international obligations

6. – (1) If the Secretary of State is satisfied that, in order to avoid a conflict between provisions of this Part and an international obligation of the United Kingdom, it would be appropriate for the Chapter I prohibition not to apply to –
(a) a particular agreement, or
(b) any agreement of a particular description,
he may by order exclude the agreement, or agreements of that description, from the Chapter I prohibition.

(2)   An order under sub-paragraph (1) may make provision for the exclusion of the agreement or agreements to which the order applies, or of such of them as may be specified, only in specified circumstances.

(3)   An order under sub-paragraph (1) may also provide that the Chapter I prohibition is to be deemed never to have applied in relation to the agreement or agreements, or in relation to such of them as may be specified.

(4)   If the Secretary of State is satisfied that, in order to avoid a conflict between provisions of this Part and an international obligation of the United Kingdom, it would be appropriate for the Chapter II prohibition not to apply in particular circumstances, he may by order provide for it not to apply in such circumstances as may be specified.

(5)   An order under sub-paragraph (4) may provide that the Chapter

II prohibition is to be deemed never to have applied in relation to specified conduct.

(6) An international arrangement relating to civil aviation and designated by an order made by the Secretary of State is to be treated as an international obligation for the purposes of this paragraph.

(7) In this paragraph and paragraph 7 "specified" means specified in the order.

Public policy

7. – (1) If the Secretary of State is satisfied that there are exceptional and compelling reasons of public policy why the Chapter I prohibition ought not to apply to –
    (a) a particular agreement, or
    (b) any agreement of a particular description,
he may by order exclude the agreement, or agreements of that description, from the Chapter I prohibition.

(2) An order under sub-paragraph (1) may make provision for the exclusion of the agreement or agreements to which the order applies, or of such of them as may be specified, only in specified circumstances.

(3) An order under sub-paragraph (1) may also provide that the Chapter I prohibition is to be deemed never to have applied in relation to the agreement or agreements, or in relation to such of them as may be specified.

(4) If the Secretary of State is satisfied that there are exceptional and compelling reasons of public policy why the Chapter II prohibition ought not to apply in particular circumstances, he may by order provide for it not to apply in such circumstances as may be specified.

(5) An order under sub-paragraph (4) may provide that the Chapter II prohibition is to be deemed never to have applied in relation to specified conduct.

Coal and steel

8. – (1) The Chapter I prohibition does not apply to an agreement which relates to a coal or steel product to the extent to which the ECSC Treaty gives the Commission exclusive jurisdiction in the matter.

(2) Sub-paragraph (1) ceases to have effect on the date on which the ECSC Treaty expires ("the expiry date").

(3)   The Chapter II prohibition does not apply to conduct which relates to a coal or steel product to the extent to which the ECSC Treaty gives the Commission exclusive jurisdiction in the matter.

(4)   Sub-paragraph (3) ceases to have effect on the expiry date.

(5)   In this paragraph –
>   "coal or steel product" means any product of a kind listed in Annex I to the ECSC Treaty; and
>   "ECSC Treaty" means the Treaty establishing the European Coal and Steel Community.

Agricultural products

9. – (1) The Chapter I prohibition does not apply to an agreement to the extent to which it relates to production of or trade in an agricultural product and –
>   (a) forms an integral part of a national market organisation;
>   (b) is necessary for the attainment of the objectives set out in Article 39 of the Treaty; or
>   (c) is an agreement of farmers or farmers' associations (or associations of such associations) belonging to a single member State which concerns –
>> (i) the production or sale of agricultural products, or
>> (ii) the use of joint facilities for the storage, treatment or processing of agricultural products,
>
>   and under which there is no obligation to charge identical prices.

(2)   If the Commission determines that an agreement does not fulfil the conditions specified by the provision for agricultural products for exclusion from Article 85(1), the exclusion provided by this paragraph ("the agriculture exclusion") is to be treated as ceasing to apply to the agreement on the date of the decision.

(3)   The agriculture exclusion does not apply to a particular agreement if the Director gives a direction under this paragraph to that effect.

(4)   If the Director is considering whether to give a direction under this paragraph, he may by notice in writing require any party to the agreement in question to give him such information in connection with the agreement as he may require.

(5)   The Director may give a direction under this paragraph only as provided in sub-paragraph (6) or (7).

(6)   If at the end of such period as may be specified in rules under

section 51 a person has failed, without reasonable excuse, to comply with a requirement imposed under sub-paragraph (4), the Director may give a direction under this paragraph.

(7)   The Director may also give a direction under this paragraph if he considers that an agreement (whether or not he considers that it infringes the Chapter I prohibition) is likely, or is intended, substantially and unjustifiably to prevent, restrict or distort competition in relation to an agricultural product.

(8)   A direction under this paragraph –
    (a)   must be in writing;
    (b)   may be made so as to have effect from a date specified in the direction (which may not be earlier than the date on which it is given).

(9)   In this paragraph –
    "agricultural product" means any product of a kind listed in Annex II to the Treaty; and
    "provision for agricultural products" means Council Regulation (EEC) No 26/62 of 4th April 1962 applying certain rules of competition to production of and trade in agricultural products.

Schedule 4
Professional Rules
PART I
EXCLUSION

General

1. – (1) To the extent to which an agreement (either on its own or when taken together with another agreement) –
    (a)   constitutes a designated professional rule,
    (b)   imposes obligations arising from designated professionals, or
    (c)   constitutes an agreement to act in accordance with such rules,
the Chapter I prohibition does not apply to the agreement.

(2)   In this Schedule –
    "designated" means designated by the Secretary of State under paragraph 2;
    "professional rules" means rules regulating a professional service or the persons providing, or wishing to provide, that service;
    "professional service" means any of the services described in Part II of this Schedule; and
    "rules" includes regulations, codes of practice and statements of principle.

Designated rules

2. – (1) The Secretary of State must establish and maintain a list designating, for the purposes of this Schedule, rules –
    (a) which are notified to him under paragraph 3; and
    (b) which, in his opinion, are professional rules.

(2) The list is to be established, and any alteration in the list is to be effected, by an order made by the Secretary of State.

(3) The designation of any rule is to have effect from such date (which may be earlier than the date on which the order listing it is made) as may be specified in that order.

Application for designation

3. – (1) Any body regulating a professional service or the persons who provide, or wish to provide, that service may apply to the Secretary of State for rules of that body to be designated.

(2) An application under this paragraph must –
    (a) be accompanied by a copy of the rules to which it relates; and
    (b) be made in the prescribed manner.

Alterations

4. – (1) A rule does not cease to be a designated professional rule merely because it is altered.

(2) If such a rule is altered (whether by being modified, revoked or replaced), the body concerned must notify the Secretary of State and the Director of the alteration as soon as is reasonably practicable.

Reviewing the list

5. – (1) The Secretary of State must send to the Director –
    (a) a copy of any order made under paragraph 2; and
    (b) a copy of the professional rules to which the order relates.

(2) The Director must –
    (a) retain any copy of a professional rule which is sent to him under sub-paragraph (1)(b) so long as the rule remains in force;
    (b) maintain a copy of the list, as altered from time to time; and
    (c) keep the list under review.

(3) If the Director considers –
    (a) that, with a view to restricting the exclusion provided by this Schedule, some or all of the rules of a particular body should no longer be designated, or

(b) that rules which are not designated should be designated, he must advise the Secretary of State accordingly.

Removal from the list

6. – (1) This paragraph applies if the Secretary of State receives advice under paragraph 5(3)(a).

(2) If it appears to the Secretary of State that another Minister of the Crown has functions in relation to the professional service concerned, he must consult that Minister.

(3) If it appears to the Secretary of State, having considered the Director's advice and the advice of any other Minister resulting from consultation under sub-paragraph (2), that the rules in question should no longer be designated, he may by order revoke their designation.

(4) Revocation of a designation is to have effect from such date as the order revoking it may specify.

Inspection

7. – (1) Any person may inspect, and take a copy of –
    (a) any entry in the list of designated professional rules as kept by the Director under paragraph 5(2); or
    (b) any copy of professional rules retained by him under paragraph 5(1).

(2) The right conferred by sub-paragraph (1) is to be exercised only –
    (a) at a time which is reasonable;
    (b) on payment of such fee as the Director may determine; and
    (c) at such offices of his as the Director may direct.

PART II
PROFESSIONAL SERVICES

Legal

8. The services of barristers, advocates or solicitors.

Medical

9. The provision of medical or surgical advice or attendance and the performance of surgical operations.

Dental

10. Any services falling within the practice of dentistry within the meaning of the Dentists Act 1984.

Ophthalmic

11. The testing of sight.

Veterinary

12. Any services which constitute veterinary surgery within the meaning of the Veterinary Surgeons Act 1966.

Nursing

13. The services of nurses.

Midwifery

14. The services of midwives.

Physiotherapy

15. The services of physiotherapists.

Chiropody

16. The services of chiropodists.

Architectural

17. The services of architects.

Accounting and auditing

18. The making or preparation of accounts or accounting records and the examination, verification and auditing of financial statements.

Insolvency

19. Insolvency services within the meaning of section 428 of the Insolvency Act 1986.

Patent agency

20. The services of registered patent agents (within the meaning of Part V of the Copyright, Designs and Patents Act 1988).

21. The services of persons carrying on for gain in the United Kingdom the business of acting as agents or other representatives for or obtaining European patents or for the purpose of conducting proceedings in relation to applications for or otherwise in connection with such patents before the European Patent Office or the comptroller and whose names appear on the European list (within the meaning of Part V of the Copyright, Designs and Patents Act 1988).

Parliamentary agency

22. The services of parliamentary agents entered in the register in either House of Parliament as agents entitled to practise both in

promoting and in opposing Bills.

Surveying

23.   The services of surveyors of land, of quantity surveyors, of surveyors of buildings or other structures and of surveyors of ships.

Engineering and technology etc

24.   The services of persons practising or employed as consultants in the field of –
> (a) civil engineering;
> (b) mechanical, aeronautical, marine, electrical or electronic engineering;
> (c) mining, quarrying, soil analysis or other forms of mineralogy or geology;
> (d) agronomy, forestry, livestock rearing or ecology;
> (e) metallurgy, chemistry, biochemistry or physics; or
> (f) any other form of engineering or technology analogous to those mentioned in sub-paragraphs (a) to (e).

Educational

25.   The provision of education or training.

Religious

26.   The services of ministers of religion.

Schedule 5
Notification Under Chapter I: Procedure

Terms used

1.   In this Schedule–
> "applicant" means the person making an application to which this Schedule applies;
> "application" means an application under section 13 or an application under section 14;
> "application for guidance" means an application under section 13;
> "application for a decision" means an application under section 14;
> "rules" means rules made by the Director under section 51; and
> "specified" means specified in the rules.

General rules about applications

2. – (1) An application must be made in accordance with rules.

(2) A party to an agreement who makes an application must take all reasonable steps to notify all other parties to the agreement of whom he is aware –

(a) that the application has been made; and
(b) as to whether it is for guidance or a decision.

(3) Notification under sub-paragraph (2) must be in the specified manner.

Preliminary investigation

3. – (1) If, after a preliminary investigation of an application, the Director considers that it is likely –

(a) that the agreement concerned will infringe the Chapter I prohibition, and
(b) that it would not be appropriate to grant the agreement an individual exemption,

he may make a decision ("a provisional decision") under this paragraph.

(2) If the Director makes a provisional decision –

(a) the Director must notify the applicant in writing of his provisional decision; and
(b) section 13(4) or (as the case may be) section 14(4) is to be taken as never having applied.

(3) When making a provisional decision, the Director must follow such procedures as may be specified.

(4) A provisional decision does not affect the final determination of an application.

(5) If the Director has given notice to the applicant under sub-paragraph (2) in respect of an application for a decision, he may continue with the application under section 14.

Procedure on application for guidance

4. When determining an application for guidance, the Director must follow such procedure as may be specified.

Procedure on application for a decision

5. – (1) When determining an application for a decision, the Director must follow such procedure as may be specified.

(2) The Director must arrange for the application to be published in such a way as he thinks most suitable for bringing it to the attention of those likely to be affected by it, unless he is satisfied that it will be sufficient for him to seek information from one or more particular persons other than the applicant.

(3)   In determining the application, the Director must take into account any representations made to him by persons other than the applicant.

Publication of decisions

6.   If the Director determines an application for a decision he must publish his decision, together with his reasons for making it, in such manner as may be specified.

Delay by the Director

7. – (1) This paragraph applies if the court is satisfied, on the application of a person aggrieved by the failure of the Director to determine an application for a decision in accordance with the specified procedure, that there has been undue delay on the part of the Director in determining the application.

(2)   The court may give such directions to the Director as it considers appropriate for securing that the application is determined without unnecessary further delay.

Schedule 6
Notification Under Chapter II: Procedure

Terms used

1.   In this Schedule –
   "applicant" means the person making an application to which this Schedule applies;
   "application" means an application under section 21 or an application under section 22;
   "application for guidance" means an application under section 21;
   "application for a decision" means an application under section 22;
   "other party", in relation to conduct of two or more persons, means one of those persons other than the applicant;
   "rules" means rules made by the Director under section 51; and
   "specified" means specified in the rules.

General rules about applications

2. – (1) An application must be made in accordance with rules.

(2)   If the conduct to which an application relates is conduct of two or more persons, the applicant must take all reasonable steps to notify all of the other parties of whom he is aware–
   (a) that the application has been made; and
   (b) as to whether it is for guidance or a decision.

(3)   Notification under sub-paragraph (2) must be in the specified manner.

Preliminary investigation

3. – (1) If, after a preliminary investigation of an application, the Director considers that it is likely that the conduct concerned will infringe the Chapter II prohibition, he may make a decision ("a provisional decision") under this paragraph.

(2) If the Director makes a provisional decision, he must notify the applicant in writing of that decision.

(3) When making a provisional decision, the Director must follow such procedure as may be specified.

(4) A provisional decision does not affect the final determination of an application.

(5) If the Director has given notice to the applicant under sub-paragraph (2) in respect of an application for a decision, he may continue with the application under section 22.

Procedure on application for guidance

4. When determining an application for guidance, the Director must follow such procedure as may be specified.

Procedure on application for a decision

5. – (1) When determining an application for a decision, the Director must follow such procedure as may be specified.

(2) The Director must arrange for the application to be published in such a way as he thinks most suitable for bringing it to the attention of those likely to be affected by it, unless he is satisfied that it will be sufficient for him to seek information from one or more particular persons other than the applicant.

(3) In determining the application, the Director must take into account any representations made to him by persons other than the applicant.

Publication of decisions

6. If the Director determines an application for a decision he must publish his decision, together with his reasons for making it, in such manner as may be specified.

Delay by the Director

7. – (1) This paragraph applies if the court is satisfied, on the application of a person aggrieved by the failure of the Director to determine an application for a decision in accordance with the specified procedure,

that there has been undue delay on the part of the Director in determining the application.

(2) The court may give such directions to the Director as it considers appropriate for securing that the application is determined without unnecessary further delay.

Schedule 7
The Competition Commission
PART I
GENERAL

Interpretation

1. In this Schedule –
    "the 1973 Act" means the Fair Trading Act 1973;
    "appeal panel member" means a member appointed under paragraph 2(1)(a);
    "Chairman" means the chairman of the Commission;
    "the Commission" means the Competition Commission;
    "Council" has the meaning given in paragraph 5;
    "general functions" means any functions of the Commission other than functions –
    (a) in connection with appeals under this Act; or
    (b) which are to be discharged by the Council;
    "member" means a member of the Commission;
    "newspaper merger reference" means a newspaper merger reference under section 59 of the 1973 Act;
    "President" has the meaning given by paragraph 4(2);
    "reporting panel member" means a member appointed under paragraph 2(1)(b);
    "secretary" means the secretary of the Commission appointed under paragraph 9; and
    "specialist panel member" means a member appointed under any of the provisions mentioned in paragraph 2(1)(d).

Membership of the Commission

2. – (1) The Commission is to consist of –
    (a) members appointed by the Secretary of State to form a panel for the purposes of the Commission's functions in relation to appeals;
    (b) members appointed by the Secretary of State to form a panel for the purposes of the Commission's general functions;
    (c) members appointed (in accordance with paragraph 15(5)) from the panel maintained under paragraph 22;
    (d) members appointed by the Secretary of State under or by virtue of –

     (i) section 12(4) or 14(8) of the Water Industry Act 1991;
     (ii) section 12(9) of the Electricity Act 1989;
     (iii) section 13(10) of the Telecommunications Act 1984;
     (iv) Article 15(9) of the Electricity (Northern Ireland) Order 1992.

(2) A person who is appointed as a member of a kind mentioned in one of paragraphs (a) to (c) of sub-paragraph (3) may also be appointed as a member of either or both of the other kinds mentioned in those paragraphs.

(3) The kinds of member are –
     (a) an appeal panel member;
     (b) a reporting panel member;
     (c) a specialist panel member.

(4) Before appointing a person who is qualified for appointment to the panel of chairmen (see paragraph 26(2)), the Secretary of State must consult the Lord Chancellor or Lord Advocate, as he considers appropriate.

(5) The validity of the Commission's proceedings is not affected by a defect in the appointment of a member.

Chairman and deputy chairmen

3. – (1) The Commission is to have a chairman appointed by the Secretary of State from among the reporting panel members.

(2) The Secretary of State may appoint one or more of the reporting panel members to act as deputy chairman.

(3) The Chairman, and any deputy chairman, may resign that office at any time by notice in writing addressed to the Secretary of State.

(4) If the Chairman (or a deputy chairman) ceases to be a member he also ceases to be Chairman (or a deputy chairman).

(5) If the Chairman is absent or otherwise unable to act, or there is no chairman, any of his functions may be performed –
     (a) if there is one deputy chairman, by him;
     (b) if there is more than one –
          (i) by the deputy chairman designated by the Secretary of State; or
          (ii) if no such designation has been made, by the deputy chairman designated by the deputy chairmen;

(c) if there is no deputy chairman able to act –
(i) by the member designated by the Secretary of State; or
(ii) if no such designation has been made, by the member designated by the Commission.

President

4. – (1) The Secretary of State must appoint one of the appeal panel members to preside over the discharge of the Commission's functions in relation to appeals.

(2) The member so appointed is to be known as the President of the Competition Commission Appeal Tribunals (but is referred to in this Schedule as "the President").

(3) The Secretary of State may not appoint a person to be the President unless that person –
(a) has a ten year general qualification within the meaning of section 71 of the Courts and Legal Services Act 1990,
(b) is an advocate or solicitor in Scotland of at least ten years' standing, or
(c) is –
(i) a member of the Bar of Northern Ireland of at least ten years' standing, or
(ii) a solicitor of the Supreme Court of Northern Ireland of at least ten years' standing,
and appears to the Secretary of State to have appropriate experience and knowledge of competition law and practice.

(4) Before appointing the President, the Secretary of State must consult the Lord Chancellor or Lord Advocate, as he considers appropriate.

(5) If the President ceases to be a member he also ceases to be President.

The Council

5. – (1) The Commission is to have a management board to be known as the Competition Commission Council (but referred to in this Schedule as "the Council").

(2) The Council is to consist of –
(a) the Chairman;
(b) the President;
(c) such other members as the Secretary of State may appoint; and
(d) the secretary.

(3) In exercising its functions under paragraphs 3 and 7 to 12 and

paragraph 5 of Schedule 8, the Commission is to act through the Council.

(4) The Council may determine its own procedure including, in particular, its quorum.

(5) The Chairman (and any person acting as Chairman) is to have a casting vote on any question being decided by the Council.

Term of office

6. – (1) Subject to the provisions of this Schedule, each member is to hold and vacate office in accordance with the terms of his appointment.

(2) A person is not to be appointed as a member for more than five years at a time.

(3) Any member may at any time resign by notice in writing addressed to the Secretary of State.

(4) The Secretary of State may remove a member on the ground of incapacity or misbehaviour.

(5) No person is to be prevented from being appointed as a member merely because he has previously been a member.

Expenses, remuneration and pensions

7. – (1) The Secretary of State shall pay to the Commission such sums as he considers appropriate to enable it to perform its functions.

(2) The Commission may pay, or make provision for paying, to or in respect of each member such salaries or other remuneration and such pensions, allowances, fees, expenses or gratuities as the Secretary of State may determine.

(3) If a person ceases to be a member otherwise than on the expiry of his term of office and it appears to the Secretary of State that there are special circumstances which make it right for him to receive compensation, the Commission may make a payment to him of such amount as the Secretary of State may determine.

(4) The approval of the Treasury is required for –
    (a) any payment under sub-paragraph (1);
    (b) any determination of the Secretary of State under sub-paragraph (2) or (3).

The Commission's powers

8.   Subject to the provisions of this Schedule, the Commission has power to do anything (except borrow money) –

    (a) calculated to facilitate the discharge of its functions; or

    (b) incidental or conducive to the discharge of its functions.

Staff

9. – (1) The Commission is to have a secretary, appointed by the Secretary of State on such terms and conditions of service as he considers appropriate.

(2)   The approval of the Treasury is required as to those terms and conditions.

(3)   Before appointing a person to be secretary, the Secretary of State must consult the Chairman and the President.

(4)   Subject to obtaining the approval of –

    (a) the Secretary of State, as to numbers, and

    (b) the Secretary of State and Treasury, as to terms and conditions of service,

the Commission may appoint such staff as it thinks appropriate.

Procedure

10. Subject to any provision made by or under this Act, the Commission may regulate its own procedure.

Application of seal and proof of instruments

11. – (1) The application of the seal of the Commission must be authenticated by the signature of the secretary or of some other person authorised for the purpose.

(2)   Sub-paragraph (1) does not apply in relation to any document which is or is to be signed in accordance with the law of Scotland.

(3)   A document purporting to be duly executed under the seal of the Commission –

    (a) is to be received in evidence; and

    (b) is to be taken to have been so executed unless the contrary is proved.

Accounts

12. – (1) The Commission must –

    (a) keep proper accounts and proper records in relation to its accounts;

(b) prepare a statement of accounts in respect of each of its financial years; and

(c) send copies of the statement to the Secretary of State and to the Comptroller and Auditor General before the end of the month of August next following the financial year to which the statement relates.

(2) The statement of accounts must comply with any directions given by the Secretary of State with the approval of the Treasury as to –

(a) the information to be contained in it,

(b) the manner in which the information contained in it is to be presented, or

(c) the methods and principles according to which the statement is to be prepared,

and must contain such additional information as the Secretary of State may with the approval of the Treasury require to be provided for informing Parliament.

(3) The Comptroller and Auditor General must –

(a) examine, certify and report on each statement received by him as a result of this paragraph; and

(b) lay copies of each statement and of his report before each House of Parliament.

(4) In this paragraph "financial year" means the period beginning with the date on which the Commission is established and ending with March 31st next, and each successive period of twelve months.

Status

13. – (1) The Commission is not to be regarded as the servant or agent of the Crown or as enjoying any status, privilege or immunity of the Crown.

(2) The Commission's property is not to be regarded as property of, or held on behalf of, the Crown.

PART II
PERFORMANCE OF THE COMMISSION'S GENERAL FUNCTIONS

Interpretation

14. In this Part of this Schedule "group" means a group selected under paragraph 15.

Discharge of certain functions by groups

15. – (1) Except where sub-paragraph (7) gives the Chairman power

to act on his own, any general function of the Commission must be performed through a group selected for the purpose by the Chairman.

(2) The group must consist of at least three persons one of whom may be the Chairman.

(3) In selecting the members of the group, the Chairman must comply with any requirement as to its constitution imposed by any enactment applying to specialist panel members.

(4) If the functions to be performed through the group relate to a newspaper merger reference, the group must, subject to sub-paragraph (5), consist of such reporting panel members as the Chairman may select.

(5) The Secretary of State may appoint one, two or three persons from the panel maintained under paragraph 22 to be members and, if he does so, the group –
> (a) must include that member or those members; and
> (b) if there are three such members, may (if the Chairman so decides) consist entirely of those members.

(6) Subject to sub-paragraphs (2) to (5), a group must consist of reporting panel members or specialist panel members selected by the Chairman.

(7) While a group is being constituted to perform a particular general function of the Commission, the Chairman may –
> (a) take such steps (falling within that general function) as he considers appropriate to facilitate the work of the group when it has been constituted; or
> (b) exercise the power conferred by section 75(5) of the 1973 Act (setting aside references).

Chairmen of groups

16. The Chairman must appoint one of the members of a group to act as the chairman of the group.

Replacement of member of group

17. – (1) If, during the proceedings of a group –
> (a) a member of the group ceases to be a member of the Commission,
> (b) the Chairman is satisfied that a member of the group will be unable for a substantial period to perform his duties as a member of the group, or

(c) it appears to the Chairman that because of a particular interest of a member of the group it is inappropriate for him to remain in the group,

the Chairman may appoint a replacement.

(2) The Chairman may also at any time appoint any reporting panel member to be an additional member of a group.

Attendance of other members

18. – (1) At the invitation of the chairman of a group, any reporting panel member who is not a member of the group may attend meetings or otherwise take part in the proceedings of the group.

(2) But any person attending in response to such an invitation may not –

(a) vote in any proceedings of the group; or
(b) have a statement of his dissent from a conclusion of the group included in a report made by them.

(3) Nothing in sub-paragraph (1) is to be taken to prevent a group, or a member of a group, from consulting any member of the Commission with respect to any matter or question with which the group is concerned.

Procedure

19. – (1) Subject to any special or general directions given by the Secretary of State, each group may determine its own procedure.

(2) Each group may, in particular, determine its quorum and determine –

(a) the extent, if any, to which persons interested or claiming to be interested in the subject-matter of the reference are allowed –

(i) to be present or to be heard, either by themselves or by their representatives;
(ii) to cross-examine witnesses; or
(iii) otherwise to take part; and

(b) the extent, if any, to which sittings of the group are to be held in public.

(3) In determining its procedure a group must have regard to any guidance issued by the Chairman.

(4) Before issuing any guidance for the purposes of this paragraph the Chairman must consult the members of the Commission.

Effect of exercise of functions by group

20. – (1) Subject to sub-paragraph (2), anything done by or in relation

to a group in, or in connection with, the performance of functions to be performed by the group is to have the same effect as if done by or in relation to the Commission.

(2) For the purposes of –
   (a) sections 56 and 73 of the 1973 Act,
   (b) section 19A of the Agricultural Marketing Act 1958,
   (c) Articles 23 and 42 of the Agricultural Marketing (Northern Ireland) Order 1982,
a conclusion contained in a report of a group is to be disregarded if the conclusion is not that of at least two-thirds of the members of the group.

Casting votes

21. The chairman of a group is to have a casting vote on any question to be decided by the group.

Newspaper merger references

22. The Secretary of State must maintain a panel of persons whom he regards as suitable for selection as members of a group constituted in connection with a newspaper merger reference.

PART III
APPEALS

Interpretation

23. In this Part of this Schedule –
   "panel of chairmen" means the panel appointed under paragraph 26; and
   "tribunal" means an appeal tribunal constituted in accordance with paragraph 27.

Training of appeal panel members

24. The President must arrange such training for appeal panel members as he considers appropriate.

Acting President

25. If the President is absent or otherwise unable to act, the Secretary of State may appoint as acting president an appeal panel member who is qualified to act as chairman of a tribunal.

Panel of tribunal chairmen

26. – (1) There is to be a panel of appeal panel members appointed by the Secretary of State for the purposes of providing chairmen of appeal tribunals established under this Part of this Schedule.

(2) A person is qualified for appointment to the panel of chairmen only if –

(a) he has a seven year general qualification within the meaning of section 71 of the Courts and Legal Services Act 1990,

(b) he is an advocate or solicitor in Scotland of at least seven years' standing, or

(c) he is –

(i) a member of the Bar of Northern Ireland of at least seven years' standing, or

(ii) a solicitor of the Supreme Court of Northern Ireland of at least seven years' standing,

and appears to the Secretary of State to have appropriate experience and knowledge of competition law and practice.

Constitution of tribunals

27. – (1) On receipt of a notice of appeal, the President must constitute an appeal tribunal to deal with the appeal.

(2) An appeal tribunal is to consist of –

(a) a chairman, who must be either the President or a person appointed by him to be chairman from the panel of chairmen; and

(b) two other appeal panel members appointed by the President.

PART IV
MISCELLANEOUS

Disqualification of members for House of Commons

28. In Part II of Schedule 1 to the House of Commons Disqualification Act 1975 (bodies of which all members are disqualified) insert at the appropriate place – "The Competition Commission".

Disqualification of members for Northern Ireland Assembly

29. In Part II of Schedule 1 to the Northern Ireland Assembly Disqualification Act 1975 (bodies of which all members are disqualified) insert at the appropriate place – "The Competition Commission".

PART V
TRANSITIONAL PROVISIONS

Interpretation

30. In this Part of this Schedule –

"commencement date" means the date on which section 45 comes into force; and

"MMC" means the Monopolies and Mergers Commission.

Chairman

31. – (1) The person who is Chairman of the MMC immediately before the commencement date is on that date to become both a member of the Commission and its chairman as if he had been duly appointed under paragraphs 2(1)(b) and 3.

(2) He is to hold office as Chairman of the Commission for the remainder of the period for which he was appointed as Chairman of the MMC and on the terms on which he was so appointed.

Deputy chairmen

32. The persons who are deputy chairmen of the MMC immediately before the commencement date are on that date to become deputy chairmen of the Commission as if they had been duly appointed under paragraph 3(2).

Reporting panel members

33. – (1) The persons who are members of the MMC immediately before the commencement date are on that date to become members of the Commission as if they had been duly appointed under paragraph 2(1)(b).

(2) Each of them is to hold office as a member for the remainder of the period for which he was appointed as a member of the MMC and on the terms on which he was so appointed.

Specialist panel members

34. – (1) The persons who are members of the MMC immediately before the commencement date by virtue of appointments made under any of the enactments mentioned in paragraph 2(1)(d) are on that date to become members of the Commission as if they had been duly appointed to the Commission under the enactment in question.

(2) Each of them is to hold office as a member for such period and on such terms as the Secretary of State may determine.

Secretary

35. The person who is the secretary of the MMC immediately before the commencement date is on that date to become the secretary of the Commission as if duly appointed under paragraph 9, on the same terms and conditions.

Council

36. – (1) The members who become deputy chairmen of the Commission under paragraph 32 are also to become members of the

Council as if they had been duly appointed under paragraph 5(2)(c).

(2) Each of them is to hold office as a member of the Council for such period as the Secretary of State determines.

Schedule 8
Appeals
PART I
GENERAL

Interpretation

1. In this Schedule –

"the chairman" means a person appointed as chairman of a tribunal in accordance with paragraph 27(2)(a) of Schedule 7;
"the President" means the President of the Competition Commission Appeal Tribunals appointed under paragraph 4 of Schedule 7;
"rules" means rules made by the Secretary of State under section 48;
"specified" means specified in rules;
"tribunal" means an appeal tribunal constituted in accordance with paragraph 27 of Schedule 7.

General procedure

2. – (1) An appeal to the Competition Commission must be made by sending a notice of appeal to the Commission within the specified period.

(2) The notice of appeal must set out the grounds of appeal in sufficient detail to indicate –
(a) under which provision of this Act the appeal is brought;
(b) to what extent (if any) the appellant contends that the decision against, or with respect to which, the appeal is brought was based on an error of fact or was wrong in law; and
(c) to what extent (if any) the appellant is appealing against the Director's exercise of his discretion in making the disputed decision.

(3) The tribunal may give an appellant leave to amend the grounds of appeal identified in the notice of appeal.

Decisions of the tribunal

3. – (1) The tribunal must determine the appeal on the merits by reference to the grounds of appeal set out in the notice of appeal.

(2) The tribunal may confirm or set aside the decision which is the subject of the appeal, or any part of it, and may –
>   (a) remit the matter to the Director,
>   (b) impose or revoke, or vary the amount of, a penalty,
>   (c) grant or cancel an individual exemption or vary any conditions or obligations imposed in relation to the exemption by the Director,
>   (d) give such directions, or take such other steps, as the Director could himself have given or taken, or
>   (e) make any other decision which the Director could himself have made.

(3) Any decision of the tribunal on an appeal has the same effect, and may be enforced in the same manner, as a decision of the Director.

(4) If the tribunal confirms the decision which is the subject of the appeal it may nevertheless set aside any finding of fact on which the decision was based.

4. – (1) A decision of the tribunal may be taken by a majority.

(2) The decision must –
>   (a) state whether it was unanimous or taken by a majority; and
>   (b) be recorded in a document which –
>   (i) contains a statement of the reasons for the decision; and
>   (ii) is signed and dated by the chairman of the tribunal.

(3) When the tribunal is preparing the document mentioned in sub-paragraph (2)(b), section 56 is to apply to the tribunal as it applies to the Director.

(4) The President must make such arrangements for the publication of the tribunal's decision as he considers appropriate.

PART II
RULES

Registrar of Appeal Tribunals
5. – (1) Rules may provide for the appointment by the Competition Commission, with the approval of the Secretary of State, of a Registrar of Appeal Tribunals.

(2) The rules may, in particular–
>   (a) specify the qualifications for appointment as Registrar; and

(b) provide for specified functions relating to appeals to be exercised by the Registrar in specified circumstances.

Notice of appeal

6.   Rules may make provision –
(a) as to the period within which appeals must be brought;
(b) as to the form of the notice of appeal and as to the information which must be given in the notice;
(c) with respect to amendment of a notice of appeal;
(d) with respect to acknowledgement of a notice of appeal.

Response to the appeal

7.   Rules may provide for the tribunal to reject an appeal if –
(a) it considers that the notice of appeal reveals no valid ground of appeal; or
(b) it is satisfied that the appellant has habitually and persistently and without any reasonable ground –
(i) instituted vexatious proceedings, whether against the same person or against different persons; or
(ii) made vexatious applications in any proceedings.

Pre-hearing reviews and preliminary matters

8. – (1) Rules may make provision –
(a) for the carrying-out by the tribunal of a preliminary consideration of proceedings (a "pre-hearing review"); and
(b) for enabling such powers to be exercised in connection with a pre-hearing review as may be specified.

(2)   If rules make provision of the kind mentioned in sub-paragraph (1), they may also include –
(a) provision for security; and
(b) supplemental provision.

(3)   In sub-paragraph (2) "provision for security" means provision authorising a tribunal carrying out a pre-hearing review under the rules, in specified circumstances, to make an order requiring a party to the proceedings, if he wishes to continue to participate in them, to pay a deposit of an amount not exceeding such sum –
(a) as may be specified; or
(b) as may be calculated in accordance with specified provisions.

(4)   In sub-paragraph (2) "supplemental provision" means any provision as to –
(a) the manner in which the amount of such a deposit is to be determined;

(b) the consequences of non-payment of such a deposit; and

(c) the circumstances in which any such deposit, or any part of it, may be –

    (i) refunded to the person who paid it; or

    (ii) paid to another party to the proceedings.

Conduct of the hearing

9.– (1) Rules may make provision –

(a) as to the manner in which appeals are to be conducted, including provision for any hearing to be held in private if the tribunal considers it appropriate because it may be considering information of a kind to which section 56 applies;

(b) as to the persons entitled to appear on behalf of the parties;

(c) for requiring persons to attend to give evidence and produce documents and for authorising the administration of oaths to witnesses;

(d) as to the evidence which may be required or admitted in proceedings before the tribunal and the extent to which it should be oral or written;

(e) allowing the tribunal to fix time limits with respect to any aspect of the proceedings before it and to extend any time limit (whether or not it has expired);

(f) for enabling the tribunal to refer a matter back to the Director if it appears to the tribunal that the matter has not been adequately investigated;

(g) for enabling the tribunal, on the application of any party to the proceedings before it or on its own initiative –

    (i) in England and Wales or Northern Ireland, to order the disclosure between, or the production by, the parties of documents or classes of documents;

    (ii) in Scotland, to order such recovery or inspection of documents as might be ordered by a sheriff;

(h) for the appointment of experts for the purposes of any proceedings before the tribunal;

    (i) for the award of costs or expenses, including any allowances payable to persons in connection with their attendance before the tribunal;

    (j) for taxing or otherwise settling any costs or expenses directed to be paid by the tribunal and for the enforcement of any such direction.

(2) A person who without reasonable excuse fails to comply with –

(a) any requirement imposed by virtue of sub-paragraph (1)(c), or

(b) any requirement with respect to the disclosure, production, recovery or inspection of documents which is imposed by virtue of sub-paragraph (1)(g),

is guilty of an offence and liable on summary conviction to a fine not exceeding level 3 on the standard scale.

Interest

10. – (1) Rules may make provision –

(a) as to the circumstances in which the tribunal may order that interest is payable;

(b) for the manner in which and the periods by reference to which interest is to be calculated and paid.

(2) The rules may, in particular, provide that compound interest is to be payable if the tribunal –

(a) upholds a decision of the Director to impose a penalty, or

(b) does not reduce a penalty so imposed by more than a specified percentage,

but in such a case the rules may not provide that interest is to be payable in respect of any period before the date on which the appeal was brought.

Fees

11. – (1) Rules may provide –

(a) for fees to be chargeable in respect of specified costs of proceedings before the tribunal;

(b) for the amount of such costs to be determined by the tribunal.

(2) Any sums received in consequence of rules under this paragraph are to be paid into the Consolidated Fund.

Withdrawing an appeal

12. Rules may make provision –

(a) that a party who has brought an appeal may not withdraw it without the leave of –

(i) the tribunal, or

(ii) in specified circumstances, the President or the Registrar;

(b) for the tribunal to grant leave to withdraw the appeal on such conditions as it considers appropriate;

(c) enabling the tribunal to publish any decision which it could have made had the appeal not been withdrawn;

(d) as to the effect of withdrawal of an appeal;

(e) as to any procedure to be followed if parties to proceedings on an appeal agree to settle.

Interim orders

13. – (1) Rules may provide for the tribunal to make an order ("an interim order") granting, on an interim basis, any remedy which the tribunal would have power to grant in its final decision.

(2)   An interim order may, in particular, suspend the effect of a decision made by the Director or vary the conditions or obligations attached to an exemption.

(3)   Rules may also make provision giving the tribunal powers similar to those given to the Director by section 35.

Miscellaneous

14.   Rules may make provision –
> (a) for a person who is not a party to proceedings on an appeal to be joined in those proceedings;
> (b) for appeals to be consolidated on such terms as the tribunal thinks appropriate in such circumstances as may be specified.

Schedule 9
Director's Rules
General

1.   In this Schedule –
> "application for guidance" means an application for guidance under section 13 or 21;
> "application for a decision" means an application for a decision under section 14 or 22;
> "guidance" means guidance given under section 13 or 21;
> "rules" means rules made by the Director under section 51; and
> "specified" means specified in rules.

Applications

2.   Rules may make provision –
> (a) as to the form and manner in which an application for guidance or an application for a decision must be made;
> (b) for the procedure to be followed in dealing with the application;
> (c) for the application to be dealt with in accordance with a timetable;
> (d) as to the documents and information which must be given to the Director in connection with the application;
> (e) requiring the applicant to give such notice of the application, to such other persons, as may be specified;
> (f)   as to the consequences of a failure to comply with any rule made by virtue of sub-paragraph (e);

(g) as to the procedure to be followed when the application is subject to the concurrent jurisdiction of the Director and a regulator.

Provisional decisions

3.   Rules may make provision as to the procedure to be followed by the Director when making a provisional decision under paragraph 3 of Schedule 5 or paragraph 3 of Schedule 6.

Guidance

4.   Rules may make provision as to –
(a) the form and manner in which guidance is to be given;
(b) the procedure to be followed if –
(i) the Director takes further action with respect to an agreement after giving guidance that it is not likely to infringe the Chapter I prohibition; or
(ii) the Director takes further action with respect to conduct after giving guidance that it is not likely to infringe the Chapter II prohibition.

Decisions

5. – (1) Rules may make provision as to –
(a) the form and manner in which notice of any decision is to be given;
(b) the person or persons to whom the notice is to be given;
(c) the manner in which the Director is to publish a decision;
(d) the procedure to be followed if –
(i) the Director takes further action with respect to an agreement after having decided that it does not infringe the Chapter I prohibition; or
(ii) the Director takes further action with respect to conduct after having decided that it does not infringe the Chapter II prohibition.

(2)   In this paragraph "decision" means a decision of the Director (whether or not made on an application) –
(a) as to whether or not an agreement has infringed the Chapter I prohibition, or
(b) as to whether or not conduct has infringed the Chapter II prohibition,
and, in the case of an application for a decision under section 14 which includes a request for an individual exemption, includes a decision as to whether or not to grant the exemption.

Individual exemptions

6.   Rules may make provision as to –

(a) the procedure to be followed by the Director when deciding whether, in accordance with section 5 –
    (i) to cancel an individual exemption that he has granted,
    (ii) to vary or remove any of its conditions or obligations, or
    (iii) to impose additional conditions or obligations;
(b) the form and manner in which notice of such a decision is to be given.

7.   Rules may make provision as to –
(a) the form and manner in which an application under section 4(6) for the extension of an individual exemption is to be made;
(b) the circumstances in which the Director will consider such an application;
(c) the procedure to be followed by the Director when deciding whether to grant such an application;
(d) the form and manner in which notice of such a decision is to be given.

Block exemptions
8.   Rules may make provision as to –
(a) the form and manner in which notice of an agreement is to be given to the Director under subsection (1) of section 7;
(b) the procedure to be followed by the Director if he is acting under subsection (2) of that section;
(c) as to the procedure to be followed by the Director if he cancels a block exemption.

Parallel exemptions
9.   Rules may make provision as to –
(a) the circumstances in which the Director may –
    (i) impose conditions or obligations in relation to a parallel exemption,
    (ii) vary or remove any such conditions or obligations,
    (iii) impose additional conditions or obligations, or
    (iv) cancel the exemption;
(b) as to the procedure to be followed by the Director if he is acting under section 10(5);
(c) the form and manner in which notice of a decision to take any of the steps in sub-paragraph (a) is to be given;
(d) the circumstances in which an exemption may be cancelled with retrospective effect.

Section 11 exemptions
10. Rules may, with respect to any exemption provided by regulations

made under section 11, make provision similar to that made with respect to parallel exemptions by section 10 or by rules under paragraph 9.

Directions withdrawing exclusions

11. Rules may make provision as to the factors which the Director may take into account when he is determining the date on which a direction given under paragraph 4(1) of Schedule 1 or paragraph 2(3) or 9(3) of Schedule 3 is to have effect.

Disclosure of information

12. – (1) Rules may make provision as to the circumstances in which the Director is to be required, before disclosing information given to him by a third party in connection with the exercise of any of the Director's functions under Part I, to give notice, and an opportunity to make representations, to the third party.

(2) In relation to the agreement (or conduct) concerned, "third party" means a person who is not a party to the agreement (or who has not engaged in the conduct).

Applications under section 47

13. Rules may make provision as to –
   (a) the period within which an application under section 47(1) must be made;
   (b) the procedure to be followed by the Director in dealing with the application;
   (c) the person or persons to whom notice of the Director's response to the application is to be given.

Enforcement

14. Rules may make provision as to the procedure to be followed when the Director takes action under any of sections 32 to 41 with respect to the enforcement of the provisions of this Part.

Schedule 10
Regulators
PART I
MONOPOLIES

1. The amendments of the Fair Trading Act 1973 made by sections 66 and 67 of this Act are to have effect, not only in relation to the jurisdiction of the Director under the provisions amended, but also in relation to the jurisdiction under those provisions of each of the following –
   (a) the Director General of Telecommunications;
   (b) the Director General of Electricity Supply;

(c) the Director General of Electricity Supply for Northern Ireland;

(d) the Director General of Water Services;

(e) the Rail Regulator;

(f) the Director General of Gas Supply; and

(g) the Director General of Gas for Northern Ireland.

PART II
THE PROHIBITIONS

Telecommunications

2. – (1) In consequence of the repeal by this Act of provisions of the Competition Act 1980, the functions transferred by subsection (3) of section 50 of the Telecommunications Act 1984 (functions under 1973 and 1980 Acts) are no longer exercisable by the Director General of Telecommunications.

(2) Accordingly, that Act is amended as follows.

(3) In section 3 (general duties of Secretary of State and Director), in subsection (3)(b), for "section 50" substitute "section 50(1) or (2)".

(4) In section 3, after subsection (3A), insert –

"(3B) Subsections (1) and (2) above do not apply in relation to anything done by the Director in the exercise of functions assigned to him by section 50(3) below ("Competition Act functions").
(3C) The Director may nevertheless, when exercising any Competition Act function, have regard to any matter in respect of which a duty is imposed by subsection (1) or (2) above ("a general matter"), if it is a matter to which the Director General of Fair Trading could have regard when exercising that function; but that is not to be taken as implying that, in relation to any of the matters mentioned in subsection (3) or (3A) above, regard may not be had to any general matter."

(5) Section 50 is amended as follows.

(6) For subsection (3) substitute –

"(3) The Director shall be entitled to exercise, concurrently with the Director General of Fair Trading, the functions of that Director under the provisions of Part I of the Competition Act 1998 (other than sections 38(1) to (6) and 51), so far as relating to –

(a) agreements, decisions or concerted practices of the kind mentioned in section 2(1) of that Act, or

    (b) conduct of the kind mentioned in section 18(1) of that
    Act,
which relate to commercial activities connected with
telecommunications.
(3A) So far as necessary for the purposes of, or in connection
with, the provisions of subsection (3) above, references in Part I
of the Competition Act 1998 to the Director General of Fair
Trading are to be read as including a reference to the Director
(except in sections 38(1) to (6), 51, 52(6) and (8) and 54 of that
Act and in any other provision of that Act where the context
otherwise requires)."

(7) In subsection (4), omit paragraph (c) and the "and" immediately
after it.

(8) In subsection (5), omit "or (3)".

(9) In subsection (6), for paragraph (b) substitute –
    "(b) Part I of the Competition Act 1998 (other than sections
    38(1) to (6) and 51),".

(10) In subsection (7), omit "or the 1980 Act".

Gas

3. – (1) In consequence of the repeal by this Act of provisions of the
Competition Act 1980, the functions transferred by subsection (3) of
section 36A of the Gas Act 1986 (functions with respect to competition)
are no longer exercisable by the Director General of Gas Supply.

(2) Accordingly, that Act is amended as follows.

(3) In section 4 (general duties of Secretary of State and Director),
after subsection (3), insert –
    "(3A) Subsections (1) to (3) above and section 4A below do not
    apply in relation to anything done by the Director in the exercise
    of functions assigned to him by section 36A below ("Competition
    Act functions").
    (3B) The Director may nevertheless, when exercising any
    Competition Act function, have regard to any matter in respect
    of which a duty is imposed by any of subsections (1) to (3)
    above or section 4A below, if it is a matter to which the Director
    General of Fair Trading could have regard when exercising that
    function."

(4) Section 36A is amended as follows.

(5) For subsection (3) substitute –
"(3) The Director shall be entitled to exercise, concurrently with the Director General of Fair Trading, the functions of that Director under the provisions of Part I of the Competition Act 1998 (other than sections 38(1) to (6) and 51), so far as relating to –
(a) agreements, decisions or concerted practices of the kind mentioned in section 2(1) of that Act, or
(b) conduct of the kind mentioned in section 18(1) of that Act,
which relate to the carrying on of activities to which this subsection applies.
(3A) So far as necessary for the purposes of, or in connection with, the provisions of subsection (3) above, references in Part I of the Competition Act 1998 to the Director General of Fair Trading are to be read as including a reference to the Director (except in sections 38(1) to (6), 51, 52(6) and (8) and 54 of that Act and in any other provision of that Act where the context otherwise requires)."

(6) In subsection (5) –
(a) for "transferred by", in each place, substitute "mentioned in";
(b) after paragraph (b), insert "and";
(c) omit paragraph (d) and the "and" immediately before it.

(7) In subsection (6), omit "or (3)".

(8) In subsection (7), for paragraph (b) substitute –
"(b) Part I of the Competition Act 1998 (other than sections 38(1) to (6) and 51),".

(9) In subsection (8) –
(a) omit "or under the 1980 Act";
(b) for "or (3) above" substitute "above and paragraph 1 of Schedule 10 to the Competition Act 1998".

(10) In subsection (9), omit "or the 1980 Act".

(11) In subsection (10), for the words from "transferred" to the end substitute "mentioned in subsection (2) or (3) above."

Electricity
4. – (1) In consequence of the repeal by this Act of provisions of the Competition Act 1980, the functions transferred by subsection (3) of

section 43 of the Electricity Act 1989 (functions with respect to competition) are no longer exercisable by the Director General of Electricity Supply.

(2) Accordingly, that Act is amended as follows.

(3) In section 3 (general duties of Secretary of State and Director), after subsection (6), insert –
> "(6A)Subsections (1) to (5) above do not apply in relation to anything done by the Director in the exercise of functions assigned to him by section 43(3) below ("Competition Act functions").
> (6B) The Director may nevertheless, when exercising any Competition Act function, have regard to any matter in respect of which a duty is imposed by any of subsections (1) to (5) above ("a general matter"), if it is a matter to which the Director General of Fair Trading could have regard when exercising that function; but that is not to be taken as implying that, in the exercise of any function mentioned in subsection (6) above, regard may not be had to any general matter."

(4) Section 43 is amended as follows.

(5) For subsection (3) substitute –
> "(3) The Director shall be entitled to exercise, concurrently with the Director General of Fair Trading, the functions of that Director under the provisions of Part I of the Competition Act 1998 (other than sections 38(1) to (6) and 51), so far as relating to –
> > (a) agreements, decisions or concerted practices of the kind mentioned in section 2(1) of that Act, or
> > (b) conduct of the kind mentioned in section 18(1) of that Act,
> which relate to commercial activities connected with the generation, transmission or supply of electricity.
> (3A) So far as necessary for the purposes of, or in connection with, the provisions of subsection (3) above, references in Part I of the Competition Act 1998 to the Director General of Fair Trading are to be read as including a reference to the Director (except in sections 38(1) to (6), 51, 52(6) and (8) and 54 of that Act and in any other provision of that Act where the context otherwise requires)."

(6) In subsection (4), omit paragraph (c) and the "and" immediately after it.

(7) In subsection (5), omit "or (3)".

(8) In subsection (6), for paragraph (b) substitute –
"(b) Part I of the Competition Act 1998 (other than sections 38(1) to (6) and 51),".

(9) In subsection (7), omit "or the 1980 Act".

Water

5. – (1) In consequence of the repeal by this Act of provisions of the Competition Act 1980, the functions exercisable by virtue of subsection (3) of section 31 of the Water Industry Act 1991 (functions of Director with respect to competition) are no longer exercisable by the Director General of Water Services.

(2) Accordingly, that Act is amended as follows.

(3) In section 2 (general duties with respect to water industry), in subsection (6)(a), at the beginning, insert "subject to subsection (6A) below".

(4) In section 2, after subsection (6), insert –
"(6A) Subsections (2) to (4) above do not apply in relation to anything done by the Director in the exercise of functions assigned to him by section 31(3) below ("Competition Act functions").
(6B) The Director may nevertheless, when exercising any Competition Act function, have regard to any matter in respect of which a duty is imposed by any of subsections (2) to (4) above, if it is a matter to which the Director General of Fair Trading could have regard when exercising that function."

(5) Section 31 is amended as follows.

(6) For subsection (3) substitute –
"(3) The Director shall be entitled to exercise, concurrently with the Director General of Fair Trading, the functions of that Director under the provisions of Part I of the Competition Act 1998 (other than sections 38(1) to (6) and 51), so far as relating to –
(a) agreements, decisions or concerted practices of the kind mentioned in section 2(1) of that Act, or
(b) conduct of the kind mentioned in section 18(1) of that Act,
which relate to commercial activities connected with the supply of water or securing a supply of water or with the provision or securing of sewerage services."

(7) In subsection (4) –
    (a) for "to (3)" substitute "and (2)";
    (b) omit paragraph (c) and the "and" immediately before it.

(8) After subsection (4), insert –
    "(4A) So far as necessary for the purposes of, or in connection with, the provisions of subsection (3) above, references in Part I of the Competition Act 1998 to the Director General of Fair Trading are to be read as including a reference to the Director (except in sections 38(1) to (6), 51, 52(6) and (8) and 54 of that Act and in any other provision of that Act where the context otherwise requires)."

(9) In subsection (5), omit "or in subsection (3) above".

(10) In subsection (6), omit "or in subsection (3) above".

(11) In subsection (7), omit "or (3)".

(12) In subsection (8), for paragraph (b) substitute –
    "(b) Part I of the Competition Act 1998 (other than sections 38(1) to (6) and 51),".

(13) In subsection (9), omit "or the 1980 Act".

Railways
6. – (1) In consequence of the repeal by this Act of provisions of the Competition Act 1980, the functions transferred by subsection (3) of section 67 of the Railways Act 1993 (respective functions of the Regulator and the Director etc) are no longer exercisable by the Rail Regulator.

(2) Accordingly, that Act is amended as follows.

(3) In section 4 (general duties of the Secretary of State and the Regulator), after subsection (7), insert –
    "(7A) Subsections (1) to (6) above do not apply in relation to anything done by the Regulator in the exercise of functions assigned to him by section 67(3) below ("Competition Act functions").
    (7B) The Regulator may nevertheless, when exercising any Competition Act function, have regard to any matter in respect of which a duty is imposed by any of subsections (1) to (6) above, if it is a matter to which the Director General of Fair Trading could have regard when exercising that function."

(4)   Section 67 is amended as follows.

(5)   For subsection (3) substitute –
   "(3)   The Regulator shall be entitled to exercise, concurrently with the Director, the functions of the Director under the provisions of Part I of the Competition Act 1998 (other than sections 38(1) to (6) and 51), so far as relating to –
      (a) agreements, decisions or concerted practices of the kind mentioned in section 2(1) of that Act, or
      (b) conduct of the kind mentioned in section 18(1) of that Act,
   which relate to the supply of railway services.
   (3A)   So far as necessary for the purposes of, or in connection with, the provisions of subsection (3) above, references in Part I of the Competition Act 1998 to the Director are to be read as including a reference to the Regulator (except in sections 38(1) to (6), 51, 52(6) and (8) and 54 of that Act and in any other provision of that Act where the context otherwise requires)."

(6)   In subsection (4), omit paragraph (c) and the "and" immediately after it.

(7)   In subsection (6)(a), omit "or (3)".

(8)   In subsection (8), for paragraph (b) substitute –
   "(b)   Part I of the Competition Act 1998 (other than sections 38(1) to (6) and 51),".

(9)   In subsection (9) –
      (a) omit "or under the 1980 Act";
      (b) for "or (3) above" substitute "above and paragraph 1 of Schedule 10 to the Competition Act 1998".

PART III
THE PROHIBITIONS: NORTHERN IRELAND

Electricity

7. – (1) In consequence of the repeal by this Act of provisions of the Competition Act 1980, the functions transferred by paragraph (3) of Article 46 of the Electricity (Northern Ireland) Order 1992 (functions with respect to competition) are no longer exercisable by the Director General of Electricity Supply for Northern Ireland.

(2)   Accordingly, that Order is amended as follows.

(3) In Article 6 (general duties of the Director), after paragraph (2), add –

> "(3) Paragraph (1) does not apply in relation to anything done by the Director in the exercise of functions assigned to him by Article 46(3) ("Competition Act functions").
>
> (4) The Director may nevertheless, when exercising any Competition Act function, have regard to any matter in respect of which a duty is imposed by paragraph (1) ("a general matter"), if it is a matter to which the Director General of Fair Trading could have regard when exercising that function; but that is not to be taken as implying that, in the exercise of any function mentioned in Article 4(7) or paragraph (2), regard may not be had to any general matter."

(4) Article 46 is amended as follows.

(5) For paragraph (3) substitute –

> "(3) The Director shall be entitled to exercise, concurrently with the Director General of Fair Trading, the functions of that Director under the provisions of Part I of the Competition Act 1998 (other than sections 38(1) to (6) and 51), so far as relating to –
>
>> (a) agreements, decisions or concerted practices of the kind mentioned in section 2(1) of that Act, or
>> (b) conduct of the kind mentioned in section 18(1) of that Act,
>
> which relate to commercial activities connected with the generation, transmission or supply of electricity.
>
> (3A) So far as necessary for the purposes of, or in connection with, the provisions of paragraph (3), references in Part I of the Competition Act 1998 to the Director General of Fair Trading are to be read as including a reference to the Director (except in sections 38(1) to (6), 51, 52(6) and (8) and 54 of that Act and in any other provision of that Act where the context otherwise requires)."

(6) In paragraph (4), omit sub-paragraph (c) and the "and" immediately after it.

(7) In paragraph (5), omit "or (3)".

(8) In paragraph (6), for sub-paragraph (b) substitute –

> "(b) Part I of the Competition Act 1998 (other than sections 38(1) to (6) and 51),".

(9) In paragraph (7), omit "or the 1980 Act".

Gas

8. – (1) In consequence of the repeal by this Act of provisions of the Competition Act 1980, the functions transferred by paragraph (3) of Article 23 of the Gas (Northern Ireland) Order 1996 (functions with respect to competition) are no longer exercisable by the Director General of Gas for Northern Ireland.

(2) Accordingly, that Order is amended as follows.

(3) In Article 5 (general duties of the Department and Director), after paragraph (4), insert –
> "(4A) Paragraphs (2) to (4) do not apply in relation to anything done by the Director in the exercise of functions assigned to him by Article 23(3) ("Competition Act functions").
> (4B) The Director may nevertheless, when exercising any Competition Act function, have regard to any matter in respect of which a duty is imposed by any of paragraphs (2) to (4), if it is a matter to which the Director General of Fair Trading could have regard when exercising that function."

(4) Article 23 is amended as follows.

(5) For paragraph (3) substitute –
> "(3) The Director shall be entitled to exercise, concurrently with the Director General of Fair Trading, the functions of that Director under the provisions of Part I of the Competition Act 1998 (other than sections 38(1) to (6) and 51), so far as relating to –
> > (a) agreements, decisions or concerted practices of the kind mentioned in section 2(1) of that Act, or
> > (b) conduct of the kind mentioned in section 18(1) of that Act,
> connected with the conveyance, storage or supply of gas.
> (3A) So far as necessary for the purposes of, or in connection with, the provisions of paragraph (3), references in Part I of the Competition Act 1998 to the Director General of Fair Trading are to be read as including a reference to the Director (except in sections 38(1) to (6), 51, 52(6) and (8) and 54 of that Act and in any other provision of that Act where the context otherwise requires)."

(6) In paragraph (4) –
> (a) for "transferred by", in each place, substitute "mentioned in";
> (b) after sub-paragraph (b), insert "and";
> (c) omit sub-paragraph (d) and the "and" immediately before it.

(7) In paragraph (5), omit "or (3)".

(8) In paragraph (6), for sub-paragraph (b) substitute –
"(b) Part I of the Competition Act 1998 (other than sections 38(1) to (6) and 51),".

(9) In paragraph (7) –
(a) omit "or under the 1980 Act";
(b) for "or (3)" substitute "and paragraph 1 of Schedule 10 to the Competition Act 1998".

(10) In paragraph (8), omit "or the 1980 Act".

(11) In paragraph (9), for the words from "transferred" to the end substitute "mentioned in paragraph (2) or (3)."

PART IV
UTILITIES: MINOR AND CONSEQUENTIAL AMENDMENTS

The Telecommunications Act 1984 (c 12)

9. – (1) The Telecommunications Act 1984 is amended as follows.

(2) In section 13 (licence modification references to Competition Commission), for subsections (9) and (10) substitute –
"(9) The provisions mentioned in subsection (9A) are to apply in relation to references under this section as if –
(a) the functions of the Competition Commission in relation to those references were functions under the Fair Trading Act 1973 (in this Act referred to as "the 1973 Act");
(b) the expression "merger reference" included a reference under this section;
(c) in section 70 of the 1973 Act –
(i) references to the Secretary of State were references to the Director, and
(ii) the reference to three months were a reference to six months.
(9A) The provisions are –
(a) sections 70 (time limit for report on merger) and 85 (attendance of witnesses and production of documents) of the 1973 Act;
(b) Part II of Schedule 7 to the Competition Act 1998 (performance of the Competition Commission's general functions); and
(c) section 24 of the Competition Act 1980 (modification of provisions about performance of such functions).

(10) For the purposes of references under this section, the Secretary of State is to appoint not less than three members of the Competition Commission.

(10A) In selecting a group to perform the Commission's functions in relation to any such reference, the chairman of the Commission must select up to three of the members appointed under subsection (10) to be members of the group."

(3) In section 14, omit subsection (2) (which falls with the repeal of the Restrictive Trade Practices Act 1976).

(4) In section 16 (securing compliance with licence conditions), in subsection (5), after paragraph (a), omit "or" and after paragraph (b), insert "or

(c) that the most appropriate way of proceeding is under the Competition Act 1998."

(5) In section 50 (functions under 1973 and 1980 Acts), after subsection (6), insert –

"(6A) Section 93B of the 1973 Act (offences of supplying false or misleading information) is to have effect so far as relating to functions exercisable by the Director by virtue of –

(a) subsection (2) above and paragraph 1 of Schedule 10 to the Competition Act 1998, or

(b) paragraph 1 of Schedule 2 to the Deregulation and Contracting Out Act 1994,

as if the reference in section 93B(1)(a) to the Director General of Fair Trading included a reference to the Director."

(6) In section 95 (modification by orders under other enactments) –

(a) in subsection (1), omit "or section 10(2)(a) of the 1980 Act";

(b) in subsection (2) –

(i) after paragraph (a), insert "or";

(ii) omit paragraph (c) and the "or" immediately before it;

(c) in subsection (3), omit "or the 1980 Act".

(7) In section 101(3) (general restrictions on disclosure of information) –

(a) omit paragraphs (d) and (e) (which refer to the Restrictive Trade Practices Act 1976 and the Resale Prices Act 1976);

(b) after paragraph (m), insert –

"(n) the Competition Act 1998".

(8) At the end of section 101, insert –

"(6) Information obtained by the Director in the exercise of functions which are exercisable concurrently with the Director

275

General of Fair Trading under Part I of the Competition Act 1998 is subject to sections 55 and 56 of that Act (disclosure) and not to subsections (1) to (5) of this section."

The Gas Act 1986 (c. 44)

10. – (1) The Gas Act 1986 is amended as follows.

(2) In section 24 (modification references to the Competition Commission), for subsection (7) substitute –

"(7)   The provisions mentioned in subsection (7A) are to apply in relation to references under this section as if –

(a) the functions of the Competition Commission in relation to those references were functions under the Fair Trading Act 1973;

(b) the expression "merger reference" included a reference under this section;

(c) in section 70 of the Fair Trading Act 1973 –

(i) references to the Secretary of State were references to the Director, and

(ii) the reference to three months were a reference to six months.

(7A) The provisions are –

(a) sections 70 (time limit for report on merger) and 85 (attendance of witnesses and production of documents) of the Fair Trading Act 1973;

(b) Part II of Schedule 7 to the Competition Act 1998 (performance of the Competition Commission's general functions); and

(c) section 24 of the Competition Act 1980 (modification of provisions about performance of such functions)."

(3) In section 25, omit subsection (2) (which falls with the repeal of the Restrictive Trade Practices Act 1976).

(4) In section 27 (modification by order under other enactments) –

(a) in subsection (1), omit "or section 10(2)(a) of the Competition Act 1980";

(b) in subsection (3)(a), omit from "or" to "competition reference";

(c) in subsection (6), omit "or the said Act of 1980".

(5) In section 28 (orders for securing compliance with certain provisions), in subsection (5), after paragraph (aa), omit "or" and after paragraph (b), insert "or

(c) that the most appropriate way of proceeding is under the Competition Act 1998."

(6) In section 42(3) (general restrictions on disclosure of information) –
    (a) omit paragraphs (e) and (f) (which refer to the Restrictive Trade Practices Act 1976 and the Resale Prices Act 1976);
    (b) after paragraph (n), insert –
    "(o) the Competition Act 1998".

(7) At the end of section 42, insert –
    "(7) Information obtained by the Director in the exercise of functions which are exercisable concurrently with the Director General of Fair Trading under Part I of the Competition Act 1998 is subject to sections 55 and 56 of that Act (disclosure) and not to subsections (1) to (6) of this section."

The Water Act 1989 (c 15)

11. In section 174(3) of the Water Act 1989 (general restrictions on disclosure of information) –
    (a) omit paragraphs (d) and (e) (which refer to the Restrictive Trade Practices Act 1976 and the Resale Prices Act 1976);
    (b) after paragraph (l), insert –
    "(ll)   the Competition Act 1998".

The Electricity Act 1989 (c 29)

12. – (1) The Electricity Act 1989 is amended as follows.

(2) In section 12 (modification references to Competition Commission), for subsections (8) and (9) substitute –
    "(8) The provisions mentioned in subsection (8A) are to apply in relation to references under this section as if –
        (a) the functions of the Competition Commission in relation to those references were functions under the 1973 Act;
        (b) the expression "merger reference" included a reference under this section;
        (c) in section 70 of the 1973 Act –
            (i) references to the Secretary of State were references to the Director, and
            (ii) the reference to three months were a reference to six months.
    (8A) The provisions are –
        (a) sections 70 (time limit for report on merger) and 85 (attendance of witnesses and production of documents) of the 1973 Act;
        (b) Part II of Schedule 7 to the Competition Act 1998 (performance of the Competition Commission's general functions); and
        (c) section 24 of the 1980 Act (modification of provisions

about performance of such functions).

(9) For the purposes of references under this section, the Secretary of State is to appoint not less than eight members of the Competition Commission.

(9A) In selecting a group to perform the Commission's functions in relation to any such reference, the chairman of the Commission must select up to three of the members appointed under subsection (9) to be members of the group."

(3) In section 13, omit subsection (2) (which falls with the repeal of the Restrictive Trade Practices Act 1976).

(4) In section 15 (modification by order under other enactments) –
    (a) in subsection (1), omit paragraph (b) and the "or" immediately before it;
    (b) in subsection (2) –
        (i) after paragraph (a), insert "or";
        (ii) omit paragraph (c) and the "or" immediately before it;
    (c) in subsection (3), omit "or the 1980 Act".

(5) In section 25 (orders for securing compliance), in subsection (5), after paragraph (b), omit "or" and after paragraph (c), insert "or
    (d) that the most appropriate way of proceeding is under the Competition Act 1998."

(6) In section 43 (functions with respect to competition), after subsection (6), insert –
    "(6A) Section 93B of the 1973 Act (offences of supplying false or misleading information) is to have effect so far as relating to functions exercisable by the Director by virtue of –
        (a) subsection (2) above and paragraph 1 of Schedule 10 to the Competition Act 1998, or
        (b) paragraph 4 of Schedule 2 to the Deregulation and Contracting Out Act 1994,
    as if the reference in section 93B(1)(a) to the Director General of Fair Trading included a reference to the Director."

(7) In section 57(3) (general restrictions on disclosure of information) –
    (a) omit paragraphs (d) and (e) (which refer to the Restrictive Trade Practices Act 1976 and the Resale Prices Act 1976);
    (b) after paragraph (no), insert –
    "(nop) the Competition Act 1998".

(8) At the end of section 57, insert –
    "(7) Information obtained by the Director in the exercise of

functions which are exercisable concurrently with the Director General of Fair Trading under Part I of the Competition Act 1998 is subject to sections 55 and 56 of that Act (disclosure) and not to subsections (1) to (6) of this section."

The Water Industry Act 1991 (c 56)

13. – (1) The Water Industry Act 1991 is amended as follows.

(2)   In section 12(5) (determinations under conditions of appointment) –
   (a) after "this Act", insert "or";
   (b) omit "or the 1980 Act".

(3) In section 14 (modification references to Competition Commission), for subsections (7) and (8) substitute –
   "(7)   The provisions mentioned in subsection (7A) are to apply in relation to references under this section as if –
      (a) the functions of the Competition Commission in relation to those references were functions under the 1973 Act;
      (b) the expression "merger reference" included a reference under this section;
      (c) in section 70 of the 1973 Act –
         (i) references to the Secretary of State were references to the Director, and
         (ii) the reference to three months were a reference to six months.
   (7A) The provisions are –
      (a) sections 70 (time limit for report on merger) and 85 (attendance of witnesses and production of documents) of the 1973 Act;
      (b) Part II of Schedule 7 to the Competition Act 1998 performance of the Competition Commission's general functions); and
      (c) section 24 of the 1980 Act (modification of provisions about performance of such functions).
   (8) For the purposes of references under this section, the Secretary of State is to appoint not less than eight members of the Competition Commission.
   (8A) In selecting a group to perform the Commission's functions in relation to any such reference, the chairman of the Commission must select one or more of the members appointed under subsection (8) to be members of the group."

(4)   In section 15, omit subsection (2) (which falls with the repeal of the Restrictive Trade Practices Act 1976).

(5) In section 17 (modification by order under other enactments) –
   (a) in subsection (1), omit paragraph (b) and the "or" immediately before it;
   (b) in subsection (2) –
      (i) after paragraph (a), insert "or";
      (ii) omit paragraph (c) and the "or" immediately before it;
   (c) in subsection (4), omit "or the 1980 Act".

(6) In section 19 (exceptions to duty to enforce), after subsection (1), insert –
   "(1A) The Director shall not be required to make an enforcement order, or to confirm a provisional enforcement order, if he is satisfied that the most appropriate way of proceeding is under the Competition Act 1998."

(7) In section 19(3), after "subsection (1) above", insert "or, in the case of the Director, is satisfied as mentioned in subsection (1A) above,".

(8) In section 31 (functions of Director with respect to competition) after subsection (8), insert –
   "(8A) Section 93B of the 1973 Act (offences of supplying false or misleading information) is to have effect so far as relating to functions exercisable by the Director by virtue of –
      (a) subsection (2) above and paragraph 1 of Schedule 10 to the Competition Act 1998, or
      (b) paragraph 8 of Schedule 2 to the Deregulation and Contracting Out Act 1994,
   as if the reference in section 93B(1)(a) to the Director General of Fair Trading included a reference to the Director."

(9) After section 206(9) (restriction on disclosure of information), insert –
   "(9A) Information obtained by the Director in the exercise of functions which are exercisable concurrently with the Director General of Fair Trading under Part I of the Competition Act 1998 is subject to sections 55 and 56 of that Act (disclosure) and not to subsections (1) to (9) of this section."

(10) In Schedule 15 (disclosure of information), in Part II (enactments in respect of which disclosure may be made) –
   (a) omit the entries relating to the Restrictive Trade Practices Act 1976 and the Resale Prices Act 1976;
   (b) after the entry relating to the Railways Act 1993, insert the entry – "The Competition Act 1998".

The Water Resources Act 1991 (c. 57)

14. In Schedule 24 to the Water Resources Act 1991 (disclosure of information), in Part II (enactments in respect of which disclosure may be made) –
    (a) omit the entries relating to the Restrictive Trade Practices Act 1976 and the Resale Prices Act 1976;
    (b) after the entry relating to the Coal Industry Act 1994, insert the entry – "The Competition Act 1998".

The Railways Act 1993 (c. 43)

15. – (1) The Railways Act 1993 is amended as follows.

(2) In section 13 (modification references to the Competition Commission), for subsection (8) substitute –
    "(8) The provisions mentioned in subsection (8A) are to apply in relation to references under this section as if –
        (a) the functions of the Competition Commission in relation to those references were functions under the 1973 Act;
        (b) the expression "merger reference" included a reference under this section;
        (c) in section 70 of the 1973 Act –
            (i) references to the Secretary of State were references to the Director, and
            (ii) the reference to three months were a reference to six months.
    (8A) The provisions are –
        (a) sections 70 (time limit for report on merger) and 85 (attendance of witnesses and production of documents) of the 1973 Act;
        (b) Part II of Schedule 7 to the Competition Act 1998 (performance of the Competition Commission's general functions); and
        (c) section 24 of the Competition Act 1980 (in this Part referred to as "the 1980 Act") (modification of provisions about performance of such functions)."

(3) In section 14, omit subsection (2) (which falls with the repeal of the Restrictive Trade Practices Act 1976).

(4) In section 16 (modification by order under other enactments) –
    (a) in subsection (1), omit paragraph (b) and the "or" immediately before it;
    (b) in subsection (2) –
        (i) after paragraph (a), insert "or";
        (ii) omit paragraph (c) and the "or" immediately before it;

(c) in subsection (5), omit "or the 1980 Act".

(5) In section 22, after subsection (6), insert –
  "(6A) Neither the Director General of Fair Trading nor the Regulator may exercise, in respect of an access agreement, the powers given by section 32 (enforcement directions) or section 35(2) (interim directions) of the Competition Act 1998.
  (6B) Subsection (6A) does not apply to the exercise of the powers given by section 35(2) in respect of conduct –
    (a) which is connected with an access agreement; and
    (b) in respect of which section 35(1)(b) of that Act applies."

(6) In section 55 (orders for securing compliance), after subsection (5), insert –
  "(5A) The Regulator shall not make a final order, or make or confirm a provisional order, in relation to a licence holder or person under closure restrictions if he is satisfied that the most appropriate way of proceeding is under the Competition Act 1998."

(7) In section 55 –
  (a) in subsection (6), after "subsection (5)", insert "or (5A)";
  (b) in subsection (11), for "subsection (10)" substitute "subsections (5A) and (10)".

(8) Omit section 131 (modification of Restrictive Trade Practices Act 1976).

(9) In section 145(3) (general restrictions on disclosure of information) –
  (a) omit paragraphs (d) and (e) (which refer to the Restrictive Trade Practices Act 1976 and the Resale Prices Act 1976);
  (b) after paragraph (q), insert –
    "(qq) the Competition Act 1998."

(10) After section 145(6), insert –
  "(6A) Information obtained by the Regulator in the exercise of functions which are exercisable concurrently with the Director General of Fair Trading under Part I of the Competition Act 1998 is subject to sections 55 and 56 of that Act (disclosure) and not to subsections (1) to (6) of this section."

The Channel Tunnel Rail Link Act 1996 (c 61)
16. – (1) The Channel Tunnel Rail Link Act 1996 is amended as follows.

(2) In section 21 (duties as to exercise of regulatory functions), in

subsection (6), at the end of the paragraph about regulatory functions, insert "other than any functions assigned to him by virtue of section 67(3) of that Act ("Competition Act functions").

(7) The Regulator may, when exercising any Competition Act function, have regard to any matter to which he would have regard if –

(a) he were under the duty imposed by subsection (1) or (2) above in relation to that function; and

(b) the matter is one to which the Director General of Fair Trading could have regard if he were exercising that function."

(3) In section 22 (restriction of functions in relation to competition etc), for subsection (3) substitute –

"(3) The Rail Regulator shall not be entitled to exercise any functions assigned to him by section 67(3) of the Railways Act 1993 (by virtue of which he exercises concurrently with the Director General of Fair Trading certain functions under Part I of the Competition Act 1998 so far as relating to matters connected with the supply of railway services) in relation to –

(a) any agreements, decisions or concerted practices of the kind mentioned in section 2(1) of that Act that have been entered into or taken by, or

(b) any conduct of the kind mentioned in section 18(1) of that Act that has been engaged in by,

a rail link undertaker in connection with the supply of railway services, so far as relating to the rail link."

PART V
MINOR AND CONSEQUENTIAL AMENDMENTS: NORTHERN IRELAND

The Electricity (Northern Ireland) Order 1992

17. – (1) The Electricity (Northern Ireland) Order 1992 is amended as follows.

(2) In Article 15 (modification references to Competition Commission), for paragraphs (8) and (9) substitute –

"(8) The provisions mentioned in paragraph (8A) are to apply in relation to references under this Article as if –

(a) the functions of the Competition Commission in relation to those references were functions under the 1973 Act;

(b) "merger reference" included a reference under this Article;

(c) in section 70 of the 1973 Act –

(i) references to the Secretary of State were references to the Director, and

(ii) the reference to three months were a reference to six months.

(8A) The provisions are –

(a) sections 70 (time limit for report on merger) and 85 (attendance of witnesses and production of documents) of the 1973 Act;

(b) Part II of Schedule 7 to the Competition Act 1998 (performance of the Competition Commission's general functions); and

(c) section 24 of the 1980 Act (modification of provisions about performance of such functions).

(9) The Secretary of State may appoint members of the Competition Commission for the purposes of references under this Article.

(9A) In selecting a group to perform the Commission's functions in relation to any such reference, the chairman of the Commission must select up to three of the members appointed under paragraph (9) to be members of the group."

(3) In Article 16, omit paragraph (2) (which falls with the repeal of the Restrictive Trade Practices Act 1976).

(4) In Article 18 (modification by order under other statutory provisions) –

(a) in paragraph (1), omit sub-paragraph (b) and the "or" immediately before it;

(b) in paragraph (2) –

(i) after sub-paragraph (a), insert "or";

(ii) omit sub-paragraph (c) and the "or" immediately before it;

(c) in paragraph (3), omit "or the 1980 Act".

(5) In Article 28 (orders for securing compliance), in paragraph (5), after sub-paragraph (b), omit "or" and after sub-paragraph (c), insert "or

(d) that the most appropriate way of proceeding is under the Competition Act 1998."

(6) In Article 46 (functions with respect to competition), after paragraph (6), insert –

"(6A) Section 93B of the 1973 Act (offences of supplying false or misleading information) is to have effect so far as relating to functions exercisable by the Director by virtue of –

(a) paragraph (2) and paragraph 1 of Schedule 10 to the Competition Act 1998, or
(b) paragraph 5 of Schedule 2 to the Deregulation and Contracting Out Act 1994,
as if the reference in section 93B(1)(a) to the Director General of Fair Trading included a reference to the Director."

(7) In Article 61(3) (general restrictions on disclosure of information) –
(a) omit sub-paragraphs (f) and (g) (which refer to the Restrictive Trade Practices Act 1976 and the Resale Prices Act 1976);
(b) after sub-paragraph (t), add –
"(u) the Competition Act 1998".

(8) At the end of Article 61, insert –
"(7) Information obtained by the Director in the exercise of functions which are exercisable concurrently with the Director General of Fair Trading under Part I of the Competition Act 1998 is subject to sections 55 and 56 of that Act (disclosure) and not to paragraphs (1) to (6)."

(9) In Schedule 12, omit paragraph 16 (which amends the Restrictive Trade Practices Act 1976).

The Gas (Northern Ireland) Order 1996
18. – (1) The Gas (Northern Ireland) Order 1996 is amended as follows.

(2) In Article 15 (modification references to the Competition Commission), for paragraph (9) substitute –
"(9) The provisions mentioned in paragraph (9A) are to apply in relation to references under this Article as if –
(a) the functions of the Competition Commission in relation to those references were functions under the 1973 Act;
(b) "merger reference" included a reference under this Article;
(c) in section 70 of the 1973 Act –
(i) references to the Secretary of State were references to the Director, and
(ii) the reference to three months were a reference to six months.
(9A) The provisions are –
(a) sections 70 (time limit for report on merger) and 85 (attendance of witnesses and production of documents) of the 1973 Act;
(b) Part II of Schedule 7 to the Competition Act 1998

(performance of the Competition Commission's general functions); and

(c) section 24 of the 1980 Act (modification of provisions about performance of such functions)."

(3)   In Article 16, omit paragraph (2) (which falls with the repeal of the Restrictive Trade Practices Act 1976).

(4)   In Article 18 (modification by order under other statutory provisions) –

(a) in paragraph (1), omit sub-paragraph (b) and the "or" immediately before it;

(b) in paragraph (3) –

(i) after sub-paragraph (a), insert "or";

(ii) omit sub-paragraph (c) and the "or" immediately before it;

(c) in paragraph (5), omit "or the 1980 Act".

(5)   In Article 19 (orders for securing compliance), in paragraph (5), after sub-paragraph (b), omit "or" and after sub-paragraph (c), insert "or

(d) that the most appropriate way of proceeding is under the Competition Act 1998."

(6)   In Article 44(4) (general restrictions on disclosure of information) –

(a) omit sub-paragraphs (f) and (g) (which refer to the Restrictive Trade Practices Act 1976 and the Resale Prices Act 1976);

(b) after sub-paragraph (u), add –

"(v) the Competition Act 1998".

(7)   At the end of Article 44, insert –

"(8)   Information obtained by the Director in the exercise of functions which are exercisable concurrently with the Director General of Fair Trading under Part I of the Competition Act 1998 is subject to sections 55 and 56 of that Act (disclosure) and not to paragraphs (1) to (7)."

Schedule 11
Interpretation of Section 55

Relevant functions

1.   In section 55(3) "relevant functions" means any function under –

(a) Part I or any enactment repealed in consequence of Part I;

(b) the Fair Trading Act 1973 (c 41) or the Competition Act 1980 (c 21);

(c) the Estate Agents Act 1979 (c 38);

(d) the Telecommunications Act 1984 (c 12);

(e) the Gas Act 1986 (c 44) or the Gas Act 1995 (c 45);

(f) the Gas (Northern Ireland) Order 1996;

(g) the Airports Act 1986 (c 31) or Part IV of the Airports (Northern Ireland) Order 1994;

(h) the Financial Services Act 1986 (c 60);

(i) the Electricity Act 1989 (c 29) or the Electricity (Northern Ireland) Order 1992;

(j) the Broadcasting Act 1990 (c 42) or the Broadcasting Act 1996 (c 55);

(k) the Courts and Legal Services Act 1990 (c 41);

(l) the Water Industry Act 1991 (c 56), the Water Resources Act 1991 (c 57), the Statutory Water Companies Act 1991 (c 58), the Land Drainage Act 1991 (c 59) and the Water Consolidation (Consequential Provisions) Act 1991 (c 60);

(m) the Railways Act 1993 (c 43);

(n) the Coal Industry Act 1994 (c 21);

(o) the EC Competition Law (Articles 88 and 89) Enforcement Regulations 1996;

(p) any subordinate legislation made (whether before or after the passing of this Act) for the purpose of implementing Council Directive No 91/440/EEC of 29th July 1991 on the development of the Community's railways, Council Directive No 95/18/EC of 19th June 1995 on the licensing of railway undertakings or Council Directive No 95/19/EC of 19th June 1995 on the allocation of railway infrastructure capacity and the charging of infrastructure fees.

Designated persons

2.   In section 55(3) "designated person" means any of the following –

(a) the Director;

(b) the Director General of Telecommunications;

(c) the Independent Television Commission;

(d) the Director General of Gas Supply;

(e) the Director General of Gas for Northern Ireland;

(f) the Civil Aviation Authority;

(g) the Director General of Water Services;

(h) the Director General of Electricity Supply;

(i) the Director General of Electricity Supply for Northern Ireland;

(j) the Rail Regulator;

(k) the Director of Passenger Rail Franchising;

(l) the International Rail Regulator;

(m) the Authorised Conveyancing Practitioners Board;

(n) the Scottish Conveyancing and Executry Services Board;
(o) the Coal Authority;
(p) the Monopolies and Mergers Commission;
(q) the Competition Commission;
(r) the Securities and Investments Board;
(s) any Minister of the Crown or any Northern Ireland department.

Schedule 12
Minor and Consequential Amendments

The Fair Trading Act 1973 (c 41)

1. – (1) The Fair Trading Act 1973 is amended as follows.

(2) Omit section 4 and Schedule 3 (which make provision in respect of the Monopolies and Mergers Commission).

(3) Omit –
    (a) section 10(2),
    (b) section 54(5),
    (c) section 78(3),
    (d) paragraph 3(1) and (2) of Schedule 8,
(which fall with the repeal of the Restrictive Trade Practices Act 1976).

(4) In section 10 (supplementary provisions about monopoly situations), in subsection (8), for "to (7)" substitute "and (3) to (7)".

(5) In sections 35 and 37 to 41, for "the Restrictive Practices Court", in each place, substitute "a relevant Court".

(6) After section 41, insert –
    "41A In this Part of this Act, "relevant Court", in relation to proceedings in respect of a course of conduct maintained in the course of a business, means any of the following courts in whose jurisdiction that business is carried on –
        (a) in England and Wales or Northern Ireland, the High Court;
        (b) in Scotland, the Court of Session."

(7) In section 42 (appeals from decisions or orders of courts under Part III) –
    (a) in subsection (1), at the end, add "; but this subsection is subject to subsection (3) of this section";
    (b) in subsection (2)(b), after "Scotland," insert "from the sheriff court"; and

(c) after subsection (2), add –
"(3) A decision or order of the Court of Session as the relevant Court may be reviewed, whether on a question of fact or on a question of law, by reclaiming to the Inner House."

(8) Omit section 45 (power of the Director to require information about complex monopoly situations).

(9) In section 81 (procedure in carrying out investigations) –
(a) in subsection (1) –
(i) in the words before paragraph (a), omit from "and the Commission" to "of this Act)";
(ii) in paragraph (b), omit "or the Commission, as the case may be," and "or of the Commission";
(b) in subsection (2), omit "or the Commission" and "or of the Commission"; and
(c) in subsection (3), omit from "and, in the case," to "85 of this Act" and "or the Commission, as the case may be,".

(10) In section 85 (attendance of witnesses and production of documents on investigations by Competition Commission of references under the Fair Trading Act 1973), in subsection (1)(b) –
(a) after "purpose", insert "(i)";
(b) after the second "notice", insert "or
(ii) any document which falls within a category of document which is specified, or described, in the notice,".

(11) In section 85, in subsection (1)(c), after "estimates" (in both places), insert "forecasts".

(12) In section 85, after subsection (1), insert –
"(1A) For the purposes of subsection (1) above –
(a) "document" includes information recorded in any form;
(b) the power to require the production of documents includes power to take copies of, or extracts from, any document produced; and
(c) in relation to information recorded otherwise than in legible form, the power to require it to be produced includes power to require it to be produced in legible form, so far as the means to do so are within the custody or under the control of the person on whom the requirement is imposed."

(13) In section 85(2), for "any such investigation" substitute "an investigation of the kind mentioned in subsection (1)".

(14) In section 133 (general restrictions on disclosure of information), in subsection (2)(a), after "the Coal Industry Act 1994" insert "or the Competition Act 1998".

(15) In section 135(1) (financial provisions) –
    (a) in the words before paragraph (a) and in paragraph (b), omit "or the Commission"; and
    (b) omit paragraph (a).

The Energy Act 1976 (c 76)

2.   In the Energy Act 1976, omit section 5 (temporary relief from restrictive practices law in relation to certain agreements connected with petroleum).

The Estate Agents Act 1979 (c 38)

3.   In section 10(3) of the Estate Agents Act 1979 (restriction on disclosure of information), in paragraph (a) –
    (a) omit "or the Restrictive Trade Practices Act 1976"; and
    (b) after "the Coal Industry Act 1994", insert "or the Competition Act 1998".

The Competition Act 1980 (c 21)

4. – (1) The Competition Act 1980 is amended as follows.

(2) In section 11(8) (public bodies and other persons referred to the Commission), omit paragraph (b) and the "and" immediately before it.

(3) For section 11(9) (which makes provision for certain functions of the Competition Commission under the Fair Trading Act 1973 to apply in relation to references under the Competition Act 1980) substitute –
    "(9) The provisions mentioned in subsection (9A) are to apply in relation to a reference under this section as if –
        (a) the functions of the Competition Commission under this section were functions under the Fair Trading Act 1973;
        (b) the expression "merger reference" included a reference to the Commission under this section; and
        (c) in paragraph 20(2)(a) of Schedule 7 to the Competition Act 1998, the reference to section 56 of the Fair Trading Act 1973 were a reference to section 12 below.
    (9A) The provisions are –
        (a) sections 70 (time limit for report on merger), 84 (public interest) and 85 (attendance of witnesses and production of documents) of the Fair Trading Act 1973; and
        (b) Part II of Schedule 7 to the Competition Act 1998

(performance of the Competition Commission's general functions)."

(4) In section 13 (investigation of prices directed by Secretary of State) –
    (a) in subsection (1), omit from "but the giving" to the end;
    (b) for subsection (6) substitute –

"(6)   For the purposes of an investigation under this section the Director may, by notice in writing signed by him –

    (a) require any person to produce –
        (i) at a time and a place specified in the notice,
        (ii) to the Director or to any person appointed by him for the purpose,

any documents which are specified or described in the notice and which are documents in his custody or under his control and relating to any matter relevant to the investigation; or

    (b) require any person carrying on any business to –
        (i) furnish to the Director such estimates, forecasts, returns or other information as may be specified or described in the notice; and
        (ii) specify the time, manner and form in which any such estimates, forecasts, returns or information are to be furnished.

(7) No person shall be compelled, for the purpose of any investigation under this section –

    (a) to produce any document which he could not be compelled to produce in civil proceedings before the High Court or, in Scotland, the Court of Session; or
    (b) in complying with any requirement for the furnishing of information, to give any information which he could not be compelled to give in evidence in such proceedings.

(8) Subsections (6) to (8) of section 85 of the Fair Trading Act 1973 (enforcement provisions relating to notices requiring production of documents etc) shall apply in relation to a notice under subsection (6) above as they apply in relation to a notice under section 85(1) but as if, in section 85(7), for the words from "any one" to "the Commission" there were substituted "the Director.""

(5) In section 15 (special provisions for agricultural schemes) omit subsections (2)(b), (3) and (4).

(6) In section 16 (reports), omit subsection (3).

(7) In section 17 (publication etc of reports) –
    (a) in subsections (1) and (3) to (5), omit "8(1)";
    (b) in subsection (2), omit "8(1) or"; and
    (c) in subsection (6), for "sections 9, 10 or" substitute "section".

(8) In section 19(3) (restriction on disclosure of information), omit paragraphs (d) and (e).

(9) In section 19(3), after paragraph (q), insert –
    "(r) the Competition Act 1998".

(10) In section 19(5)(a), omit "or in anything published under section 4(2)(a) above".

(11) Omit section 22 (which amends the Fair Trading Act 1973).

(12) In section 24(1) (modifications of provisions about performance of Commission's functions), for from "Part II" to the first "Commission" substitute "Part II of Schedule 7 to the Competition Act 1998 (performance of the Competition Commission's general functions)".

(13) Omit sections 25 to 30 (amendments of the Restrictive Trade Practices Act 1976).

(14) In section 31 (orders and regulations) –
    (a) omit subsection (2); and
    (b) in subsection (3), omit "10".

(15) In section 33 (short title etc) –
    (a) in subsection (2), for "sections 2 to 24" substitute "sections 11 to 13 and sections 15 to 24";
    (b) omit subsections (3) and (4).

Magistrates' Courts (Northern Ireland) Order 1981 (SI 1981/1675 (NI 26))
5. In Schedule 6 to the Magistrates' Courts (Northern Ireland) Order 1981, omit paragraphs 42 and 43 (which amend the Restrictive Trade Practices Act 1976).
Agricultural Marketing (Northern Ireland) Order 1982 (SI 1982/1080 (NI 12))

6. In Schedule 8 to the Agricultural Marketing (Northern Ireland) Order 1982 –
    (a) omit the entry relating to paragraph 16(2) of Schedule 3 to the Fair Trading Act 1973; and

(b) in the entry relating to the Competition Act 1980 –
(i) for "sections" substitute "section";
(ii) omit "and 15(3)".

The Airports Act 1986 (c 31)
7. – (1) The Airports Act 1986 is amended as follows.

(2) In section 44 (which makes provision about references by the CAA to the Competition Commission), for subsection (3) substitute –
"(3) The provisions mentioned in subsection (3A) are to apply in relation to references under this section as if –
(a) the functions of the Competition Commission in relation to those references were functions under the 1973 Act;
(b) the expression "merger reference" included a reference under this section;
(c) in section 70 of the 1973 Act –
(i) references to the Secretary of State were references to the CAA, and
(ii) the reference to three months were a reference to six months.
(3A) The provisions are –
(a) sections 70 (time limit for report on merger) and 85 (attendance of witnesses and production of documents) of the 1973 Act;
(b) Part II of Schedule 7 to the Competition Act 1998 (performance of the Competition Commission's general functions); and
(c) section 24 of the 1980 Act (modification of provisions about performance of such functions)."

(3) In section 45, omit subsection (3) (which falls with the repeal of the Restrictive Trade Practices Act 1976).

(4) In section 54 (orders under the 1973 Act or 1980 Act modifying or revoking conditions) –
(a) in subsection (1), omit "or section 10(2)(a) of the 1980 Act";
(b) in subsection (3), omit paragraph (c) and the "or" immediately before it;
(c) in subsection (4), omit "or the 1980 Act".

(5) In section 56 (co-ordination of exercise of functions by CAA and Director General of Fair Trading), in paragraph (a)(ii), omit "or the 1980 Act".

The Financial Services Act 1986 (c 60)

8. In Schedule 11 to the Financial Services Act 1986, in paragraph 12 –
    (a) in sub-paragraph (1), omit "126";
    (b) omit sub-paragraph (2).

The Companies Consolidation (Consequential Provisions) (Northern Ireland) Order 1986 (SI 1986/1035 (NI 9))

9. In Part II of Schedule 1 to the Companies Consolidation (Consequential Provisions)(Northern Ireland) Order 1986, omit the entries relating to the Restrictive Trade Practices Act 1976 and the Resale Prices Act 1976.

The Consumer Protection Act 1987 (c. 43)

10. In section 38(3) of the Consumer Protection Act 1987 (restrictions on disclosure of information) –
    (a) omit paragraphs (e) and (f); and
    (b) after paragraph (o), insert –
       "(p)   the Competition Act 1998."

The Channel Tunnel Act 1987 (c. 53)

11. In section 33 of the Channel Tunnel Act 1987 –
    (a) in subsection (2), omit paragraph (c) and the "and" immediately before it;
    (b) in subsection (5), omit paragraphs (b) and (c).

The Road Traffic (Consequential Provisions) Act 1988 (c. 54)

12. In Schedule 3 to the Road Traffic (Consequential Provisions) Act 1988 (consequential amendments), omit paragraph 19.

The Companies Act 1989 (c. 40)

13. In Schedule 20 to the Companies Act 1989 (amendments about mergers and related matters), omit paragraphs 21 to 24.

The Broadcasting Act 1990 (c. 42)

14. – (1) The Broadcasting Act 1990 is amended as follows.

(2) In section 193 (modification of networking arrangements in consequence of reports under competition legislation) –
    (a) in subsection (2), omit paragraph (c) and the "and" immediately before it;
    (b) in subsection (4), omit "or the Competition Act 1980".

(3) In Schedule 4 (which makes provision for references to the Director or the Competition Commission in respect of networking arrangements), in paragraph 4, for sub-paragraph (7) substitute –

"(7) The provisions mentioned in sub-paragraph (7A) are to apply in relation to references under this paragraph as if –

(a) the functions of the Competition Commission in relation to those references were functions under the Fair Trading Act 1973;

(b) the expression "merger reference" included a reference under this paragraph.

(7A) The provisions are –

(a) section 85 of the Fair Trading Act 1973 (attendance of witnesses and production of documents);

(b) Part II of Schedule 7 to the Competition Act 1998 (performance of the Competition Commission's general functions); and

(c) section 24 of the Competition Act 1980 (modification of provisions about performance of such functions)."

The Tribunals and Inquiries Act 1992 (c. 53)

15. In Schedule 1 to the Tribunals and Inquiries Act 1992 (tribunals under the supervision of the Council on Tribunals), after paragraph 9, insert –

"Competition 9A. An appeal tribunal established under section 48 of the Competition Act 1998."

The Osteopaths Act 1993 (c. 21)

16. Section 33 of the Osteopaths Act 1993 (competition and anti-competitive practices) is amended as follows –

(a) in subsection (4), omit paragraph (b) and the "or" immediately before it;

(b) in subsection (5), omit "or section 10 of the Act of 1980".

The Chiropractors Act 1994 (c. 17)

17. Section 33 of the Chiropractors Act 1994 (competition and anti-competitive practices) is amended as follows –

(a) in subsection (4), omit paragraph (b) and the "or" immediately before it;

(b) in subsection (5), omit "or section 10 of the Act of 1980".

The Coal Industry Act 1994 (c 21)

18. In section 59(4) of the Coal Industry Act 1994 (information to be kept confidential by the Coal Authority) –

(a) omit paragraphs (e) and (f); and

(b) after paragraph (m), insert –

"(n) the Competition Act 1998."

The Deregulation and Contracting Out Act 1994 (c 40)

19. – (1) The Deregulation and Contracting Out Act 1994 is amended as follows.

(2)   Omit –
    (a) section 10 (restrictive trade practices: non-notifiable agreements); and
    (b) section 11 (registration of commercially sensitive information).

(3)   In section 12 (anti-competitive practices: competition references), omit subsections (1) to (6).

(4)   In Schedule 4, omit paragraph 1.

(5)   In Schedule 11 (miscellaneous deregulatory provisions: consequential amendments), in paragraph 4, omit sub-paragraphs (3) to (7).

The Airports (Northern Ireland) Order 1994 (SI 1994/426 (NI 1))

20. – (1) The Airports (Northern Ireland) Order 1994 is amended as follows.

(2)   In Article 35 (which makes provision about references by the CAA to the Competition Commission), for paragraph (3) substitute –
    "(3)   The provisions mentioned in paragraph (3A) are to apply in relation to references under Article 34 as if –
        (a) the functions of the Competition Commission in relation to those references were functions under the 1973 Act;
        (b) the expression "merger reference" included a reference under that Article;
        (c) in section 70 of the 1973 Act –
            (i) references to the Secretary of State were references to the Director, and
            (ii) the reference to three months were a reference to six months.
    (3A) The provisions are –
        (a) sections 70 (time limit for report on merger) and 85 (attendance of witnesses and production of documents) of the 1973 Act;
        (b) Part II of Schedule 7 to the Competition Act 1998 (performance of the Competition Commission's general functions); and
        (c) section 24 of the 1980 Act (modification of provisions about performance of such functions)."

(3)   In Article 36, omit paragraph (3) (which falls with the repeal of the Restrictive Trade Practices Act 1976).

(4)   In Article 45 (orders under the 1973 Act or 1980 Act modifying or revoking conditions) –
> (a) in paragraph (1), omit "or section 10(2)(a) of the 1980 Act";
> (b) in paragraph (3), omit sub-paragraph (c) and the "or" immediately before it;
> (c) in paragraph (4), omit "or the 1980 Act".

(5)   In Article 47 (co-ordination of exercise of functions by CAA and Director of Fair Trading), in paragraph (a)(ii), omit "or the 1980 Act".

(6)   In Schedule 9, omit paragraph 5 (which amends the Restrictive Trade Practices Act 1976).

The Broadcasting Act 1996 (c 55)
21.   In section 77 of the Broadcasting Act 1996 (which modifies the Restrictive Trade Practices Act 1976 in its application to agreements relating to Channel 3 news provision), omit subsection (2).

Schedule 13
Transitional Provisions and Savings
PART I
GENERAL

Interpretation
1. – (1) In this Schedule –
> "RPA" means the Resale Prices Act 1976;
> "RTPA" means the Restrictive Trade Practices Act 1976;
> "continuing proceedings" has the meaning given by paragraph 15;
> "the Court" means the Restrictive Practices Court;
> "Director" means the Director General of Fair Trading;
> "document" includes information recorded in any form;
> "enactment date" means the date on which this Act is passed;
> "information" includes estimates and forecasts;
> "interim period" means the period beginning on the enactment date and ending immediately before the starting date;
> "prescribed" means prescribed by an order made by the Secretary of State;
> "regulator" means any person mentioned in paragraphs (a) to (g) of paragraph 1 of Schedule 10;
> "starting date" means the date on which section 2 comes into force;

"transitional period" means the transitional period provided for in Chapters III and IV of Part IV of this Schedule.

(2) Sections 30, 44, 51, 53, 55, 56, 57 and 59(3) and (4) and paragraph 12 of Schedule 9 ("the applied provisions") apply for the purposes of this Schedule as they apply for the purposes of Part I of this Act.

(3) Section 2(5) applies for the purposes of any provisions of this Schedule which are concerned with the operation of the Chapter I prohibition as it applies for the purposes of Part I of this Act.

(4) In relation to any of the matters in respect of which a regulator may exercise powers as a result of paragraph 35(1), the applied provisions are to have effect as if references to the Director included references to the regulator.

(5) The fact that to a limited extent the Chapter I prohibition does not apply to an agreement, because a transitional period is provided by virtue of this Schedule, does not require those provisions of the agreement in respect of which there is a transitional period to be disregarded when considering whether the agreement infringes the prohibition for other reasons.

General power to make transitional provision and savings

2. – (1) Nothing in this Schedule affects the power of the Secretary of State under section 75 to make transitional provisions or savings.

(2) An order under that section may modify any provision made by this Schedule.

Advice and information

3 – (1) The Director may publish advice and information explaining provisions of this Schedule to persons who are likely to be affected by them.

(2) Any advice or information published by the Director under this paragraph is to be published in such form and manner as he considers appropriate.

PART II
DURING THE INTERIM PERIOD

Block exemptions

4. – (1) The Secretary of State may, at any time during the interim period, make one or more orders for the purpose of providing block exemptions which are effective on the starting date.

(2)   An order under this paragraph has effect as if properly made under section 6.

Certain agreements to be non-notifiable agreements

5.   An agreement which –
    (a) is made during the interim period, and
    (b) satisfies the conditions set out in paragraphs (a), (c) and (d) of section 27A(1) of the RTPA,
is to be treated as a non–notifiable agreement for the purposes of RTPA.

Application of RTPA during the interim period

6.   In relation to agreements made during the interim period –
    (a) the Director is no longer under the duty to take proceedings imposed by section 1(2)(c) of the RTPA but may continue to do so;
    (b) section 21 of that Act has effect as if subsections (1) and (2) were omitted; and
    (c) section 35(1) of that Act has effect as if the words "or within such further time as the Director may, upon application made within that time, allow" were omitted.

Guidance

7. – (1) Sub-paragraphs (2) to (4) apply in relation to agreements made during the interim period.

(2)   An application may be made to the Director in anticipation of the coming into force of section 13 in accordance with directions given by the Director and such an application is to have effect on and after the starting date as if properly made under section 13.

(3)   The Director may, in response to such an application –
    (a) give guidance in anticipation of the coming into force of section 2; or
    (b) on and after the starting date, give guidance under section 15 as if the application had been properly made under section 13.

(4)   Any guidance so given is to have effect on and after the starting date as if properly given under section 15.

PART III
ON THE STARTING DATE

Applications which fall

8. – (1) Proceedings in respect of an application which is made to the

Court under any of the provisions mentioned in sub-paragraph (2), but which is not determined before the starting date, cease on that date.

(2) The provisions are –
(a) sections 2(2), 35(3), 37(1) and 40(1) of the RTPA and paragraph 5 of Schedule 4 to that Act;
(b) section 4(1) of the RTPA so far as the application relates to an order under section 2(2) of that Act; and
(c) section 25(2) of the RPA.

(3) The power of the Court to make an order for costs in relation to any proceedings is not affected by anything in this paragraph or by the repeals made by section 1.

Orders and approvals which fall
9. – (1) An order in force immediately before the starting date under –
(a) section 2(2), 29(1), 30(1), 33(4), 35(3) or 37(1) of the RTPA; or
(b) section 25(2) of the RPA,
ceases to have effect on that date.

(2) An approval in force immediately before the starting date under section 32 of the RTPA ceases to have effect on that date.

PART IV
ON AND AFTER THE STARTING DATE
Chapter I
General

Duty of Director to maintain register etc.
10. – (1) This paragraph applies even though the relevant provisions of the RTPA are repealed by this Act.

(2) The Director is to continue on and after the starting date to be under the duty imposed by section 1(2)(a) of the RTPA to maintain a register in respect of agreements –
(a) particulars of which are, on the starting date, entered or filed on the register;
(b) which fall within sub-paragraph (4);
(c) which immediately before the starting date are the subject of proceedings under the RTPA which do not cease on that date by virtue of this Schedule; or
(d) in relation to which a court gives directions to the Director after the starting date in the course of proceedings in which a question arises as to whether an agreement was, before that date –

(i) one to which the RTPA applied;

(ii) subject to registration under that Act;

(iii) a non–notifiable agreement for the purposes of that Act.

(3)   The Director is to continue on and after the starting date to be under the duties imposed by section 1(2)(a) and (b) of the RTPA of compiling a register of agreements and entering or filing certain particulars in the register, but only in respect of agreements of a kind referred to in paragraph (b), (c) or (d) of sub–paragraph (2).

(4)   An agreement falls within this sub–paragraph if –

(a) it is subject to registration under the RTPA but –

(i) is not a non–notifiable agreement within the meaning of section 27A of the RTPA, or

(ii) is not one to which paragraph 5 applies;

(b) particulars of the agreement have been provided to the Director before the starting date; and

(c) as at the starting date no entry or filing has been made in the register in respect of the agreement.

(5)   Sections 23 and 27 of the RTPA are to apply after the starting date in respect of the register subject to such modifications, if any, as may be prescribed.

(6) In sub–paragraph (2)(d) "court" means –

(a) the High Court;

(b) the Court of Appeal;

(c) the Court of Session;

(d) the High Court or Court of Appeal in Northern Ireland; or

(e) the House of Lords.

RTPA section 3 applications

11. – (1) Even though section 3 of the RTPA is repealed by this Act, its provisions (and so far as necessary that Act) are to continue to apply, with such modifications (if any) as may be prescribed –

(a) in relation to a continuing application under that section; or

(b) so as to allow an application to be made under that section on or after the starting date in respect of a continuing application under section 1(3) of the RTPA.

(2) "Continuing application" means an application made, but not determined, before the starting date.

RTPA section 26 applications

12. – (1) Even though section 26 of the RTPA is repealed by this Act,

its provisions (and so far as necessary that Act) are to continue to apply, with such modifications (if any) as may be prescribed, in relation to an application which is made under that section, but not determined, before the starting date.

(2) If an application under section 26 is determined on or after the starting date, this Schedule has effect in relation to the agreement concerned as if the application had been determined immediately before that date.

Right to bring civil proceedings

13. – (1) Even though section 35 of the RTPA is repealed by this Act, its provisions (and so far as necessary that Act) are to continue to apply in respect of a person who, immediately before the starting date, has a right by virtue of section 27ZA or 35(2) of that Act to bring civil proceedings in respect of an agreement (but only so far as that right relates to any period before the starting date or, where there are continuing proceedings, the determination of the proceedings).

(2) Even though section 25 of the RPA is repealed by this Act, the provisions of that section (and so far as necessary that Act) are to continue to apply in respect of a person who, immediately before the starting date, has a right by virtue of subsection (3) of that section to bring civil proceedings (but only so far as that right relates to any period before the starting date or, where there are continuing proceedings, the determination of the proceedings).

Chapter II
Continuing Proceedings

The general rule

14. – (1) The Chapter I prohibition does not apply to an agreement at any time when the agreement is the subject of continuing proceedings under the RTPA.

(2) The Chapter I prohibition does not apply to an agreement relating to goods which are the subject of continuing proceedings under section 16 or 17 of the RPA to the extent to which the agreement consists of exempt provisions.

(3) In sub-paragraph (2) "exempt provisions" means those provisions of the agreement which would, disregarding section 14 of the RPA, be –

    (a) void as a result of section 9(1) of the RPA; or
    (b) unlawful as a result of section 9(2) or II of the RPA.

(4) If the Chapter I prohibition does not apply to an agreement because of this paragraph, the provisions of, or made under, the RTPA or the RPA are to continue to have effect in relation to the agreement.

(5) The repeals made by section 1 do not affect –
    (a) continuing proceedings; or
    (b) proceedings of the kind referred to in paragraph 11 or 12 of this Schedule which are continuing after the starting date.

Meaning of "continuing proceedings"

15. – (1) For the purposes of this Schedule "continuing proceedings" means proceedings in respect of an application made to the Court under the RTPA or the RPA, but not determined, before the starting date.

(2) But proceedings under section 3 or 26 of the RTPA to which paragraph 11 or 12 applies are not continuing proceedings.

(3) The question whether (for the purposes of Part III, or this Part, of this Schedule) an application has been determined is to be decided in accordance with sub-paragraphs (4) and (5).

(4) If an appeal against the decision on the application is brought, the application is not determined until –
    (a) the appeal is disposed of or withdrawn; or
    (b) if as a result of the appeal the case is referred back to the Court –
        (i) the expiry of the period within which an appeal ("the further appeal") in respect of the Court's decision on that reference could have been brought had this Act not been passed; or
        (ii) if later, the date on which the further appeal is disposed of or withdrawn.

(5) Otherwise, the application is not determined until the expiry of the period within which any party to the application would have been able to bring an appeal against the decision on the application had this Act not been passed.

RTPA section 4 proceedings

16. Proceedings on an application for an order under section 4 of the RTPA are also continuing proceedings if –
    (a) leave to make the application is applied for before the starting date but the proceedings in respect of that application for leave are not determined before that date; or

303

(b) leave to make an application for an order under that section is granted before the starting date but the application itself is not made before that date.

RPA section 16 or 17 proceedings

17. Proceedings on an application for an order under section 16 or 17 of the RPA are also continuing proceedings if –

(a) leave to make the application is applied for before the starting date but the proceedings in respect of that application for leave are not determined before that date; or

(b) leave to make an application for an order under section 16 or 17 of the RPA is granted before the starting date, but the application itself is not made before that date.

Continuing proceedings which are discontinued

18. – (1) On an application made jointly to the Court by all the parties to any continuing proceedings, the Court must, if it is satisfied that the parties wish it to do so, discontinue the proceedings.

(2) If, on an application under sub-paragraph (1) or for any other reason, the Court orders the proceedings to be discontinued, this Schedule has effect (subject to paragraphs 21 and 22) from the date on which the proceedings are discontinued as if they had never been instituted.

Chapter III
The Transitional Period

The general rule

19. – (1) Except where this Chapter or Chapter IV provides otherwise, there is a transitional period, beginning on the starting date and lasting for one year, for any agreement made before the starting date.

(2) The Chapter I prohibition does not apply to an agreement to the extent to which there is a transitional period for the agreement.

(3) The Secretary of State may by regulations provide for sections 13 to 16 and Schedule 5 to apply with such modifications (if any) as may be specified in the regulations, in respect of applications to the Director about agreements for which there is a transitional period.

Cases for which there is no transitional period

20. – (1) There is no transitional period for an agreement to the extent to which, immediately before the starting date, it is –

(a) void under section 2(1) or 35(1)(a) of the RTPA;

(b) the subject of an order under section 2(2) or 35(3) of the RTPA; or

(c) unlawful under section 1, 2 or 11 of the RPA or void under section 9 of that Act.

(2)   There is no transitional period for an agreement to the extent to which, before the starting date, a person has acted unlawfully for the purposes of section 27ZA(2) or (3) of the RTPA in respect of the agreement.

(3)   There is no transitional period for an agreement to which paragraph 25(4) applies.

(4)   There is no transitional period for –

(a) an agreement in respect of which there are continuing proceedings, or

(b) an agreement relating to goods in respect of which there are continuing proceedings,

to the extent to which the agreement is, when the proceedings are determined, void or unlawful.

Continuing proceedings under the RTPA

21. In the case of an agreement which is the subject of continuing proceedings under the RTPA, the transitional period begins –

(a) if the proceedings are discontinued, on the date of discontinuance;

(b) otherwise, when the proceedings are determined.

Continuing proceedings under the RPA

22. – (1) In the case of an agreement relating to goods which are the subject of continuing proceedings under the RPA, the transitional period for the exempt provisions of the agreement begins –

(a) if the proceedings are discontinued, on the date of discontinuance;

(b) otherwise, when the proceedings are determined.

(2)   In sub-paragraph (1) "exempt provisions" has the meaning given by paragraph 14(3).

Provisions not contrary to public interest

23. – (1) To the extent to which an agreement contains provisions which, immediately before the starting date, are provisions which the Court has found not to be contrary to the public interest, the transitional period lasts for five years.

(2)   Sub-paragraph (1) is subject to paragraph 20(4).

(3) To the extent to which an agreement which on the starting date is the subject of continuing proceedings is, when the proceedings are determined, found by the Court not to be contrary to the public interest, the transitional period lasts for five years.

Goods

24. – (1) In the case of an agreement relating to goods which, immediately before the starting date, are exempt under section 14 of the RPA, there is a transitional period for the agreement to the extent to which it consists of exempt provisions.

(2) Sub-paragraph (1) is subject to paragraph 20(4).

(3) In the case of an agreement relating to goods –
    (a) which on the starting date are the subject of continuing proceedings, and
    (b) which, when the proceedings are determined, are found to be exempt under section 14 of the RPA,
there is a transitional period for the agreement, to the extent to which it consists of exempt provisions.

(4) In each case, the transitional period lasts for five years.

(5) In sub-paragraphs (1) and (3) "exempt provisions" means those provisions of the agreement which would, disregarding section 14 of the RPA, be –
    (a) void as a result of section 9(1) of the RPA; or
    (b) unlawful as a result of section 9(2) or 11 of the RPA.

Transitional period for certain agreements

25. – (1) This paragraph applies to agreements –
    (a) which are subject to registration under the RTPA but which –
        (i) are not non-notifiable agreements within the meaning of section 27A of the RTPA, or
        (ii) are not agreements to which paragraph 5 applies; and
    (b) in respect of which the time for furnishing relevant particulars as required by or under the RTPA expires on or after the starting date.

(2) "Relevant particulars" means –
    (a) particulars which are required to be furnished by virtue of section 24 of the RTPA; or
    (b) particulars of any variation of an agreement which are required to be furnished by virtue of sections 24 and 27 of the RTPA.

(3) There is a transitional period of one year for an agreement to which this paragraph applies if –
>(a) relevant particulars are furnished before the starting date; and
>(b) no person has acted unlawfully (for the purposes of section 27ZA(2) or (3) of the RTPA) in respect of the agreement.

(4) If relevant particulars are not furnished by the starting date, section 35(1)(a) of the RTPA does not apply in relation to the agreement (unless sub-paragraph (5) applies).

(5) This sub-paragraph applies if a person falling within section 27ZA(2) or (3) of the RTPA has acted unlawfully for the purposes of those subsections in respect of the agreement.

Special cases

26. – (1) In the case of an agreement in respect of which –
>(a) a direction under section 127(2) of the Financial Services Act 1986 ("the 1986 Act") is in force immediately before the starting date, or
>(b) a direction under section 194A(3) of the Broadcasting Act 1990 ("the 1990 Act") is in force immediately before the starting date,

the transitional period lasts for five years.

(2) To the extent to which an agreement is the subject of a declaration –
>(a) made by the Treasury under section 127(3) of the 1986 Act, and
>(b) in force immediately before the starting date,

the transitional period lasts for five years.

(3) Sub-paragraphs (1) and (2) do not affect the power of –
>(a) the Treasury to make a declaration under section 127(2) of the 1986 Act (as amended by Schedule 2 to this Act),
>(b) the Secretary of State to make a declaration under section 194A of the 1990 Act (as amended by Schedule 2 to this Act),

in respect of an agreement for which there is a transitional period.

Chapter IV
The Utilities

General

27. In this Chapter "the relevant period" means the period beginning with the starting date and ending immediately before the fifth anniversary of that date.

Electricity

28. – (1) For an agreement to which, immediately before the starting date, the RTPA does not apply by virtue of a section 100 order, there is a transitional period –

    (a) beginning on the starting date; and

    (b) ending at the end of the relevant period.

(2) For an agreement which is made at any time after the starting date and to which, had the RTPA not been repealed, that Act would not at the time at which the agreement is made have applied by virtue of a section 100 order, there is a transitional period –

    (a) beginning on the date on which the agreement is made; and

    (b) ending at the end of the relevant period.

(3) For an agreement (whether made before or after the starting date) which, during the relevant period, is varied at any time in such a way that it becomes an agreement which, had the RTPA not been repealed, would at that time have been one to which that Act did not apply by virtue of a section 100 order, there is a transitional period –

    (a) beginning on the date on which the variation is made; and

    (b) ending at the end of the relevant period.

(4) If an agreement for which there is a transitional period as a result of sub-paragraph (1), (2) or (3) is varied during the relevant period, the transitional period for the agreement continues if, had the RTPA not been repealed, the agreement would have continued to be one to which that Act did not apply by virtue of a section 100 order.

(5) But if an agreement for which there is a transitional period as a result of sub-paragraph (1), (2) or (3) ceases to be one to which, had it not been repealed, the RTPA would not have applied by virtue of a section 100 order, the transitional period ends on the date on which the agreement so ceases.

(6) Sub-paragraph (3) is subject to paragraph 20.

(7) In this paragraph and paragraph 29 –

    "section 100 order" means an order made under section 100 of the Electricity Act 1989; and

expressions which are also used in Part I of the Electricity Act 1989 have the same meaning as in that Part.

Electricity: power to make transitional orders

29. – (1) There is a transitional period for an agreement (whether made before or after the starting date) relating to the generation, transmission

or supply of electricity which –

    (a) is specified, or is of a description specified, in an order ("a transitional order") made by the Secretary of State (whether before or after the making of the agreement but before the end of the relevant period); and

    (b) satisfies such conditions as may be specified in the order.

(2) A transitional order may make provision as to when the transitional period in respect of such an agreement is to start or to be deemed to have started.

(3) The transitional period for such an agreement ends at the end of the relevant period.

(4) But if the agreement –

    (a) ceases to be one to which a transitional order applies, or

    (b) ceases to satisfy one or more of the conditions specified in the transitional order,

the transitional period ends on the date on which the agreement so ceases.

(5) Before making a transitional order, the Secretary of State must consult the Director General of Electricity Supply and the Director.

(6) The conditions specified in a transitional order may include conditions which refer any matter to the Secretary of State for determination after such consultation as may be so specified.

(7) In the application of this paragraph to Northern Ireland, the reference in sub-paragraph (5) to the Director General of Electricity Supply is to be read as a reference to the Director General of Electricity Supply for Northern Ireland.

Gas

30. – (1) For an agreement to which, immediately before the starting date, the RTPA does not apply by virtue of section 62 or a section 62 order, there is a transitional period –

    (a) beginning on the starting date; and

    (b) ending at the end of the relevant period.

(2) For an agreement which is made at any time after the starting date and to which, had the RTPA not been repealed, that Act would not at the time at which the agreement is made have applied by virtue of section 62 or a section 62 order, there is a transitional period –

    (a) beginning on the date on which the agreement is made; and

(b) ending at the end of the relevant period.

(3)   For an agreement (whether made before or after the starting date) which, during the relevant period, is varied at any time in such a way that it becomes an agreement which, had the RTPA not been repealed, would at that time have been one to which that Act did not apply by virtue of section 62 or a section 62 order, there is a transitional period –
     (a) beginning on the date on which the variation is made; and
     (b) ending at the end of the relevant period.

(4)   If an agreement for which there is a transitional period as a result of sub-paragraph (1), (2) or (3) is varied during the relevant period, the transitional period for the agreement continues if, had the RTPA not been repealed, the agreement would have continued to be one to which that Act did not apply by virtue of section 62 or a section 62 order.

(5)   But if an agreement for which there is a transitional period as a result of sub-paragraph (1), (2) or (3) ceases to be one to which, had it not been repealed, the RTPA would not have applied by virtue of section 62 or a section 62 order, the transitional period ends on the date on which the agreement so ceases.

(6)   Sub-paragraph (3) also applies in relation to a modification which is treated as an agreement made on or after 28th November 1985 by virtue of section 62(4).

(7)   Sub-paragraph (3) is subject to paragraph 20.

(8)   In this paragraph and paragraph 31 –
     "section 62" means section 62 of the Gas Act 1986;
     "section 62 order" means an order made under section 62.

Gas: power to make transitional orders

31. – (1) There is a transitional period for an agreement of a description falling within section 62(2)(a) and (b) or section 62(2A)(a) and (b) which –
     (a) is specified, or is of a description specified, in an order ("a transitional order") made by the Secretary of State (whether before or after the making of the agreement but before the end of the relevant period); and
     (b) satisfies such conditions as may be specified in the order.

(2)   A transitional order may make provision as to when the transitional period in respect of such an agreement is to start or to be deemed to have started.

(3)   The transitional period for such an agreement ends at the end of the relevant period.

(4)   But if the agreement –
(a) ceases to be one to which a transitional order applies, or
(b) ceases to satisfy one or more of the conditions specified in the transitional order,
the transitional period ends on the date when the agreement so ceases.

(5)   Before making a transitional order, the Secretary of State must consult the Director General of Gas Supply and the Director.

(6)   The conditions specified in a transitional order may include –
(a) conditions which are to be satisfied in relation to a time before the coming into force of this paragraph;
(b) conditions which refer any matter (which may be the general question whether the Chapter I prohibition should apply to a particular agreement) to the Secretary of State, the Director or the Director General of Gas Supply for determination after such consultation as may be so specified.

Gas: Northern Ireland

32. – (1) For an agreement to which, immediately before the starting date, the RTPA does not apply by virtue of an Article 41 order, there is a transitional period –
(a) beginning on the starting date; and
(b) ending at the end of the relevant period.

(2)   For an agreement which is made at any time after the starting date and to which, had the RTPA not been repealed, that Act would not at the time at which the agreement is made have applied by virtue of an Article 41 order, there is a transitional period –
(a) beginning on the date on which the agreement is made; and
(b) ending at the end of the relevant period.

(3)   For an agreement (whether made before or after the starting date) which, during the relevant period, is varied at any time in such a way that it becomes an agreement which, had the RTPA not been repealed, would at that time have been one to which that Act did not apply by virtue of an Article 41 order, there is a transitional period –
(a) beginning on the date on which the variation is made; and
(b) ending at the end of the relevant period.

(4)   If an agreement for which there is a transitional period as a result

of sub-paragraph (1), (2) or (3) is varied during the relevant period, the transitional period for the agreement continues if, had the RTPA not been repealed, the agreement would have continued to be one to which that Act did not apply by virtue of an Article 41 order.

(5) But if an agreement for which there is a transitional period as a result of sub-paragraph (1), (2) or (3) ceases to be one to which, had it not been repealed, the RTPA would not have applied by virtue of an Article 41 order, the transitional period ends on the date on which the agreement so ceases.

(6) Sub-paragraph (3) is subject to paragraph 20.

(7) In this paragraph and paragraph 33 –
   "Article 41 order" means an order under Article 41 of the Gas (Northern Ireland) Order 1996;
   "Department" means the Department of Economic Development.

Gas: Northern Ireland – power to make transitional orders
33. – (1) There is a transitional period for an agreement of a description falling within Article 41(1) which –
   (a) is specified, or is of a description specified, in an order ("a transitional order") made by the Department (whether before or after the making of the agreement but before the end of the relevant period); and
   (b) satisfies such conditions as may be specified in the order.
(2) A transitional order may make provision as to when the transitional period in respect of such an agreement is to start or to be deemed to have started.

(3) The transitional period for such an agreement ends at the end of the relevant period.

(4) But if the agreement –
   (a) ceases to be one to which a transitional order applies, or
   (b) ceases to satisfy one or more of the conditions specified in the transitional order,
the transitional period ends on the date when the agreement so ceases.

(5) Before making a transitional order, the Department must consult the Director General of Gas for Northern Ireland and the Director.

(6) The conditions specified in a transitional order may include conditions which refer any matter (which may be the general question

whether the Chapter I prohibition should apply to a particular agreement) to the Department for determination after such consultation as may be so specified.

Railways

34. – (1) In this paragraph –

"section 131" means section 131 of the Railways Act 1993 ("the 1993 Act");

"section 131 agreement" means an agreement –

(a) to which the RTPA does not apply immediately before the starting date by virtue of section 131(1); or

(b) in respect of which a direction under section 131(3) is in force immediately before that date;

"non-exempt agreement" means an agreement relating to the provision of railway services (whether made before or after the starting date) which is not a section 131 agreement; and

"railway services" has the meaning given by section 82 of the 1993 Act.

(2) For a section 131 agreement there is a transitional period of five years.

(3) There is a transitional period for a non-exempt agreement to the extent to which the agreement is at any time before the end of the relevant period required or approved –

(a) by the Secretary of State or the Rail Regulator in pursuance of any function assigned or transferred to him under or by virtue of any provision of the 1993 Act;

(b) by or under any agreement the making of which is required or approved by the Secretary of State or the Rail Regulator in the exercise of any such function; or

(c) by or under a licence granted under Part I of the 1993 Act.

(4) The transitional period conferred by sub-paragraph (3) –

(a) is to be taken to have begun on the starting date; and

(b) ends at the end of the relevant period.

(5) Sub-paragraph (3) is subject to paragraph 20.

(6) Any variation of a section 131 agreement on or after the starting date is to be treated, for the purposes of this paragraph, as a separate non-exempt agreement.

The regulators

35. – (1) Subject to sub-paragraph (3), each of the regulators may exercise, in respect of sectoral matters and concurrently with the

Director, the functions of the Director under paragraph 3, 7, 19(3), 36, 37, 38 or 39.

(2)   In sub-paragraph (1) "sectoral matters" means –
(a) in the case of the Director General of Telecommunications, the matters referred to in section 50(3) of the Telecommunications Act 1984;
(b) in the case of the Director General of Gas Supply, the matters referred to in section 36A(3) and (4) of the Gas Act 1986;
(c) in the case of the Director General of Electricity Supply, the matters referred to in section 43(3) of the Electricity Act 1989;
(d) in the case of the Director General of Electricity Supply for Northern Ireland, the matters referred to in Article 46(3) of the Electricity (Northern Ireland) Order 1992;
(e) in the case of the Director General of Water Services, the matters referred to in section 31(3) of the Water Industry Act 1991;
(f) in the case of the Rail Regulator, the matters referred to in section 67(3) of the Railways Act 1993;
(g) in the case of the Director General of Gas for Northern Ireland, the matters referred to in Article 23(3) of the Gas (Northern Ireland) Order 1996.

(3)   The power to give directions in paragraph 7(2) is exercisable by the Director only but if the Director is preparing directions which relate to a matter in respect of which a regulator exercises concurrent jurisdiction, he must consult that regulator.

(4)   Consultations conducted by the Director before the enactment date, with a view to preparing directions which have effect on or after that date, are to be taken to satisfy sub-paragraph (3).

(5)   References to enactments in sub-paragraph (2) are to the enactments as amended by or under this Act.

Chapter V
Extending the Transitional Period

36. – (1) A party to an agreement for which there is a transitional period may apply to the Director, not less than three months before the end of the period, for the period to be extended.

(2)   The Director may (on his own initiative or on an application under sub-paragraph (1)) –
(a) extend a one-year transitional period by not more than twelve months;

(b) extend a transitional period of any period other than one year by not more than six months.

(3) An application under sub-paragraph (1) must – ·
(a) be in such form as may be specified; and
(b) include such documents and information as may be specified.

(4) If the Director extends the transitional period under this paragraph, he must give notice in such form, and to such persons, as may be specified.

(5) The Director may not extend a transitional period more than once.

(6) In this paragraph –
"person" has the same meaning as in Part I; and
"specified" means specified in rules made by the Director under section 51.

Chapter VI
Terminating the Transitional Period

General
37. – (1) Subject to sub-paragraph (2), the Director may by a direction in writing terminate the transitional period for an agreement, but only in accordance with paragraph 38.

(2) The Director may not terminate the transitional period, nor exercise any of the powers in paragraph 38, in respect of an agreement which is excluded from the Chapter I prohibition by virtue of any of the provisions of Part I of this Act other than paragraph 1 of Schedule 1 or paragraph 2 or 9 of Schedule 3.

Circumstances in which the Director may terminate the transitional period
38. – (1) If the Director is considering whether to give a direction under paragraph 37 ("a direction"), he may in writing require any party to the agreement concerned to give him such information in connection with that agreement as he may require.

(2) If at the end of such period as may be specified in rules made under section 51, a person has failed, without reasonable excuse, to comply with a requirement imposed under sub-paragraph (1), the Director may give a direction.

(3) The Director may also give a direction if he considers –

(a) that the agreement would, but for the transitional period or a relevant exclusion, infringe the Chapter I prohibition; and

(b) that he would not be likely to grant the agreement an unconditional individual exemption.

(4) For the purposes of sub-paragraph (3) an individual exemption is unconditional if no conditions or obligations are imposed in respect of it under section 4(3)(a).

(5) In this paragraph –
"person" has the same meaning as in Part I;
"relevant exclusion" means an exclusion under paragraph 1 of Schedule 1 or paragraph 2 or 9 of Schedule 3.

Procedural requirements on giving a paragraph 37 direction

39. – (1) The Director must specify in a direction under paragraph 37 ("a direction") the date on which it is to have effect (which must not be less than 28 days after the direction is given).

(2) Copies of the direction must be given to –
(a) each of the parties concerned, and
(b) the Secretary of State,
not less than 28 days before the date on which the direction is to have effect.

(3) In relation to an agreement to which a direction applies, the transitional period (if it has not already ended) ends on the date specified in the direction unless, before that date, the direction is revoked by the Director or the Secretary of State.

(4) If a direction is revoked, the Director may give a further direction in respect of the same agreement only if he is satisfied that there has been a material change of circumstance since the revocation.

(5) If, as a result of paragraph 24(1) or (3), there is a transitional period in respect of provisions of an agreement relating to goods –
(a) which immediately before the starting date are exempt under section 14 of the RPA, or
(b) which, when continuing proceedings are determined, are found to be exempt under section 14 of the RPA,
the period is not affected by paragraph 37 or 38.

PART V
THE FAIR TRADING ACT 1973

References to the Monopolies and Mergers Commission

40. – (1) If, on the date on which the repeal by this Act of a provision mentioned in sub-paragraph (2) comes into force, the Monopolies and Mergers Commission has not completed a reference which was made to it before that date, continued consideration of the reference may include consideration of a question which could not have been considered if the provision had not been repealed.

(2) The provisions are –
    (a) sections 10(2), 54(5) and 78(3) and paragraph 3(1) and (2) of Schedule 8 to the Fair Trading Act 1973 (c 41);
    (b) section 11(8)(b) of the Competition Act 1980 (c 21);
    (c) section 14(2) of the Telecommunications Act 1984 (c 12);
    (d) section 45(3) of the Airports Act 1986 (c 31);
    (e) section 25(2) of the Gas Act 1986 (c 44);
    (f) section 13(2) of the Electricity Act 1989 (c 29);
    (g) section 15(2) of the Water Industry Act 1991 (c 56);
    (h) article 16(2) of the Electricity (Northern Ireland) Order 1992;
    (i) section 14(2) of the Railways Act 1993 (c 43);
    (j) article 36(3) of the Airports (Northern Ireland) Order 1994;
    (k) article 16(2) of the Gas (Northern Ireland) Order 1996.

Orders under Schedule 8

41. – (1) In this paragraph –
    "the 1973 Act" means the Fair Trading Act 1973;
    "agreement" means an agreement entered into before the date on which the repeal of the limiting provisions comes into force;
    "the order" means an order under section 56 or 73 of the 1973 Act;
    "the limiting provisions" means sub-paragraph (1) or (2) of paragraph 3 of Schedule 8 to the 1973 Act (limit on power to make orders under paragraph 1 or 2 of that Schedule) and includes any provision of the order included because of either of those sub-paragraphs; and
    "transitional period" means the period which –
        (a) begins on the day on which the repeal of the limiting provisions comes into force; and
        (b) ends on the first anniversary of the starting date.

(2) Sub-paragraph (3) applies to any agreement to the extent to which it would have been unlawful (in accordance with the provisions of the order) but for the limiting provisions.

(3) As from the end of the transitional period, the order is to have effect in relation to the agreement as if the limiting provisions had never had effect.

Part III of the Act

42. – (1) The repeals made by section 1 do not affect any proceedings in respect of an application which is made to the Court under Part III of the Fair Trading Act 1973, but is not determined, before the starting date.

(2) The question whether (for the purposes of sub-paragraph (1)) an application has been determined is to be decided in accordance with sub-paragraphs (3) and (4).

(3) If an appeal against the decision on the application is brought, the application is not determined until –
>   (a) the appeal is disposed of or withdrawn; or
>   (b) if as a result of the appeal the case is referred back to the Court –
>>   (i) the expiry of the period within which an appeal ("the further appeal") in respect of the Court's decision on that reference could have been brought had this Act not been passed; or
>>   (ii) if later, the date on which the further appeal is disposed of or withdrawn.

(4) Otherwise, the application is not determined until the expiry of the period within which any party to the application would have been able to bring an appeal against the decision on the application had this Act not been passed.

(5) Any amendment made by Schedule 12 to this Act which substitutes references to a relevant Court for references to the Court is not to affect proceedings of the kind referred to in sub-paragraph (1).

PART VI

THE COMPETITION ACT 1980

Undertakings

43. – (1) Subject to sub-paragraph (2), an undertaking accepted by the Director under section 4 or 9 of the Competition Act 1980 ceases to have effect on the coming into force of the repeal by this Act of that section.

(2) If the undertaking relates to an agreement which on the starting date is the subject of continuing proceedings, the undertaking continues

to have effect for the purposes of section 29 of the Competition Act 1980 until the proceedings are determined.

Application of sections 25 and 26

44. The repeals made by section 1 do not affect –
>   (a) the operation of section 25 of the Competition Act 1980 in relation to an application under section 1(3) of the RTPA which is made before the starting date;
>   (b) an application under section 26 of the Competition Act 1980 which is made before the starting date.

PART VII
MISCELLANEOUS

Disclosure of information

45. – (1) Section 55 of this Act applies in relation to information which, immediately before the starting date, is subject to section 41 of the RTPA as it applies in relation to information obtained under or as a result of Part I.

(2) But section 55 does not apply to any disclosure of information of the kind referred to in sub-paragraph (1) if the disclosure is made –
>   (a) for the purpose of facilitating the performance of functions of a designated person under the Control of Misleading Advertisements Regulations 1988; or
>   (b) for the purposes of any proceedings before the Court or of any other legal proceedings under the RTPA or the Fair Trading Act 1973 or the Control of Misleading Advertisements Regulations 1988.

(3) Section 56 applies in relation to information of the kind referred to in sub-paragraph (1) if particulars containing the information have been entered or filed on the special section of the register maintained by the Director under, or as a result of, section 27 of the RTPA or paragraph 10 of this Schedule.

(4) Section 55 has effect, in relation to the matters as to which section 41(2) of the RTPA had effect, as if it contained a provision similar to section 41(2).

The Court

46. If it appears to the Lord Chancellor that a person who ceases to be a non-judicial member of the Court as a result of this Act should receive compensation for loss of office, he may pay to him out of moneys provided by Parliament such sum as he may with the approval of the Treasury determine.

Schedule 14
Repeals and Revocations
PART I
REPEALS

Chapter	Short title	Extent of repeal
1973 c 41.	The Fair Trading Act 1973.	Section 4.
		Section 10(2).
		Section 45.
		Section 54(5).
		Section 78(3).
		In section 81(1), in the words before paragraph (a), from "and the Commission" to "of this Act)"; in paragraph (b), "or the Commission, as the case may be" and "or of the Commission"; in subsection (2), "or the Commission" and "or of the Commission" and in subsection (3), from "and, in the case," to "85 of this Act", and "or the Commission, as the case may be,".
		In section 83, in subsection (1) "Subject to subsection (1A) below" and subsection (1A).
		In section 135(1), in the words before paragraph (a) and in paragraph (b), "or the Commission", and paragraph (a).
		Schedule 3.
		In Schedule 8, paragraph 3(1) and (2).

1976 c 33.	The Restrictive Practices Court Act 1976.	The whole Act.
1976 c 34.	The Restrictive Trade Practices Act 1976.	The whole Act.
1976 c 53.	The Resale Prices Act 1976.	The whole Act.
1976 c 76.	The Energy Act 1976.	Section 5.
1977 c 19.	The Restrictive Trade Practices Act 1977.	The whole Act.
1977 c 37.	The Patents Act 1977.	Sections 44 and 45.
1979 c 38.	The Estate Agents Act 1979.	In section 10(3), "or the Restrictive Trade Practices Act 1976."
1980 c 21.	The Competition Act 1980.	Sections 2 to 10. In section 11(8), paragraph (b) and the "and" immediately before it. In section 13(1), from "but the giving" to the end. In section 15, subsections (2)(b), (3) and (4). Section 16(3). In section 17, "8(1)" in subsections (1) and (3) to (5) and in subsection (2) "8(1) or". In section 19(3), paragraph (d).

		In section 19(5)(a), "or in anything published under section 4(2)(a) above".
		Section 22.
		Sections 25 to 30.
		In section 31, subsection (2) and "10" in subsection (3).
		Section 33(3) and (4).
1984 c 12.	The Telecommunications Act 1984.	Section 14(2).
		In section 16(5), the "or" immediately after paragraph (a).
		In section 50(4), paragraph (c) and the "and" immediately after it.
		In section 50(5), "or (3)".
		In section 50(7), "or the 1980 Act".
		In section 95(1), "or section 10(2)(a) of the 1980 Act".
		In section 95(2), paragraph (c) and the "or" immediately before it.
		In section 95(3), "or the 1980 Act".
		In section 101(3), paragraphs (d) and (e).

1986 c 31.	The Airports Act 1986.	Section 45(3).
		In section 54(1), "or section 10(2)(a) of the 1980 Act".
		In section 54(3), paragraph (c) and the "or" immediately before it.
		In section 54(4), "or the 1980 Act".
		In section 56(a)(ii), "or the 1980 Act".
1986 c 44.	The Gas Act 1986.	Section 25(2).
		In section 27(1), "or section 10(2)(a) of the Competition Act 1980".
		In section 27(3)(a), from "or" to "competition reference".
		In section 27(6), "or the said Act of 1980".
		In section 28(5), the "or" immediately after paragraph (aa).
		In section 36A(5), paragraph (d) and the "and" immediately before it.
		In section 36A(6), "or (3)".
		In section 36A(8), "or under the 1980 Act".

		In section 36A(9), "or the 1980 Act".
		In section 42(3), paragraphs (e) and (f).
1986 c 60.	The Financial Services Act 1986.	Section 126.
1987 c 43.	The Consumer Protection Act 1986.	In section 38(3), paragraphs (e) and (f).
1987 c 53.	The Channel Tunnel Act 1987	In section 33(2), paragraph (c) and the "and" mmediately before it.
		In section 33(5), paragraphs (b) and (c).
1988 c 54.	The Road Traffic (Consequential Provisions) Act 1988.	In Schedule 3, paragraph 19.
1989 c 15.	The Water Act 1989.	In section 174(3), paragraphs (d) and (e).
1989 c 29.	The Electricity Act 1989.	Section 13(2).
		In section 15(1), paragraph (b) and the "or" immediately before it.
		In section 15(2), paragraph (c) and the "or" immediately before it.
		In section 15(3), "or the 1980 Act".
		In section 25(5), the "or" immediately after paragraph (b).

		In section 43(4), paragraph (c) and the "and" immediately after it.
		In section 43(5), "or (3)".
		In section 43(7), "or the 1980 Act".
		In section 57(3), paragraphs (d) and (e).
1989 c 40.	The Companies Act 1989.	In Schedule 20, paragraphs 21 to 24.
1990 c 42.	The Broadcasting Act 1990.	In section 193(2), paragraph (c) and the "and" immediately before it.
		In section 193(4), "or the Competition Act 1980".
1991 c 56.	The Water Industry Act 1991.	In section 12(5), "or the 1980 Act".
		Section 15(2).
		In section 17(1), paragraph (b) and the "or" immediately before it.
		In section 17(2), paragraph (c) and the "or" immediately before it.
		In section 17(4), "or the 1980 Act".
		In section 31(4), paragraph (c) and the "and" immediately before it.

		In section 31(5), "or in subsection (3) above".
		In section 31(6), "or in subsection (3) above".
		In section 31(7), "or (3)".
		In section 31(9), "or the 1980 Act".
		In Part II of Schedule 15, the entries relating to the Restrictive Trade Practices Act 1976 and the Resale Prices Act 1976.
1991 c 57.	The Water Resources Act 1991.	In Part II of Schedule 24, the entries relating to the Restrictive Trade Practices Act 1976 and the Resale Prices Act 1976.
1993 c 21.	The Osteopaths Act 1993.	In section 33(4), paragraph (b) and the "or" immediately before it.
		In section 33(5), "or section 10 of the Act of 1980".
1993 c 43.	The Railways Act 1993.	Section 14(2).
		In section 16(1), paragraph (b) and the "or" immediately before it.
		In section 16(2), paragraph (c) and the "or" immediately before it.

		In section 16(5), "or the 1980 Act".
		In section 67(4), paragraph (c) and the "and" immediately after it.
		In section 67(6)(a), "or (3)".
		In section 67(9), "or under the 1980 Act".
		Section 131.
		In section 145(3), paragraphs (d) and (e).
1994 c 17.	The Chiropractors Act 1994.	In section 33(4), paragraph (b) and the "or" immediately before it.
		In section 33(5), "or section 10 of the Act of 1980".
1994 c 21.	The Coal Industry Act 1994.	In section 59(4), paragraphs (e) and (f).
1994 c 40.	The Deregulation and Contracting Out Act 1994.	Sections 10 and 11.
		In section 12, subsections (1) to (6).
		In Schedule 4, paragraph 1.
		In Schedule 11, in paragraph 4, sub-paragraphs (3) to (6).
1996 c 55.	The Broadcasting Act 1996.	Section 77(2).

PART II
REVOCATIONS

Reference	Title	Extent of revocation
SI 1981/1675 (NI 26).	The Magistrates' Courts (Northern Ireland) Order 1981.	In Schedule 6, paragraphs 42 and 43.
SI 1982/1080 (NI 12).	The Agricultural Marketing (Northern Ireland) Order 1982.	In Schedule 8, the entry relating to paragraph 16(2) of Schedule 3 to the Fair Trading Act 1973 and in the entry relating to the Competition Act 1980, "and 15(3)".
SI 1986/1035 (N.I.9).	The Companies Consolidation (Consequential Provisions) (Northern Ireland) Order 1986.	In Part II of Schedule 1, the entries relating to the Restrictive Trade Practices Act 1976 and the Resale Prices Act 1976.
SI 1992/231 (N.I.1).	The Electricity (Northern Ireland) Order 1992.	Article 16(2). In Article 18– (a) in paragraph (1), sub-paragraph (b) and the "or" immediately before it; (b) in paragraph (2), sub-paragraph (c) and the "or" immediately before it; (c) in paragraph (3) "or the 1980 Act". In Article 28(5), the "or" immediately after sub-paragraph (b). In Article 46– (a) in paragraph (4), sub-paragraph (c) and the "and" immediately after it; (b) in paragraph (5), "or (3)";

		(c) in paragraph (7), "or the 1980 Act".
		Article 61(3)(f) and (g).
		In Schedule 12, paragraph 16.
SI 1994/426 (N.I.1).	The Airports (Northern Ireland) Order 1994.	Article 36(3).
		In Article 45–
		(a) in paragraph (1), "or section 10(2)(a) of the 1980 Act"; (b) in paragraph (3), sub-paragraph (c) and the "or" immediately before it; (c) in paragraph (4), "or the 1980 Act".
		In Article 47(a)(ii), "or the 1980 Act".
		In Schedule 9, paragraph 5.
SI 1996/275 (N.I.2).	The Gas (Northern Ireland) Order 1996.	Article 16(2).
		In Article 18– (a) in paragraph (1), sub-paragraph (b) and the "or" immediately before it; (b) in paragraph (3), sub-paragraph (c) and the "or" immediately before it; (c) in paragraph (5), "or the 1980 Act".
		In Article 19(5), the "or" immediately after sub-paragraph (b).

		In Article 23– (a) in paragraph (4), sub-paragraph (d) and the "and" immediately before it; (b) in paragraph (5), "or (3)"; (c) in paragraph (7), "or under the 1980 Act"; (d) in paragraph (8), "or the 1980 Act". Article 44(4)(f) and (g).

Crown Copyright material reproduced with the permission of the Controller of Her Majesty's Stationery Office.

Table of Cases

Table of Statutes

Table of Statutory Instruments

European Legislation

1957 Treaty of Rome

EC Merger Regulation (4064/89)   4.34

Index

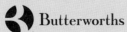

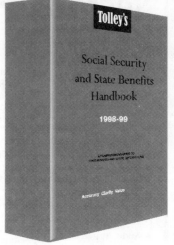
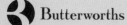

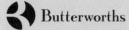

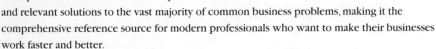
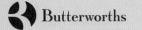

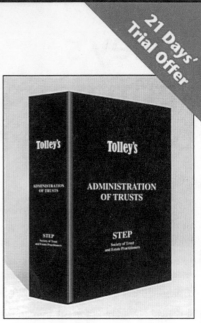
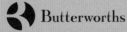